A Post-Eman...

Is... ookhan Ph.D
Associate Professor of History and
Historian Writer in Residence
College of the Virgin Islands

Addison Wesley Longman Limited,
Edinburgh Gate, Harlow,
Essex CM20 2JE, England
and Associated Companies throughout the world

Carlong Publishers (Caribbean) Limited
PO Box 489
Kingston 10
33 Second Street
Newport West
Kingston 13
Jamaica

Lexicon Trinidad Limited,
Boundary Road,
San Juan,
Trinidad

© Isaac Dookhan 1975
All rights reserved. No part of this publication may be
reproduced, stored in a retrieval system, or transmitted
in any form or by any means, electronic, mechanical,
photocopying, recording, or otherwise, without
the prior written permission of the Publishers.

First published by Collins Educational 1975
This impression published by Longman Group UK Ltd 1988
Ninth impression 1997

Produced by Longman Asia Limited, Hong Kong.
PPLC/09

ISBN 0-582-02803-5

Acknowledgement
The Examination Questions on pages 177 to 184
have been reproduced by permission of the
University of Cambridge Local Examination
Syndicate and the University of London, School
Examinations Department.

A Post-Emancipation History of the West Indies

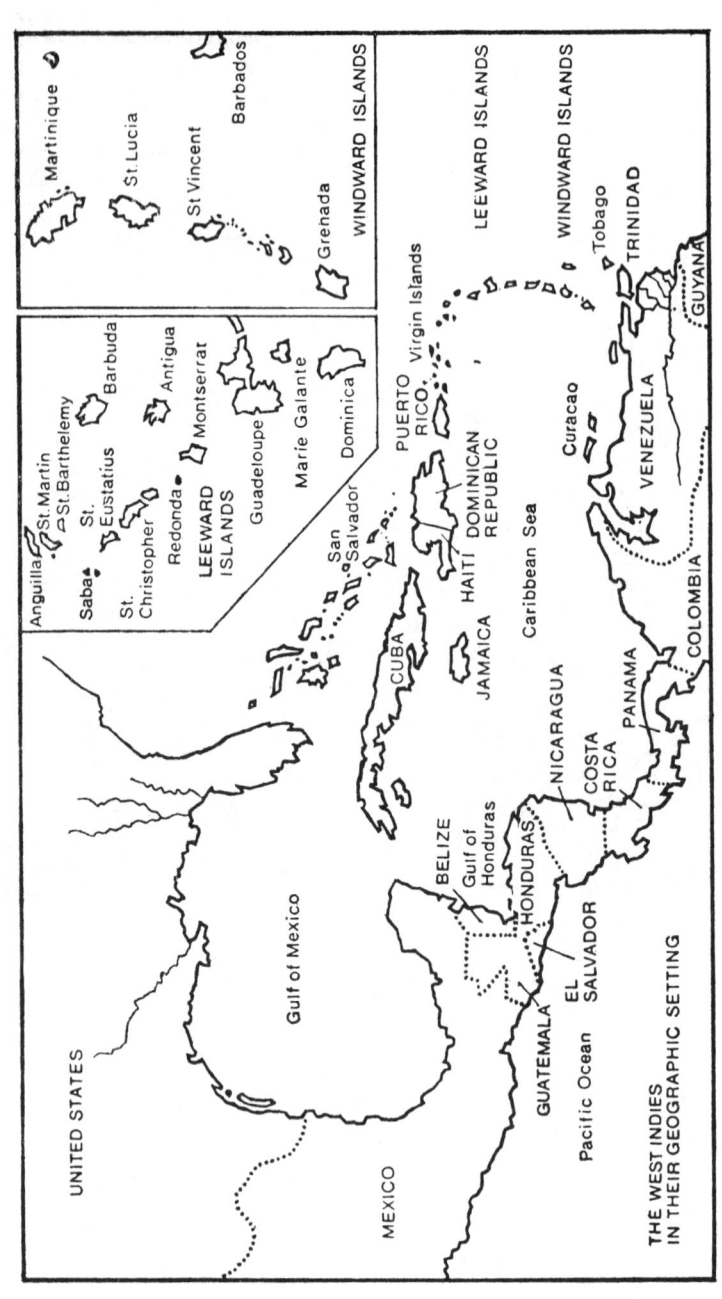

Contents

Preface 7

1. The Economic Background 9

The Labour Situation 10 *The Establishment of the Peasantry* 11 *The Post-Emancipation Financial Problem* 13 *Free Trade and the Sugar Duties Act of 1846* 15 *Beet Sugar Competition* 17 *Improvements in the Sugar Industry in the later nineteenth century* 19 *British Response to West Indian Economic Problems: (a) The Select Committee of Enquiry, 1847-8* 21 *(b) The Royal Commission of 1882-3* 22 *(c) The Royal Commission of 1896-7* 25 *Economic Diversification in the nineteenth century* 27 *The Economic Pattern to the 1930s* 28 *The Labour Unrest of the 1930s* 30 *The Moyne Commission, 1938-9* 34 *The British West Indian Sugar Industry since the Second World War* 37 *Economic Diversification in the twentieth century* 39 *Conclusion* 42

2. Immigration and Emigration 44

Conditions giving rise to Immigration in the British West Indies 45 *Immigration of Europeans, West Indians and Africans* 46 *Chinese and East Indian Immigration* 49 *Reasons why Indians Emigrated* 51 *Recruitment and Trans-Oceanic Transportation of Indian Immigrants* 53 *Working and Living Conditions of Immigrants* 55 *The Termination of Indian Indentured Labour* 59 *Overall Impact of Immigration* 60 *Emigration from the British West Indies* 63 *The Impact of Emigration on the West Indies* 65 *Conclusion* 66

3. The Public Welfare 68

Establishing Education, 1834-45: The Negro Education Grant and the Mico Charity 69 *Developments in Education, 1845-1900* 71 *Developments in Education in the twentieth century* 73 *Problems of Education since Emancipation* 75 *Transportation and Communication* 76 *Health and Medical Services* 79 *Current Health Problems* 82 *Social Welfare* 83 *Conclusion* 87

4. Organization for Development 89

A. Trade Unions: Early Beginnings 90 *Later Developments and Influences* 92 *Growth of Trade Unions* 93 *Difficulties Experienced by Trade Unions* 97 *Achievements of Trade Unions* 98 *B. Political Parties: The Background to the Development of Political Parties* 99 *The*

Rise of Political Parties: (a) Jamaica 100   *(b) Trinidad* 101   *(c) Guyana* 102   *(d) Barbados* 103   *(e) Leeward and Windward Islands* 104   *Characteristics of Political Parties* 107   *Scope of Political Party Activities* 108   *Problems Encountered by Political Parties* 109   *The Relationship between Political Parties and Trade Unions* 110   *Conclusion* 111

5. Constitutional Changes   112

The Passing of the Old Representative System 113   *The British West Indies under Crown Colony Government* 114   *Stages in the Constitutional Evolution of the British West Indies* 116 *Constitutional Development in the British West Indies: (a) Jamaica* 119   *(b) Trinidad* 120   *(c) Guyana* 123   *(d) Barbados* 125   *(e) The Leeward and Windward Islands* 127   *Associated Statehood* 128   *The Aftermath of Independence* 129   *Conclusion* 133

6. Closer Association   135

Attempts at Unification up to 1900 136   *The Leeward Islands Federation of 1674* 139   *The Leeward Islands Federation of 1871* 140   *Proposals for Closer Union in the West Indies after 1871* 142   *Conditions Retarding the Adoption of Federation* 144   *Conditions promoting Federation in the twentieth century* 161   *Steps towards the Federation of 1958* 146   *The Federation of the West Indies* 148   *Causes for the Failure and Collapse of the Federation of the West Indies* 151   *Regional Co-operation and Integration* 152   *Conclusion* 156

7. The United States and the Caribbean   158

Reasons for United States Interest in the Caribbean 158   *United States Involvement in the Caribbean in the nineteenth century* 160   *Extension of United States Influence in the twentieth century* 162   *Impact of the United States presence on the Caribbean* 165   *Local Response to the United States in the Caribbean* 168   *Conclusion* 170

List of Short Note Topics	172
A Select Bibliography	175
Examination Questions	177
Index	185

Preface

This book has been prepared as the sequel to my previous publication entitled *A Pre-Emancipation History of the West Indies*, and it is designed to serve the same general purpose of assisting students to prepare for particular examinations.

Like the earlier work, this study has been divided into seven parts, each one treating a particular aspect of West Indian history. They are, The Economic Background; Immigration and Emigration; The Public Welfare; Organization for Development; Constitutional Changes; Closer Association; The United States and the Caribbean. Except for the last chapter, the emphasis is on the history of the British West Indies from emancipation to the present time. The chapters as well as their sub-divisions have been developed from examination syllabuses, though a few subjects have been expanded beyond requirements to give them fuller and more complete treatment.

The plan of this book has been based on the general organization of the *Pre-Emancipation History*. Accordingly, some subjects have been treated in essay-form, while only the essential information has been given in others to afford students the opportunity to develop them.

Although detailed and in-depth study has been given to the various topics, this should not preclude students from consulting other books, both general and specialized, on West Indian history. Some of the most important of these titles have been included in the select bibliography at the end of the book.

A number of revision questions have been provided at the end of each chapter, and students are strongly advised to answer these questions after they have mastered the content of the chapter. The same method should be applied to the list of examination questions given towards the end of the book, which have been selected from specified examination papers for the General Certificate of Education, Ordinary Level. These questions have been designed to cover the subject as comprehensively as possible.

In order to avoid confusion, the name Guyana, given to the only British South American possession since its independence in 1966, has been used throughout this study instead of its colonial designation of British Guiana.

I wish to thank those West Indian history teachers who were consulted when this work was under preparation and who gave their advice freely and frankly as to how it could be improved. Also, I would like to express my gratitude to all my students at the College of the Virgin Islands on whom I tested many of my ideas and who gave me the benefit of their more familiar knowledge of current West Indian events and personalities. This book is dedicated to all of them.

College of the Virgin Islands
April, 1975

1. The Economic Background

Before emancipation every aspect of life in the West Indies was circumscribed by the plantation system and the masses of the people were slaves subject to the whims and fancy of their owners. After emancipation the slaves became free to choose the nature of their future occupation, and their response constituted a revolutionary departure from past practice.

A fundamental development during the post-emancipation period was the exodus of ex-slaves from the estates mostly to set themselves up as peasant proprietors. The movement created a labour shortage which threatened the imminent collapse of the sugar industry, already in decline and now suffering from a shortage of capital and from foreign colonial cane sugar and European beet sugar competition.

To avoid ruin planters sought to introduce immigrant labour from Europe, Africa and Asia, and to effect certain technical improvements to reduce the cost of production. Their efforts could not avert economic depression a major consequence of which was diversification to escape from over-reliance on sugar cane monoculture. Consequently, other agricultural crops such as bananas, cocoa and arrowroot were developed, mineral resources exploited and, more recently, industry and tourism promoted.

Agricultural diversification was given point by the rise of a West Indian peasantry which produced not only food crops but cash crops also. Peasant farming begun by ex-slaves was boosted considerably by the East Indians who had succeeded them as plantation labourers but who later became farmers themselves.

The emancipation of slaves and their exodus from the estates led not only to the development of peasant farming and immigration, but it also affected other related aspects of colonial life, namely, the provision of social services, the rise of trade unions and political parties, the system of colonial government, and eventually co-operation and association among the various colonies. The post-emancipation period was essentially one of adjustment to discover social, economic and political forms most appropriate to the West Indian situation. The spirit of independence aroused by the act of emancipation was directed towards the end of colonialism and against its resurgence in any new form.

1. The Labour Situation

With emancipation in 1838, slaves became free to choose the nature of their future existence. They were free to continue in the employment of their former masters, or they could exploit employment opportunities other than plantation wage labour in which the vast majority of them were then engaged.

In the years immediately following emancipation many of the ex-slaves chose to remain on the estates because of their attachment to their homes and provision grounds, because of the availability of certain services such as medical treatment which was granted free of charge, and because they hoped thereby to escape an uncertain future. Nevertheless, many others wanted to dissociate themselves at any cost from the 'symbol of enslavement.'

Among the newly-emancipated people, plantation labour was regarded as inadequate to satisfy the range of expectations created by emancipation. Labourers now had to be paid for their services, and many employers either lacked the funds or were short of money of small denominations to do so. Existing statistics show slight wage fluctuations over a period of time as well as variations among the several colonies; in any case they indicate that wages were extremely low. Daily wages of first class field labour in 1842, for which year statistics are available for most colonies, were 1/0½ to 1/7 in Antigua, 1/3 in Barbados, 10½d. in Grenada, 1/6 in Jamaica, 6d. in Montserrat, 10d. to 1/10 in St. Lucia, 8d. to 2/- in St. Vincent, 8d. to 1/- in Tobago, 2/1 in Trinidad, and 1/8 to 2/- in Guyana. As will be explained later, many ex-slaves from the smaller, highly populated islands sought employment through emigration to Guyana and the larger islands like Trinidad where the wages were higher.

In addition to low wages, the labouring population continued to experience the brutal and degrading conditions of slavery since many employers were unable or disinclined to adjust to the new situation of freedom. Heavy rentals on plantation houses and provision grounds, and evictions for non-payment of rents in an effort to enforce labour were accompanied by the destruction of provision grounds and the killing or maiming of livestock belonging to labourers.

Several alternative forms of employment were available to those who sought to abandon plantation labour. Women could become housewives or set themselves up in occupations such as sewing, handicraft, peddling, or petty-shopkeeping. Children could take advantage of available educational facilities and go to school. Men could engage in local small-scale trading in clothing and foodstuffs by setting up shops near to estates or in villages. Such occupation would naturally appeal to those who lacked the industry or skill to be artisans or farmers.

Ex-slaves who already had the benefit of previous training and experience were attracted into skilled trades where the financial rewards were between two and four times better than in plantation agriculture in several colonies. For example, the daily wages for artisans were 1/9 in Grenada in 1839, up to 6/- in Jamaica in 1841, between 4/2 and 5/8 in Guyana in 1844, and 8d. to 1/6 in Tobago, 1/2 to 1/9 in Dominica, and 2/1 in Barbados in 1845. In 1844 there were as many as 12,348 artisans in Barbados, 17,496 in Jamaica, 5,987 in Guyana and 2,521 in Antigua.

Among those who abandoned full-time employment on the estates, however, the largest number was attracted towards subsistence peasant agriculture, since agriculture was what most of them were accustomed to. The response of a large number of ex-slaves to the new opportunities for farming was an understandable reluctance to work on the estates. Consequently, there was a voluntary exodus of ex-slaves from the estates principally to small holdings acquired either by purchase, rental or illegal occupation.

2. The Establishment of the Peasantry

A number of conditions led ex-slaves to leave the estates and establish themselves as independent cultivators. These were the desire for personal liberty and landownership, insecurity of tenure on the estates, high rents on estate houses, low wages, familiarity with agriculture, and availability of land for cultivation.

The loss of plantation labourers to peasant farming was greatest numerically in Jamaica, Trinidad and Guyana where there were large areas of unoccupied land available for ex-slaves to set themselves up as peasant proprietors. In the smaller islands where there were large populations and less available land, the drift was less intense though the rate varied from island to island. It was greatest in Tobago, Grenada, St. Vincent, Montserrat and Nevis, and least in Antigua, St. Kitts and Barbados; St. Lucia and Dominica fell between the two extremes.

The peasantry grew as plantations were abandoned as a result of the fall in sugar prices in London from 33/8 per cwt. in 1838, to 23/8 per cwt. in 1847, and to 21/5 per cwt. in 1854. Between 1838 and 1848 as many as 14 sugar and 465 coffee estates in Jamaica, and 40 estates in Trinidad were abandoned; in Guyana 72 sugar estates were abandoned between 1838 and 1850.

The lower profitability of sugar also resulted in a fall in the price of land; depending on the quality and location, the price per acre in the 1840s ranged from as low as £4 to £20 in Jamaica, and £1.5 to £13 in Trinidad to as high as £40 to £80 in Antigua, and £60 to £200 in Barbados. By pooling their financial resources, acquired through thrift and industry, ex-slaves could buy abandoned estates, subdivide them, and establish themselves as peasant proprietors. In Jamaica, some secured the assistance of Baptist ministers in their attempts to bargain with landowners and to secure land. Co-operative activity of this kind among ex-slaves stimulated the growth of free villages many of which were haphazardly founded and unplanned.

Holdings were acquired mainly by purchase; lease-holding was of secondary importance and confined more or less to islands such as Antigua, St. Kitts and Barbados where there was little available idle land. In addition, a substantial number of labourers came into 'possession' of land by squatting on Crown lands or on patented property lying idle in colonies such as Guyana, Trinidad, Dominica and St. Lucia. Squatters disregarded official warnings to desist from such practice because they knew that it was difficult for them to be brought to justice.

Available statistics show that the number of peasant freeholds in Jamaica increased from 2,114 in 1838, to 27,379 in 1845, and to about 50,000 in 1861. In Trinidad, the number of proprietors increased from about 2,000 in 1832 to over 7,000 in 1849, while in Guyana about 15,000 ex-slaves owned 4,506 acres of land in 1842, increased to over 40,000 ex-slaves on 17,000 acres divided into 9,979 smallholdings in 1848; and by 1851 there were 11,152 freeholds. In Tobago, there were 658 freeholds in 1845, increased to 2,367 in 1853, and in Grenada the increase was from 1,943 to 3,571 during the same period. In Barbados, the number of freeholds rose from 26 in 1842 to about 1,630 in 1845; in St. Kitts there were 2,864 freeholds and 2,307 leaseholds in 1844, while in St. Lucia freeholds increased from 100 in 1841, to 1,345 in 1845, to 1,920 in 1849, and to 2,343 in 1853.

Peasant holdings varied in quality, but most of them were marginal land, inaccessible to markets, unsurveyed and uncleared. Plots ranged in size from as small as one half to as large as fifty acres, and they were used for growing ground provisions, fruits and vegetables, for rearing livestock such as cattle, sheep, goats, pigs and poultry, or for burning charcoal. Peasants also cultivated cash crops such as tobacco, bananas, ginger, arrowroot, cocoa, coffee, coconuts, logwood, pimentos and even sugar cane. By so doing they diversified the basic monoculture pattern of cultivation in the West Indies. Where plots were small, peasants engaged in part-time work on nearby estates in order to supplement their earnings, or combined agriculture with activities like fishing and shopkeeping. Cash crops were generally sold through the big producers while surplus food was sold in the village or town markets by the peasants themselves or through middlemen higglers. Some goods were also sold by itinerant hawkers and hucksters.

Peasant ownership was not allowed to develop unmolested by the colonial plantocracy. Governments imposed burdensome regulations on the acquisition of Crown lands and refused to survey them as a preliminary to peasant settlement, levied heavy and discriminatory taxation on smallholdings, and required incredibly costly licences for selling sugar and coffee and for making charcoal. Besides, laws were passed restricting the movement of labourers both within a particular colony and among the various West Indian colonies.

Of importance too was the metayer (or metairie) system which many planters lacking money to pay wages adopted to prevent the drift of labourers from the estates. Metayer was a system of land tenure in which the proprietor formed a partnership with his labourers for the cultivation of his land. First adopted in St. Lucia it spread to the different colonies especially after 1847 and assumed real importance in St. Lucia, Montserrat, Tobago, Grenada and Nevis. The most usual practice was for the proprietor to furnish the land, mills, carts and draft animals and the labourer to provide labour. Of the produce the proprietor took half the sugar together with the skimmings and molasses while the labourer obtained the other half of the sugar and some rum. The proprietor was responsible for marketing all sugar. The system enabled many properties to be maintained which must otherwise have been abandoned, but it operated against the interests of the labourers, did not prevent their drift from the estates, and eventually yielded to the older system of direct management and wage labour.

3. The Post-Emancipation Financial Problem

The fall in sugar prices after 1838 and the disappearance of profits led many marginal estates to cease production and contributed to the growing indebtedness of planters. Cultivation was confined to the most suitable lands, but the costs of production were increasing due to mismanagement, to the need to pay labourers' wages, as well as to the introduction of labour-saving devices such as ploughs and harrows to do the work of ex-slaves leaving the estates. The £17 million obtained by British West Indian slave-owners under the Act of Emancipation as slave compensation was used to purchase some agricultural implements but most of it went to liquidate debts previously contracted.

Meanwhile, the traditional sources of credit were drying up, such as from consignee merchants in Britain who had been accustomed to market the West Indian produce and provide credit; advances were limited to the barest necessities as planters' indebtedness increased. Even during more prosperous times, few estate owners had been able to accumulate enough savings for times of hardship; soon after emancipation only the financially sound could rely on the traditional sources of credit for investment purposes.

The Colonial Bank of the West Indies had been chartered in 1836 to give financial assistance to planters, and it established branches in most of the British West Indian colonies. However, it was forbidden to make substantial loans to sugar estates, and it undertook only normal banking operations such as accepting deposits, dealing in bills of exchange and providing some working expenses. Loans for long term capital improvement were impossible for it to provide, and its very high discount rate might have seriously hindered development. Other local banks such as the Bank of British Guiana (1836) and the Planters' Bank of Jamaica (1839) followed the practice of the influential Colonial Bank and refused to lend money on the security of sugar estates.

The removal of preferences on British West Indian produce through the equalization of duties on British West Indian, British East Indian and foreign colonial sugars entering the British market after 1846 (discussed more fully below) increased the financial burden of many planters. Then in 1847-8 a serious commercial crisis in Britain due to unsound financial speculation resulted in the liquidation of eighteen merchant houses engaged in West Indian trade and finance. Their collapse entailed the failure of many of their branches or agents in the West Indies including the West India Bank in Barbados and the Planters' Bank in Jamaica. Many bills drawn by planters on agents in Britain were dishonoured on their arrival and were returned to their drawers, thus adding to their losses.

Various methods were adopted to deal with the financial crisis. In order to reduce production costs a new source of cheap and efficient labour was sought and found in East Indian immigration. Factory operations were rationalized and mechanized: steam mills replaced animal mills, central factories were constructed to serve several estates, and new equipment such as vacuum pans and centrifugals were installed. In the fields, improved varieties of sugar cane were cultivated, and newer techniques of field operations were implemented where necessary including the more widespread use of ploughs and harrows, fertilizers, and drainage and irrigation schemes.

The amalgamation of small estates into larger, well-managed commercial enterprises allowed for more efficient use of existing factory equipment, available labour supplies and marketing facilities. As more acreage was obtained through consolidation, costs could be lowered by concentrating cultivation on the most productive parts. More importantly, consolidated estates found it easier to obtain credit and introduce cost-saving changes.

For many estates amalgamation was hindered by their debt liabilities which made their sale difficult. To deal with this problem special courts were established under the West Indies Encumbered Estates Act passed by the British Parliament in 1854 and adopted by the British West Indian colonies through appropriate enabling legislation. Only Barbados, St. Lucia, Trinidad and Guyana did not adopt it on the ground that prevailing laws were adequate. The Act permitted the sale by judicial decree of any estate which was crippled by mortgages and other liens. The proceeds of the sale were distributed among the interested parties, and the purchaser received a title free from any encumbrances. By 1874, 155 estates had been sold under Encumbered Estates Acts at prices amounting to $249,015. Most of the purchasers were non-resident British companies.

In addition to the above methods, sugar producers sought more favourable markets in the United States since transportation costs were lower and prices better, even though duties tended to be unstable. Also, after 1846 many colonial governments employed skilled engineers to advise planters on improved manufacturing techniques thus indirectly encouraging capital investment. Some governments even established Departments of Agriculture to give advice and assistance to planters interested in improving production methods, and to discover, through experimentation, new strains of staples more suited to West Indian soils and climates.

4. Free Trade and the Sugar Duties Act of 1846

Before 1825 the British West Indies enjoyed an almost complete monopoly of the British market for their muscovado sugar due to the differential tariff in Britain on sugar imports from the various sources. Thus prohibitively high duties were levied on foreign colonial sugars, followed by a lower rate on British East Indian sugars, and with the lowest rate imposed on the British West Indian product. From 1825, however, the tariff structure was remodelled progressively reducing the British West Indian advantage and alternately increasing the competitive advantage of sugar from other British and foreign sources.

In 1825 Mauritian muscovado was allowed to enter Britain at the same tariff as British West Indian muscovado, and ten years later muscovado from the British East Indies was similarly treated. During the period 1836–44, the British sugar duties experienced an almost annual modification, though for most of the time British colonial muscovado paid duties of 24/- a cwt., while foreign muscovado paid 63/- a cwt. Then in 1844, foreign muscovado was introduced into Britain at 34/- a cwt., providing it could be certified as the produce of free labour only. The following year the duties on both British colonial and foreign free-labour sugar were lowered by approximately 10/- per cwt.

The importation of foreign colonial and British East Indian sugars at lower rates of duty naturally increased their ability to compete effectively against the British West Indian product. Their production increased – for example, in Mauritius from 10,481 tons in 1825 to 127,324 tons in 1855, and in Cuba from 162,425 tons in 1841 to 392,000 tons in 1855 – which helped to reduce the price of sugar. The net result for the British West Indian sugar producer was to reduce his profits and to drive marginal estates out of production.

The greatest blow to the British West Indian producers was given with the passing by the British Parliament of the Sugar Duties Act of 1846. It swept away the prohibitory duties on refined sugar from foreign sources, abolished existing discriminations against slave-grown sugar, and provided for a rapid reduction in the preference given to colonial sugar by the equalization of duties placed on foreign and British colonial produce. The Act provided that such equalization should be effected by 1851, but in response to the request of British West Indians, this did not in fact take place until 1854.

As a necessary corollary to the Sugar Duties Act, in 1849 the British Parliament repealed the Navigation Acts which had been in existence since the second half of the seventeenth century, partly on the grounds of policy and partly as a concession to British West Indian demands. The effect was to enable the British West Indies to exploit other markets than the British with the result that there was a growing market with such countries as France and the United States.

An immediate consequence of the Sugar Duties Act was the cessation of credit advances by British merchants to West Indian sugar producers, thereby obstructing the ordinary processes of cultivation and severely curtailing the introduction of machinery. By further limiting planters' ability to pay wages, it contributed to the exodus of labourers from the estates. When it was compounded with the financial and commercial crises of the next two years, the results were serious in terms of the abandonment of estates and the fall of London sugar prices – from 34/5 a cwt. in 1846 to 21/1 in 1854 – due to competition from British East Indian and foreign sources.

However, the Sugar Duties Act did not result in the collapse of the British West Indian sugar industry and trade. Indeed, by stimulating the more efficient use of available ex-slave labour, by encouraging the large-scale importation of indentured labour, and by leading to the introduction of labour-saving devices, the result was an increase in the annual average sugar exports from the British West Indies to all countries from 3,419,000 cwt. in 1853–5, to 4,774,000 cwt. in 1868–70. The Crimean War (1854–6) in Europe had the effect of increasing the price of sugar per cwt. in London from 21/1 in 1854 to 35/2 in 1857, and although the price dropped thereafter, events relating to the American Civil War maintained it at a level higher than the 1854 price until 1866 when it fell to 20/3 a cwt.

Another condition which operated in favour of British West Indian sugar after 1854 was that different qualities of sugar were taxed differently when imported into Britain. In order to protect the British refining industry the highest duties were paid on imported refined sugar while successively lower duties were charged on partially refined and unrefined muscovado sugars such as were produced in the British West Indies. This advantage disappeared only after 1874 when all sugars were admitted into Britain free of all duties. As a result some West Indian estates were abandoned, while those which survived sought more satisfactory markets in the United States for their produce.

Sugar remained free of duty in Britain from 1874 until 1901 when a customs duty of 4/2 a cwt. was imposed equally on all sugars from all sources. These duties were changed from time to time until 1919 when differential duties were imposed in favour of British colonial sugar, thereby reversing the policy in force since 1854.

5. Beet Sugar Competition

The cultivation of beet root for sugar production on a commercial basis was first encouraged in continental Europe during the Napoleonic Wars in an attempt to overcome the shortage of cane sugar created by wartime disruption. After the war ended in 1815 beet sugar production collapsed, but after a shaky revival was again flourishing in countries like France, Germany and Austria by the middle of the nineteenth century. Progress thereafter was rapid; whereas in 1859–60 world beet sugar production amounted to 451,584 tons, by 1894–5 it had increased to 4,725,800 tons. During the second half of the nineteenth century European beet sugar posed a serious threat to the prosperity of British West Indian cane sugar. Not only was it exported to Britain, but it also satisfied the continental market thereby shutting off British re-exports of West Indian cane sugar.

Beet root produced not only sugar but also cattle feed from its residue and a cheap spirit from its molasses. It facilitated crop rotation, employed a large working population, and unlike sugar cane could be stored for months without spoiling. Beet sugar production enjoyed certain advantages over the production of cane sugar. It was subsidized through government bounties which allowed for technological and scientific improvements in production, boosted production and enabled beet sugar to be sold cheaper than the cost of production. Between 1884 and 1894 bounties on beet per ton were £1 in Germany and £5 in France; in 1896 both were doubled. Improvements increased the sugar content of beets from 8 percent in 1870, to 11 percent in 1884, and to 17 percent in 1918. The cost of producing beet sugar and cane sugar was about equal, but European beet sugar sold in Britain had the advantage of lower freight rates. Thus the freightage to Britain on a ton of beet sugar from Europe was 6/- compared with £2 on a ton of cane sugar from the West Indies. Lower prices made beet sugar more popular among British consumers, including sugar refiners and confectioners, though it also had the reputation of being of a superior quality to West Indian cane sugar.

An increasing amount of beet sugar was imported into Britain during the later nineteenth century rising from 80,027 tons in 1865, to 305,000 tons in 1878, to 559,000 tons in 1884, and to 1,362,000 tons in 1900.

THE SUGAR TRADE, 1884-1900 (In Thousands of Tons)

B.W.I. Sugar Exports		Sugar Imports into Britain			
		Cane Sugar		Beet Sugar	
Year	Amount	B.W.I.	Other Areas		Total
1884	329	168	414	559	1,141
1885	283	138	423	562	1,123
1886	256	99	367	586	1,052
1887	336	108	331	772	1,211
1888	299	106	468	661	1,235
1889	289	94	376	855	1,325
1890	298	67	216	987	1,270
1891	264	54	298	1,001	1,353
1892	279	75	311	958	1,344
1893	273	61	307	1,009	1,377
1894	260	85	239	1,087	1,411
1895	236	85	243	1,169	1,497
1896	206	72	226	1,144	1,442
1897	254	47	228	1,159	1,434
1898	289	41	235	1,117	1,393
1899	244	39	106	1,258	1,403
1900	238	37	113	1,362	1,512

This increase, of course, was achieved at the expense of cane sugar. Between 1865 and 1878, the importation of British West Indian cane sugar into Britain increased from 176,593 to 191,960 tons, but the increased imports were not commensurate with the increase in consumption. In any case, by 1884 imports had dropped to 168,000 tons, and by 1900 to 37,000 tons.

In order to overcome the depression in the British market, British West Indian cane sugar producers turned to the United States. Even there, however, they met with competition from beet sugar, imports of which from Germany alone increased from 200,000 tons in 1887 to 717,170 tons in 1897. Besides, United States consumers were less inclined towards British West Indian muscovado, and after the Spanish-American War in 1898, Cuban and Puerto Rican sugar entered into competition against other West Indian sugar.

Apart from destroying the cane sugar market, beet sugar competition led to a fall in the price of cane sugar. Between 1870 and 1878, for example, cane sugar prices fell by about 1/3 a cwt.; in 1884 alone prices fell from 20/- to 13/- a cwt.; and by 1897 prices were down to 10/- a cwt. The fall in prices naturally affected profits which on the best estates fell from an average of £7.15s. a ton in 1882 to only 6/- a ton in 1897. The declining profitability of cane sugar contributed to the abandonment of several estates: 58 sugar estates ceased production between 1875 and 1878, while 38 others were advertised for sale during the latter year. By 1886 two-thirds of the sugar cultivation of St. Vincent had been abandoned.

Beginning in 1897, action taken to deal with beet sugar competition affected the British West Indian sugar industry. In that year, the United States Congress placed countervailing duties on bounty-fed beet sugar imported into the country, to the full extent of the bounty, in order to protect the United States sugar industry. Within a year, United States imports of German beet sugar dropped from 717,170 tons to 17,000 tons thereby giving West Indian sugar 35/- per ton more in the United States market. Then in 1902 the Brussels Convention was signed by which beet sugar countries agreed to cease subsidizing beet sugar production, and Britain agreed to prohibit the importation of bounty-fed beet sugar or to subject it to a duty equal to or higher than the bounty, for the next five years. By 1909 British West Indian exports of cane sugar into Britain had increased to 129,000 tons.

6. Improvements in the Sugar Industry in the later nineteenth century

Improvements were made in the sugar industry though for various reasons changes came very slowly and were subject to limitations:

(a) The system of crushing canes was improved by the introduction of double and even triple crushing in the mills. This enabled 75 to 80 percent extraction of juice compared with only 50 to 60 percent by the old-fashioned mills. The further adoption of the maceration and diffusion process whereby the megasse was shredded into small pieces and steam or warm water applied to it to dissolve all the sucrose, made possible almost perfect extraction. However, the changes were introduced mostly in Guyana and Trinidad and rarely in other islands.

(b) The use of steam-power increased milling efficiency, while the adoption of multi-tubular boilers eased fuel difficulties. However, the scarcity of water and the expenses involved in installing new engines were deterrents to these changes which were limited to the most prosperous estates in the most important sugar-producing colonies.

(c) The use of the vacuum pan invented as early as 1813 facilitated speedier evaporation in the conversion of syrup to sugar. The development of the 'triple effect' in the late 1880s allowed three pans to use the same steam power. This method was also costly and was more or less confined to the large estates in Trinidad and Guyana. Elsewhere it was rarely used; by the end of the nineteenth century there were only nine vacuum pans in Barbados and one in St. Kitts-Nevis.

(d) The invention of the centrifugal in 1837 led to a big improvement in the drainage of molasses from sugar crystals; a much drier sugar could be obtained, and bags replaced hogsheads as containers at a much reduced cost. The centrifugal was the most widely adopted improvement because it could be easily installed.

(e) Central factories were created to process the sugar cane of several estates thus moving away from the system where every estate, however small, had its own factory. The first central factory was established in Martinique in 1847 but despite the recommendation of the Select Committee of 1847-8 it was not until between 1871 and 1873 that central factories were established in Trinidad and St. Lucia. They reduced the cost of production by 50 percent, but even so they were not generally adopted until the twentieth century following the recommendation of the Royal Commission of 1897. The spirit of independence and pride of the small proprietors and the economic depression after 1884 were mainly responsible for the delay.

(f) Some improvement in sugar cane cultivation took place with the wider use of manures and fertilizers to restore the organic content and fertility of the soil. Imported manures were expensive, but by 1885 guano from the Morant and Pedro Cays was being used in Jamaica, while Antiguan planters obtained their supplies of guano

from Redonda. Reduction in the price of fertilizers, especially sulphate of ammonia in the 1890s, made them more readily available. However, manures and fertilizers were indiscriminately used without proper soil analysis.
(g) By the end of the nineteenth century the steam plough was being used for tillage in some colonies, but the use of the hoe in field work was still as common as during slavery.
(h) Experts were advocating improved varieties of cane but no systematic work was started until the creation of the West Indian Department of Agriculture in 1898.

The transportation of canes from field to mill suffered from insufficient carts and punts and from the unintelligent care of animals.

7. British Response to West Indian Economic Problems

Although the British Government cannot be held fully responsible for the economic problems facing the British West Indies after 1838, nevertheless some of the troubles facing the colonies were due to action taken by it. Indirectly, it contributed to the drift of labourers from the estates by the Colonial Office's approval of colonial legislation which caused hardship to the newly-emancipated people. More directly, its implementation of free trade principles aggravated the financial crisis facing the colonies. Attempts were made to deal with some of the problems. The approach generally taken was the appointment of special committees or commissions to investigate particular or general areas of West Indian concern and to recommend appropriate actions to be taken to improve the situation. The most important were:

(a) *The Select Committee of Enquiry, 1847–8*

Following the passing of the Sugar Duties Act of 1846 and the commercial crisis of 1847, a Select Committee of Enquiry was appointed under the chairmanship of Lord George Bentinck, chief spokesman of the sugar interests in the British Parliament, to enquire into the condition of sugar and coffee planting in the West Indies.

The Committee heard an enormous amount of evidence from West Indians who pleaded for an extension of colonial preferences, and the exclusion of foreign slave-grown sugar from the British market. Its report, adopted by a majority vote, recommended that British colonial sugar be given a preference of 10/- per cwt., over foreign sugar for six years. The British Government, however, refused to accept the recommendation, but the date for the equalization of duties between colonial and foreign sugars under the Sugar Duties Act of 1846 was postponed from 1851 to 1854.

Other measures were adopted to relieve the critical situation in the

West Indies as depicted by the Committee. West Indian sugar was admitted for use in British distilleries, and the duties on colonial rum entering Britain were considerably reduced. The colonies were allowed to remove the differential duties which they had been compelled hitherto to levy on foreign imported goods. Restrictions on immigration were relaxed and Parliament granted the interest on £500,000 to be raised by the West Indies, for immigration and public works. In addition, £155,000 was advanced immediately to Trinidad and Guyana for the same purpose, at 4 percent interest which was at least 2 percent lower than what the colonies would have paid on their own security. The period of payment of certain long-outstanding loans amounting to nearly £800,000 was further extended. These debts included the slave insurrection loan to Jamaica in 1831, and the hurricane loans to Barbados, St. Lucia and Tobago in 1832, and to Antigua, Montserrat and Nevis in 1843. Finally, steps were taken to reduce the administrative expenditure of colonies such as Trinidad and Guyana which were major sufferers from the crises of the mid-1840s.

(b) *The Royal Commission of 1882–3*

The backward economic condition of the British West Indies during the second half of the nineteenth century led to the appointment of a Royal Commission in December 1882 to inquire fully into the public finances of Jamaica, all of the British Leeward Islands, and the Windward Islands of St. Lucia, St. Vincent, Grenada and Tobago. In addition, the Commission was instructed to give special consideration to the methods of raising revenue and to the manner by which the public service could be reduced without detriment to the public interest.

The Commission was composed of William Crossman and George Baden-Powell as members, and included Charles A. Harris of the Colonial Office as Secretary. The Commissioners conducted their investigations over the next four months travelling throughout the colonies and taking evidence from a wide cross-section of the population. The result was a voluminous three-part report which was submitted at various times in 1883 and 1884.

The Commissioners were convinced of the need for greater economy in all the colonies and urged joint consultation and, if necessary, joint action among them to effect this. They recognized a community of interest among the islands and believed that through co-operation uniformity and improvement of operation could be achieved in the colonial civil service, the collection of rum duties, taxation, customs duties, extraordinary expenditure, capital and labour, the administration of justice, and in postal and telegraphic communication.

A detailed examination was made by the Commissioners of the composition of each government department in the various colonies as well as of the functions of each employee. In each colony they found that the public service was beyond the financial capacity of the government to maintain. Accordingly, for Jamaica they recommended either the outright reduction of the number of government officials compatible with the maximum efficiency of their offices, or otherwise a reduction of their annual income as a means of effecting greater economy. In some cases they proposed the amalgamation of offices to reduce expenditures though the incumbents of the combined offices might be given an appropriate increase in salary. Some important offices were allowed to remain unchanged though recommendations were made whereby their efficiency could be improved.

For the Windward and Leeward Islands where the combination of offices and the reduction of salaries had already been effected, the Commissioners recommended even further trimming. But the principal method advocated to effect savings and efficiency here was political reform. For both the Leeward Islands already federated since 1871 and the Windward Islands, the Commissioners recommended the abolition of the unit governments and the creation of a common government for each group. Such unity would not only promote joint action and uniformity, but would have the additional advantage of attracting investors hitherto discouraged by the political fragmentation.

The Commissioners found the colonial civil service in an unsatisfactory condition and officials generally incompetent due primarily to low salaries and because each colony, no matter how small and poor, tried to carry on all the functions of government. They discovered a marked deficiency of capable candidates for public employment and their report exposed glaring shortcomings in the manner the public business was transacted. Their proposals for reform were designed to ensure that expenditure on salaries and establishments was at the lowest rate consistent with proper efficiency. These included the creation of one Supreme Court for the Lesser Antilles and the establishment of one or more central convict stations.

The Commissioners examined the ways and means by which revenues were raised in the various colonies and found them deficient in several respects. Accordingly, they recommended ways by which collection could be improved as well as other possible sources of additional revenue. The uniformity and simplicity of rates and kinds of internal taxes, such as on lands, animals and houses, was urged to promote investment in industries and commerce, and to avoid evasion. Differences in the tax structures of the several colonies were recommended to be abolished, and suggestions were made for more efficient budgetary appropriation of revenues.

Considering the importance of customs duties to the colonies, the Commissioners were opposed to the repeal of import duties, but favoured their reduction instead, especially on such goods as flour, fish, rice and tea. The reduction of duties would lead to a reduction in the prices of these foodstuffs and promote their consumption among the masses who were not at that time heavy consumers of such foods. In addition, the Commissioners advised higher import duties on luxuries and uniformity in the customs tariffs among the Lesser Antilles as much to facilitate steamship commerce and general mercantile intercourse as to reduce the opportunities for successful smuggling. In order to stimulate greater trade, they considered it desirable that all port charges should be, as far as possible, made uniform and simple, and that West Indian telegraphic communication with North America and Europe should be made trustworthy and continuous.

On the other hand, the Commissioners were completely in favour of abolishing export duties, especially those on staples. Export duties were objectionable on principle, especially since the West Indian colonies did not have a monopoly on the articles taxed. Besides, the duties were costly to collect, and trade was hampered by the strict rules that had to be laid down as to times and places of shipment. In the larger islands, the collection of export duties was a grave impediment in the way of steamers calling for produce, while in the smaller islands, especially in the Virgin Islands, the export duties were an unwarrantable and ruinous check on development. Export duties had the effect of forcing industrious negroes to leave the British colonies to reside in foreign islands where there were fewer restrictions on trade.

Although the Commissioners had not been instructed to study the overall economy of the colonies, they could not completely ignore general economic considerations from their investigation. For financial reasons, they were forced to comment on two important matters, namely, the operation of the West Indies Encumbered Estates Court and immigration. With regard to the Court, the Commissioners found that it was an impediment to economic development in so far as its practice of conferring priority on a consignee's lien made landed property valueless as a security for advances of capital.

Throughout the colonies the Commissioners found a shortage of labour on the estates because the negro ex-slaves preferred alternative occupations such as peasant farming or skilled crafts to plantation agriculture. Accordingly, they were of the opinion that the immigration of a sure and reliable supply of labourers from India was necessary if industries were to be introduced and expanded, and if increased revenue and prosperity were to be achieved. The Commission favoured the recruitment of immigrants on a regional basis in order to avoid unnecessary duplication of costs.

Beyond recommending the political union of the Leeward and Windward Islands, the Commissioners gave little consideration to political reform; they agreed that West Indians might be entrusted with more responsibility in the administration of local affairs, but only for Jamaica did they suggest partial elected representation and that only for local government in the parishes. They were convinced that 'as the employers and employed will be generally speaking of different races, the Imperial Government will continue to have an ultimate responsibility in the administration of these islands and must consequently retain an adequate proportion of direct power in the administration.'

The report of the Commission was not particularly noted for the success with which its recommendations were accepted and implemented. It did not result in any marked change in British policy towards the West Indies, and Britain did not adopt any immediate measures, financial or otherwise, to alleviate their destitution. Nevertheless, it did create an awareness in the British Government of some of the problems of the colonies. The policy hitherto in operation of combining offices and reducing salaries to achieve greater economy was continued, and to it was added the policy of curtailing expenditure to suit revenues. More important than this, however, was the impact which the report had upon contemporary attitudes towards federation: following the report, public opinion was expressed strongly in favour of political union among the Eastern Caribbean colonies, and the idea of an ultimate federation of the West Indies was nurtured by such comments.

(c) *The Royal Commission of 1896–7*

The last decades of the nineteenth century witnessed a weakening of the British free trade policy, the steady encroachment of Germany and the United States on Britain's overseas markets, and an increase in enthusiasm for empire. Hence, greater interest was shown by Britain in the welfare of its West Indian colonies, and another Royal Commission was appointed in 1896 by Joseph Chamberlain, the Secretary of State for the Colonies (1895–1903), who had come to regard the British West Indies as an 'undeveloped Estate' for which Britain had done nothing for centuries. The appointment of the Commission came at a time when distress in the West Indies was particularly acute and when the colonies were struggling to overcome the legacy of emancipation, heavy reliance on monoculture, British free trade, and competition from foreign cane and beet sugars. Depression was expressed in low sugar prices in Britain and in low wages, high unemployment and a cessation of investment in the West Indies. Urgent action was necessary to prevent further deterioration.

The Commission was led by Sir Henry Norman, a former governor of Jamaica (hence it is sometimes called the Norman Commission), and included Sir David Barbour, formerly Financial Secretary of India, and

Dr. D. Morris, assistant Director of Kew Gardens, as well as Sir Edward Grey and Sydney Olivier. The Commission submitted its Report in August 1897 after it had gathered evidence throughout the British West Indies and in Britain.

The Commission recognized that bounty-fed beet sugar was the cause of West Indian distress, but it did not recommend countervailing duties from fear of breaching free-trade principles. Neither did it accept a West Indian suggestion to apply a bounty system to cane sugar since this would only reduce sugar prices and so neutralize the effects of bounties. To assist the sugar industry the Commission recommended the establishment of central factories wherever suitable especially in Barbados and Antigua, and the provision of an imperial loan for this purpose.

However, the Commission was equally interested in developing alternatives to sugar production to diversify the basic sugar economy of the colonies. To this end, it recommended greater attention to the fruit trade and the settlement of the labouring population on the land as small peasant proprietors for the production of more food in order to reduce importation. So that these objectives could be achieved, it further recommended the promotion of agricultural and industrial education through the establishment of a department of economic botany to assist the small proprietors, and the improvement of inter-island and external communications.

Other minor recommendations included a grant of £20,000 for five years to the smaller islands for general expenditure, and a further grant of £30,000 to Dominica and St. Vincent for road construction and land settlement.

Following the Commission's report, Chamberlain pressed for substantial grants to the British West Indies to provide immediate relief; in March 1898 he carried a first vote of £120,000 followed by another for £41,500 in August 1898, recognized as 'necessary expenses of Empire'. The grants given to the various colonies were first used to balance their budgets and the remainder was applied to effect the recommendations of the Commission. To correct the inadequate and slow communications in the West Indies, Chamberlain obtained a subsidy for a fortnightly steamer service to improve the fruit-carrying trade with the United States, while a joint British–Canadian subsidy financed improved steamship services between the West Indies and Canada. The most important action taken, however, was the founding of the Department of Agriculture for the West Indies in Barbados in 1898 for the diversification and promotion of West Indian agriculture. In 1899, Chamberlain secured loans of over £3 million from the British Parliament for the West Indies, and he contrived to induce his colleagues to prohibit entry of bounty-fed beet sugar into Britain.

8. Economic Diversification in the nineteenth century

The production of other economic crops besides sugar was a common feature of West Indian history in the early decades of colonization before the high profitability of sugar led to an almost exclusive concentration on its production. As sugar cane expanded, the production of other commodities contracted. Even so, comparatively smaller quantities of such products as coffee, tobacco, cotton, ginger and pimento continued to be produced for export.

Despite fluctuations in the industry after 1838, sugar nevertheless remained the mainstay of the British West Indian economy. However, the difficulties it experienced suggested the adoption of alternatives in order to promote stable and progressive societies. Diversification of the economy followed in the wake of the partial abandonment of sugar cane cultivation and the growth of an independent peasantry.

Some estates which could not produce sugar cane economically changed to the cultivation of other cash crops instead of being abandoned. As a result a certain degree of crop specialization was introduced in the various colonies relating more specifically to soil potential. Abandoned estates and other lands acquired by the peasantry were given over either to food crops or, where marketing facilities permitted, to cash crops also. In this regard, the efforts of the peasants reinforced the existing pattern of cultivation.

The alternatives to sugar cane did not require heavy capital investment for machinery and a large labour force for cultivation and processing. Moreover, they could be produced economically on small plots instead of on such large estates as were necessary for sugar cane cultivation. As such they were suited to production by the peasantry.

The banana industry became important as an export commodity in Jamaica after 1869 when Captain Lorenzo Baker, an American sea-captain, took the first shipload of bananas to the United States. His action demonstrated that the fruit could be marketed in temperate climates in good condition, but any fear of trans-oceanic spoilage was removed with the invention and utilization of refrigeration. Banana cultivation spread rapidly and by 1893 there were already 113 estates cultivating it apart from the peasantry. In 1884 exports exceeded one million stems and by 1901 exports had increased eleven times despite a decrease in price from 2/- to 1/6 a stem during the same period. Around 1885 Baker and others organized the Boston Fruit Company to handle banana shipment from Jamaica, Cuba and the Dominican Republic to the United States. Then in 1899 they joined with Minor Keith who had banana interests in Costa Rica to form the United Fruit Company which henceforth controlled the Caribbean trade.

As in the pre-emancipation period Jamaica also produced large but declining quantities of coffee to which was added smaller amounts of pimento, ginger and logwood. Owing to the high cotton prices during the American Civil War (1861-5), cotton was grown again with success in Tobago, Grenada, St. Lucia, Antigua and Nevis, but with the end of the war and the return of low-priced American cotton, production soon fell away again. Of greater permanence was cocoa which ousted sugar cane from Grenada and became an important crop in Trinidad and Dominica. Arrowroot in St. Vincent and limes in Dominica replaced sugar cane in those islands. Nutmeg was planted extensively in Grenada, and coconuts were grown in most of the colonies for copra and oilmaking.

To some extent the choice of crops was determined by the geography of the land and also by the familiarity of the peasants with their cultivation. In some of the colonies, assistance was provided by Agricultural Departments in the form of technical advice on new methods of cultivation and by the provision of seeds. The establishment of the West Indian Department of Agriculture in 1898, and the Botanic Stations set up in the individual islands in conjunction with it, was to strengthen the work in these directions.

Mineral production was not of considerable importance in the nineteenth century, though some quantities of gold and diamond were mined in Guyana. Oil was discovered in Aripero, Trinidad in 1866, and bauxite deposits were found along the Demerara River in Guyana by government geologists in 1868 and 1873, but it was not until the early twentieth century that these minerals began to be commercially produced.

9. The Economic Pattern to the 1930s

Developments during the first two decades of the twentieth century were favourable to the British West Indian sugar industry. The abolition of bounties for beet sugar production by the Brussels Convention of 1902 restored confidence in cane sugar, and thereafter world production of cane sugar increased more rapidly than beet sugar. The further adoption of central factories in place of individual estate factories, such as for example in Antigua in 1904 and St. Kitts in 1912, introduced greater economy into cane sugar production. The Imperial Department of Agriculture for the West Indies assisted with the introduction of improved varieties of sugar cane. The United States market was retained, and to this was added a larger Canadian market after preferential agreements between several British West Indian colonies and Canada had been concluded in 1912 following the report of a Royal Commission to that effect two years previously. Finally, the outbreak of the First World War in August 1914 gave an added stimulus to the expansion of cane sugar by reducing beet sugar exports from Europe. The effect of the war can be seen in the rapid increase in the price of sugar per cwt. in London from 9/6 in 1913 to 24/3 in 1916.

The sugar boom continued for a few years after the war and the West Indies received greater benefits in 1919 when Britain extended preferential treatment for empire countries amounting to a reduction to one-third of full duties in the case of sugar. At the beginning of 1920 the sugar price was as high as 63/6 per cwt. and it climbed further to a record figure of 95/9 per cwt. by early summer. British West Indian sugar producers naturally took advantage of the higher prices to increase production. According to Noel Deerr, total cane sugar production increased from 74,619 tons in 1913 to 187,921 tons in 1919 in the major sugar-producing islands of Jamaica, Barbados, Trinidad, Antigua and St. Kitts-Nevis, while output in Guyana rose from 87,414 tons in 1913 to a peak of 116,244 tons in 1915 with an annual average of 106,588 tons during the war.

The prosperity was short-lived for with the return of peace European beet sugar producers quickly regained their pre-war levels of production, and in late 1920 the sugar boom collapsed. What made the situation especially difficult for the British West Indies was the small size of the open market. Special treaties gave Puerto Rico, Hawaii and the Philippines complete remission of duties in the United States market, while Cuban sugar was admitted on preferential terms. The major threat to the security given to British West Indian sugar by preferential treatment in the British and Canadian markets arose from the surplus available for the open market from Cuba and Java. Both islands enjoyed the lowest production costs in the world and during the 1920s they increased their production by over 50 percent. Because of their preferential treatment in the United States, Cubans were able to dump their surplus elsewhere leading inevitably to a fall in sugar prices. This fall led to demands for increased protection which when granted led in turn to expanded production. Between 1923 and 1929 an unmarketed surplus of 3.5 million tons had been accumulated in the world market, and a further 1.2 million tons had been added a year later.

Despite high tariffs, the United States remained an important market for British West Indian sugar. The Canadians also signed new trade agreements in 1920 and 1925 which continued and extended the preferential treatment granted West Indian products in Canada. In order to promote the sale of goods from the Empire, Britain appointed the Empire Marketing Board in 1926 and subsidized it to the amount of £1,000,000 a year. The Board was concerned with the publicity, the collection and publication of trade statistics and market information, and scientific research. It worked vigorously but was discontinued in 1933 when the Dominions proved unwilling to assist Britain with the subsidy. Even before then Britain had established the Colonial Development Fund to finance economic development in the West Indies by grants or loans.

A West Indian Sugar Commission appointed in 1929 to enquire into the depression in the sugar industry found that the main cause was competition from protective tariffs, bounties and subsidies. It could see no prospect for 'an early restoration ... of the market prices of sugar to figures which will enable the present rate of production to be maintained without loss to unprotected or unsubsidized producers.'

The Commission's report resulted in additional preferential assistance in the form of Colonial Sugar Certificates, and preferences were thereby raised to £4. 15s. a ton. However, this was still below the advantage given by the United States and France to their sugar producers. As a result of increasing production and competing tariffs, the world sugar prices continued to fall and together with labour unrest in the British West Indies, led to the International Sugar Agreement of 1937 which introduced quotas for individual exporters of sugar, both British colonial and foreign, to Britain.

As was to be expected, the fortunes of the peasantry were closely associated with those of the estates. Following the recommendations of the Royal Commission of 1897 official attention was directed towards the problems of peasant land settlement and cultivation. Land settlement schemes were extended in Jamaica, and a start was made in St. Vincent, Trinidad, Grenada, St. Lucia and Antigua over the next 20 years. However, progress was very slow and some West Indian governments even ignored the Commission's recommendations altogether.

Part of the reason for the neglect of the peasantry lay in the expansion of sugar cane cultivation after the Brussels Convention of 1902. Idle land was to be reserved for plantation agriculture rather than for peasant farming. So little had been done to develop an independent peasantry that the Royal Commission of 1929 urged the adoption of the 1897 recommendation as an essential part of the general policy for the progressive solution of West Indian problems. In addition, it strongly recommended that the peasants should be assisted with credit facilities and in the preparation and marketing of their crops. Nevertheless, it was not until the 1940s, after the labour crisis of the previous decade and another Royal Commission recommendation, that any real attempt was made to implement the recommendations.

10. The Labour Unrest of the 1930s

During the decade of the 1930s, the British West Indies were in ferment with general labour unrest manifesting itself in most of the colonies. The events were a landmark and a turning point in the history of the area. The troubles arose mainly from inadequate provision for the social, economic and political advancement of the labouring population and can be summarised as follows:

(a) Land ownership was unfairly divided; the best land was owned by absentee proprietors and the local plantocracy and worthless land was given to the peasants.

(b) For those who continued to work on the estates, wages were low; in Barbados wages averaged 2/3 a day, in Jamaica 2/6 to 3/- a day, in St. Kitts 10d. a day and in Trinidad 5/- to 12/6 a week. Moreover, the hours of work were long, the methods of discipline were harsh, and seasonal unemployment and under-employment were common.

(c) In the 1920s and early 1930s the staple products, especially sugar, had a very unfavourable world market aggravated by the Great Depression of 1929-32 in the United States. Prices were low and this was reflected in the economic condition of those who planted cash crops. Many of these people abandoned their farms and resorted to the towns where they swelled the ranks of the unemployed and aggravated the problems of city-dwelling.

Those who remained on the land as small freeholders found it increasingly difficult to compete with the agricultural methods used on the large estates, and their cost of production was therefore higher. Peasant proprietors also found that they did not have the resources to cope with the numerous tropical plant diseases or with unfavourable weather conditions.

(d) The high West Indian birth-rate aggravated the problems of overpopulation and of unemployment and under-employment. The situation was worsened because the opportunities for emigration were removed; after 1918 the United States and Central American countries closed their doors to West Indians seeking better employment opportunities there.

(e) Social services such as education and health facilities were very inadequate. Education existed mostly at the elementary level but curricula were ill-adapted to local needs, teachers were too few and badly trained, and accommodation was inadequate. Consequently only a small fraction of the children passed on to the secondary schools which also showed the same basic weaknesses. Throughout the colonies sanitation was poor, and diseases such as hookworm, venereal diseases, yaws and malaria were prevalent. Houses were dilapidated and constituted a health hazard.

(f) The people were affected by the 'revolution of rising expectations' and aspired to a higher standard of living such as existed in more advanced countries. More sophisticated tastes were acquired through contact with resident whites or through overseas service during the First World War. Other West Indians who had worked in Cuba, the

Dominican Republic and Panama wanted the higher wages earned there when they returned home.
(g) West Indian governments under the crown colony system were markedly inefficient. They were incapable of devising measures for economic development and the improvement of social services. The colonial ruling class was still dominated by *laissez-faire* thinking whereas the welfare state philosophy was being observed in more advanced societies.
(h) The 1920s and 1930s was a period of rising West Indian nationalism with an emphasis on black consciousness. The negro 'renaissance' in the United States climaxed by the formation of the National Association for the Advancement of Coloured People was partly responsible for this. Of particular importance also were the ideas and activities of Marcus Garvey, a Jamaican who had lived in the United States but had been deported back to Jamaica in 1927. Garvey was a very persuasive speaker and a dynamic leader who gained an international reputation as President of the United Negro Improvement Association. He was a staunch advocate of social reform, but more importantly he preached pride of race and of the African past, and the rejection of white values. Another stimulus to black nationalism was the philosophy of 'negritude' given expression by the French West Indian writer Aimé Césaire, which exalted the dignity and vitality of black people. These movements increased West Indian resentment against their unjust social conditions.
(i) New West Indian leaders appeared to organize the people's protest. Many of them were educated in the metropolitan countries and could draw upon the methods developed by the world labour movement. They could count on the support of British unions, the International Labour Organization, and world opinion.

The strikes and riots which resulted from the labour unrest were sometimes inspired by workingmen's associations and trade unions wherever these existed, but more often they were spontaneous outbursts of unorganized workers. Violence first started in St. Kitts in 1934 and continued into 1935. In response to the employers' refusal to increase wages striking workers moved from one estate to another attacking owners and managers. When they refused to disband, police opened fire and killed several of them. There was no retaliation against workers in St. Lucia where coal-workers on the docks went on strike, but in St. Vincent two rioters were killed.

Depression in the 1930s led to mass meetings and demonstrations among city-workers agitating for improved working conditions in Guyana. Frequent outbursts of disorder also took place among the East Indian estate workers, and in September and October 1935, there were serious disturbances on several sugar estates. Workers staged a series of strikes, set fire to cane fields and attacked police constables. However, there were no deaths. The last wave of disorder in Guyana occurred in February 1939 on the Leonora Estate and neighbouring areas where striking workers again clashed with the police, and on this occasion four labourers were killed and several others wounded.

In 1937 riots broke out in the oilfields of Trinidad under the leadership of Uriah Butler, a fiery orator. The trouble started with a sit-down strike on the property of Trinidad Leaseholds, Ltd. – operated by South African capital and where white officials were suspected of colour prejudice. Two oilfields were set on fire, and when the authorities tried to arrest Butler violence broke out and two police officers were killed. The strike spread from the oil-fields to the sugar estates and to the towns of San Fernando and Port-of-Spain where some business places were burnt. The Royal Navy and the Royal Marines were called in after 14 persons had been killed and 59 wounded. Even after order had been restored the situation was so grave that a company of British regulars was stationed in the island for a long time.

Riots in Barbados in 1937 centred on Clement Payne, a Trinidadian and self-styled 'Minister of Propaganda' whose inflammatory speeches won him a large and excited following. When the Barbadian government deported him on the ground that he had given a false declaration regarding his place of birth, riots broke out in Bridgetown, automobiles were pushed into the sea, stores were ransacked and the police were attacked. The Riot Act was read and police volunteers killed 14 and wounded 47 of the rioters.

Labour unrest began in Jamaica also in 1937 when a demonstration of unemployed workers and ex-servicemen in Kingston was broken up by the police using batons. Then in January 1938 violence erupted at the Frome factory owned by the British firm of Tate and Lyle, and when strikers attacked the estate officials, the police opened fire killing four and wounding nine. The disorder spread to the Kingston waterfront where a general strike was called. Mobs paraded the streets attacking shops and cars, and the police again used force and eight persons were killed, 171 wounded and over 700 arrested. A leading figure in the Jamaican riots was Alexander Bustamante, a moneylender and a dynamic speaker.

The wave of riots and strikes together with the death and injury of so many people attracted world-wide attention and led to major efforts to correct the injustices and remove discontent from within the society. The following can be regarded as the most important consequences of the disturbances of the 1930s:

(a) The labour unrest led to the formation of trade unions to enable concerted action among workers to achieve higher wages and better conditions of work. Within five years after the riots, there were 58

registered trade unions with a total membership of 65,000 workers in the West Indies.
(b) There was a greater awareness of the need for political reform to allow the people greater participation in the regulation of their own affairs. It was recognized that political action was a necessary prerequisite to redress economic and social grievances.
(c) Along with the demand for a greater measure of self-government, there was greater awareness of the need for a federation of the various colonies in the British West Indies. Federation was seen as the first step towards political independence.
(d) Following the uprisings, mass political parties were founded, designed in conjunction with the trade unions, to press for political, social and economic advancement. Examples of these were the People's National Party under Norman Manley in Jamaica, and the Barbados Progressive League under Grantley Adams in Barbados.
(e) The unrest of the 1930s marked the beginning of the process which saw the progressive introduction in the British West Indies of representative government based on universal adult suffrage, of self-government, and eventually of independence for several colonies.
(f) The uprising created in Britain a new concern for social and economic improvement in the colonies. A Royal Commission headed by Lord Moyne was appointed in 1938 to investigate West Indian conditions and make recommendations for their improvement. The result was the Moyne Report of 1939 which became the blueprint for British financial and technical aid for the West Indies.

11. The Moyne Commission, 1938-9

An almost immediate response of the British Government to the labour ferment in the West Indies was the appointment of a Royal Commission in August 1938 to investigate social and economic conditions and related matters in the colonies and to make recommendations. The Commission consisted of Walter Edward, Baron Moyne, as chairman, and nine other members including Sir Walter Citrine, Secretary of the British Trade Union Congress and Professor Frank Engledow who had only recently undertaken a study of agriculture in the British West Indies.

For a period of nine months from September 1938 to June 1939, the Commission took formal evidence, oral and written, from individuals and groups including many large delegations, in Britain and the West Indies. Besides the 6,000 mile journey to and from the West Indies, the Commission covered 9,000 miles in all, and heard evidence in 26 centres from 370 witnesses. In addition, it considered 789 memoranda, many of them very lengthy, as well as about 300 other communications relating to individual grievances and other matters. Witnesses included representatives of British interests in the West Indies, members of local legislative councils, representatives of trade unions, religious and youth organizations, co-operative societies, trade and commerce, agriculture and industry, education, health, transport and other social service departments.

In addition to the formal evidence, the Commission made on the spot investigations of conditions in housing, agriculture, hospitals, schools, prisons, factories, docks, lunatic and leper asylums, orphanages and land settlements. The result was a long and comprehensive report touching on all aspects of British West Indian society. It depicted the appalling state of living conditions in every sphere of life in the colonies and presented a cruel indictment of British colonial policy.

The Commission found that the problems of the West Indies were essentially economic with severe depression in industry expressing itself in widespread unemployment in urban and rural areas, and in weak public finances which made governments unable to take remedial action to improve conditions. Consequently social services were very inadequate: education required more and better trained teachers, accommodation and equipment; improvements in health called for more sufficient food supplies, balanced and nutritious diets, and the need to prevent rather than cure diseases through better housing and sanitation.

To achieve these objectives the Commission made certain specific recommendations. A major one was the establishment of a West Indian Welfare Fund to be financed by an annual grant of £1,000,000 from the Imperial Exchequer for 20 years, and the creation of a special organization under a Comptroller to administer the Fund. The objects of the Fund would be to finance schemes for the general improvement of education, health services, housing, slum clearance, the creation of labour departments, the provision of social welfare facilities, and land settlement.

The Commissioners attached great importance to the subject of health and urged the unification of the medical services of the colonies in order to promote efficiency and to attract able professionals. It recommended a fully co-ordinated inter-colonial hospital service as well as the establishment of a School of Hygiene for research, the teaching of preventive medicine, and the training of auxiliary medical personnel. In order to formulate long-term health policies, it suggested that medical schemes should be planned in consultation with other government departments. The problem of the diet of the people was important and in dealing with it public health, agricultural and education departments must co-operate.

With regard to housing, the Commission recommended controlled siting of new houses as a general measure. In urban areas, bad slum housing should be condemned and cleared without compensation except in cases of proved and extreme hardship. In rural areas, estates should provide land, including vegetable plots, for cottages or reformed ranges to be built under approved schemes financed by government at low interest rates. Furthermore, it recommended the appointment of temporary experts in building and in types of houses, and of a permanent adviser on town planning.

The main recommendations in education were the provision of more teachers and their better training, the building of more and modern schools, improvement of school equipment, and the overhauling of school curricula to make them more relevant to the West Indies. In the schools, full use should be made of films, wireless and other modern mechanical aids to learning. It also advocated the education of girls in domestic science and the development of adult education with a strong emphasis on agricultural training.

The Commission recognized the predominance of the sugar industry despite the diversification of the economy which had taken place. To assist the industry, therefore, it recommended an increase in British preferential treatment of West Indian sugar. However, this concession was dependent upon the creation of Wages Boards in the colonies to fix wages. To improve labour conditions in other ways, the Commission recommended the promotion of trade unions through legislation protecting them from actions for damages consequent on strikes, the legalization of peaceful picketing, compulsory registration of trade unions, and the audit of their funds free of charge by governments. Until trade unions were firmly established, it further proposed that Labour Departments assisted by Advisory Boards of employers' and workers' representatives should negotiate wages and conditions of employment.

Several proposals were made for the improvement of agricultural technique based on the existing pattern of land distribution including the appointment of an Inspector-General of Agriculture for the West Indies, the holding of regional Agricultural Conferences every two or three years, and the centralization of all major research and investigation at the Imperial College of Tropical Agriculture in Trinidad. It also recommended the settlement of considerable numbers of people on the land as small-holders with assistance given to improve husbandry. Mixed farming and not specialization on export crops was to be the basis of such land settlement in order to increase food production.

Because of the primacy with which the Commission considered economic development, it did not regard constitutional reform with any sense of urgency. It did not support the granting of immediate and complete self-government based on universal suffrage, and though it advocated greater representation in the legislative councils, it did not desire any drastic change in their functions. For the gradual introduction of self-government, it suggested adequate representation for all important sections and interests of the community in the executive councils, the restriction of official representation in the legislative councils to the Colonial Secretary, the Treasurer and Attorney-General, and the appointment of elected members to committees to give them an insight into the practical details of government. The Commission did not regard political federation as an appropriate means of meeting the pressing needs of the West Indies but acknowledged that it was an end towards which policy should be directed.

By the time the Commission's Report had been finished and submitted on 21 December 1939, the Second World War had begun. While in its entirety it had to wait until the end of the War to be published, the recommendations were made public, and immediate action was taken by the British Government to implement some of them. The first Colonial Development and Welfare Act was passed in 1940 granting £5,000,000 a year for the next ten years for social and economic development in the colonies, and another £500,000 for research. Sir Frank Stockdale was appointed as the first Comptroller assisted by a staff of advisers to provide West Indian governments with technical advice. The office was located in Barbados and subsequent Acts continued it in operation until 1958 when its functions were assumed by the Federal Government. Especially in the smaller colonies, the Colonial Development and Welfare Funds constituted the greatest source of public revenue to provide for essential social services.

As part of the over-all development programme for the colonies, the British Government also promoted two other organizations – the Anglo-American Caribbean Commission in 1942 and the Colonial Development Corporation in 1948. The Caribbean Commission was to engage primarily in developing and strengthening social and economic co-operation among Caribbean territories and to conduct and encourage research. The Colonial (later Commonwealth) Development Corporation was an autonomous body organized to establish and operate businesses in individual British colonies and to provide capital in fields of development where private capital could not be attracted. To accomplish these objectives, the Corporation was partly financed by the British Government and it was authorized to borrow money up to £100 million.

12. The British West Indian Sugar Industry since the Second World War

The lack of shipping facilities after the Second World War resulted in a set-back for the British West Indian sugar industry. After the war and the restoration of normal trade relations, however, sugar and rum were again in strong demand. Agricultural prosperity was restored but only temporarily as West Indians turned to industry and tourism in their search for a higher standard of living.

The preferential system was an important feature of the export marketing of sugar, a part of which was sold under the International Sugar Agreement adopted at the United Nations Sugar Conference in London in August 1953 to regulate the export of sugar from producing countries by a system of quotas. The Agreement became effective for a period of five years beginning on 1 January 1959, but it became ineffective three years later due to the inability of members to agree on quotas.

A major prop for the British West Indian sugar industry after the Second World War was the Commonwealth Sugar Agreement which offered it a protected or at least a partially sheltered market. It commenced in 1951 initially for an eight year period to allow for long-term planning, but it continued to be re-negotiated for further eight-year terms. Under the agreement British West Indian sugar was given a fixed quota in the British market and surplus in excess of the quota could be sold in Commonwealth and other world markets. Since the negotiated price under the Agreement was higher than the world market price, the arrangement offered a reasonable profit to efficient producers and brought some stability to the British West Indian sugar industry.

British West Indian sugar producers also benefited from the political and commercial break between the United States and Cuba since 1960. Part of the sugar quota previously given to Cuban producers by the United States was transferred to other Caribbean producers. This additional quota assisted some producers to remain in business.

In addition to the more favourable market, the sugar industry was aided by improvements which lowered the cost of production. Mechanization was advanced greatly as seen in the use of tractors instead of animals for ploughing and transportation. Weed-killers largely removed the need for workers engaged in hand-cleaning canes. Central factories replaced inefficient individual estate mills, while the application of fertilizers and improved varieties of sugar cane increased yields.

The sugar industry is still very important in the economy of several territories such as Guyana, Trinidad, Barbados and Jamaica. It employs large numbers of people, contributes greatly to government revenue and provides a substantial part of exports. Besides, it supports indirectly a large number of peasant farmers who cultivate sugar cane as a cash crop and sell it to nearby factories.

Despite the benefits accruing from sugar cane production, however, the industry has suffered severely within the last twenty years. In fact, sugar cane cultivation was abandoned in St. Vincent in 1962 and in St. Lucia two years later. During the decade 1956–65, total sugar production in Antigua, Grenada and St. Kitts-Nevis-Anguilla fell from 70,518 to 54,400 tons. By 1965 sugar produced in Grenada was restricted to local consumption, while Montserrat with only about 1,000 acres of sugar cane under cultivation, was using the product to make rum and syrup. Sugar cane cultivation is now being phased out in St. Kitts and Antigua and the future of the industry in Trinidad and Jamaica is uncertain.

Because it was likely to increase unemployment, mechanization in the sugar industry has not been pushed very far. Accordingly, the British West Indies are high-cost producers with little ability to compete against other sugar-producing countries. It is questionable whether lands under sugar cane are economically used or whether they can be better utilized otherwise. Besides, the entry of Britain into the European Economic Community has posed a serious threat to the future existence of the sugar industry in the British West Indies.

13. Economic Diversification in the twentieth century

Sugar production continued to be important in the overall economy of the British West Indies in the twentieth century, but since the 1930s there have been continuing attempts to find suitable alternatives to it. Diversification followed the trend begun in the nineteenth century in agriculture, but to this was added developments in forestry, mining, livestock rearing, small-scale manufacturing and tourism.

Agriculture was assisted by the work of the West Indian Department of Agriculture in Barbados and the Botanical Stations established in the several colonies in association with it. The Department and Stations worked to develop alternative crops to sugar cane suited to peasant agriculture, but they also sought to breed new strains of sugar cane to increase yields under West Indian climatic and soil conditions. In addition, they assisted farmers by introducing improved techniques of cultivation, the distribution of seeds at reasonable rates, and in the fight against plant diseases. In 1922, the Department of Agriculture was succeeded by the Imperial College of Tropical Agriculture in Trinidad.

With imperial and local government assistance, the cultivation of crops introduced during the second half of the nineteenth century was expanded. Lime cultivation spread from Dominica to St. Lucia, bananas from Jamaica to the Windward Islands, and cocoa from Trinidad and Grenada to Jamaica, St. Lucia and Dominica though to a less extent. Arrowroot production expanded in St. Vincent and bananas in Jamaica. In addition, the cultivation of cotton was reintroduced in several colonies during the first decade of the twentieth century.

Special mention should be made of rice which has been produced in large quantities in Guyana and to a less extent in Trinidad and Jamaica by East Indian peasant proprietors. Though at first grown only for domestic consumption locally in Guyana, it was soon produced in sufficient quantities to support an export market. In time, rice production became the second largest agricultural industry in Guyana where it obtained limited government assistance in mills and equipment.

Many of the British West Indian islands were once covered with dense tropical forests and these were used for construction purposes or were destroyed to make way for plantation agriculture. Twentieth-century efforts were mainly in the direction of reafforestation in order to assist in soil and water conservation. However, in the mainland territories of Guyana and Belize huge forests still exist, and though a wide variety of timbers is found in each, the greenheart of Guyana and mahogany of Belize are world famous. For some time, mainly to satisfy war-time demands, Trinidad and Guyana experimented with rubber production, but this ceased in the face of competition from East Asian countries.

In the smaller islands there has been virtually no mining activity besides stone quarrying, natural gas in Barbados, and salt-production in St. Kitts, Anguilla and the British Virgin Islands. Only in Trinidad, Guyana and Jamaica has mining been of importance. The mining of asphalt began in Trinidad in the nineteenth century, and though oil had been discovered as early as 1866, serious prospecting did not begin until 1905, and exportation did not start until 1912, two years after the Trinidad Oilfield Company Ltd. came into operation.

The bauxite industry became important in Guyana and Jamaica. Production began on the Demerara River in Guyana in 1916 when George Mackenzie, an American, organized the Demerara Bauxite Company which later became a subsidiary of the Aluminium Company of Canada. Bauxite was later discovered at Kwakwani on the Berbice River and production was undertaken by the American firm of Reynolds Company Ltd. In Jamaica, bauxite was discovered during the Second World War and mining began in 1952; three companies, one Canadian and two American, became involved in the operations.

Manganese was mined in the North West District in Guyana during the 1960s, but deposits soon petered out and the mining company ceased operations.

After the disturbances of the 1930s and more particularly after the Second World War, a large number of light industries catering to the local consumer were established in the British West Indies, especially in the larger and more populated territories. They were assisted by tax holidays, incentive legislation and import restrictions to encourage local production. A wide variety of manufactured goods were produced including cigarettes, soap, lard, matches, margarine, biscuits, bay-rum, ham and bacon, edible oil, aerated beverages, confectionery, beer and garments. Mention should be made also of printing and boat-building, the latter being of particular importance in Guyana because of the availability of timber though metal ships have also been built for local use and for export.

The waters of the Caribbean Sea, especially the area fed by the Orinoco and Amazon rivers, maintain a lively fishing industry for local consumption. The West Indies have yet to develop a fish canning industry, despite the employment in deep-sea fishing of modern motored trawlers with refrigeration facilities. Similarly, meat canning has not developed despite attempts to do so. The rearing of pigs, poultry and cattle has been undertaken at the peasant level, but in Guyana and to a less extent in Jamaica and Trinidad, where grasslands are more extensive, the cattle industry has assumed larger proportions.

The combined effect of all these industries has been to provide employment for a large number of West Indians, and more importantly, to make the region more self-sufficient by limiting importation from overseas. With reference to mining, Professor George Cumper has stated: 'The importance of these industries lies not only in the part they played in increasing and stabilising the overseas earnings of the economy, but also in their influence as pace-setters for other industries in the payment of higher wages, the improvement of training methods and the spread of mechanisation.' Small-scale manufacturing provided the means whereby local profits could be reinvested, local entrepreneurs could be trained, and the conditions for cumulative economic growth could be developed.

Tourism became a factor in West Indian economic development mainly after the Second World War with the growing affluence of North America and Europe since then. In addition, the British islands have benefited considerably from the political break between the United States and Cuba following Castro's revolution in 1959. The particular attraction of the West Indies for tourists has been their warm, sunny climate and fine beaches suited for the relaxation of a leisured class of moneyed people. Tourism has contributed considerably to the economic development of islands like Jamaica, Barbados and Antigua, and the other islands have become increasingly favourable towards it. Tourism has served to boost construction, transportation and the catering services, and by increasing cash incomes has contributed greatly to the economic well-being of large numbers of West Indians.

By the 1960s the role of agriculture in the economy of the British West Indies had been considerably reduced. It comprised an estimated 44.6 percent of the economy of the Windward Islands, and 42.4 percent of the Leewards, but only 18.5 percent in Trinidad and 20.1 percent in Jamaica. These percentages are likely to fall as more and more West Indians abandon agriculture for other occupations in their quest for higher standards of living.

Conclusion

Economic evolution during the post-emancipation period resulted in the rise of industrial production and tourism. West Indian economies, however, still rest heavily on agriculture, both plantation and peasant, for domestic consumption and the export market. Because of the low standard of living and high unemployment associated with agriculture it is unpopular among West Indians as is evident from the drift of labourers into more lucrative employment mainly associated with industry and tourism.

Apart from its greater attractiveness as a higher-income producer, industry is important for a number of other reasons. As with agriculture, it reduces reliance on foreign imports and so creates a better balance-of-payments situation in international trade. It contributes to local self-reliance and self-sufficiency and creates a greater measure of economic independence to match and reinforce the political self-government and independence of West Indian territories.

However, industry suffers from a number of problems which restrict production. It suffers from an insufficiency of trained personnel, and the trained people available have a tendency to emigrate. It finds it difficult to compete against more technologically advanced European and North American countries which can produce better quality goods at lower cost. The absence of certain basic minerals such as copper and iron limits the kind of goods that can be produced. In addition, there is a lack of cheap power; the production of hydro-electricity is practically impossible except in Guyana and there the cost is prohibitive. Capital for the introduction and expansion of industry is not easily available; as William Demas has pointed out: 'The local managers of the economy have no control over the monetary situation,' since the commercial banks are all foreign controlled.

Industrial development does not necessarily mean lower unemployment which is one of the primary objectives of Caribbean economic planning. Because of the high birth-rate and heavy unemployment, the emphasis would seem to be on labour-intensive instead of capital-intensive economic enterprise in the foreseeable future.

Revision Questions

1. What problems faced the British West Indian sugar industry between emancipation and 1930, and what measures were adopted to overcome them?
2. Why was the Sugar Duties Act passed in 1846, and what effect did it have upon the British West Indies during the following thirty years?
3. Describe the economic condition of the British West Indies at the beginning of the twentieth century.
4. How would you account for the fact that at the end of the nineteenth century the West Indies faced the prospect of financial ruin? What measures were adopted before 1939 to avert disaster?
5. Account for the strikes and riots in the West Indies in the 1930s. Describe them briefly and give their most important results.
6. What new crops and industries were developed to take the place of sugar in the West Indies since 1870?
7. What actions have the British Government taken to assist the economic development of the West Indies since emancipation?
8. What are the economic problems facing the West Indies today?

2. Immigration and Emigration

Wherever possible after emancipation the ex-slaves left the estates to seek alternative employment. Opportunities were naturally better in the larger colonies where there was more idle land for occupation and cultivation than in the smaller colonies. Planters tried by various means including coercion and co-operation to get them to remain, but in the face of declining economic conditions their attempts were not very successful. To fill the void in the labour situation thereby created they had to resort to the immigration of labourers.

In anticipation of a shortage of labour, planters had turned to immigration even before emancipation in 1838, and thereafter efforts became more determined as the shortage became more acute. With the assistance of the local legislature and the British Government, several sources were tapped to secure the required number of labourers. From the smaller over-populated West Indian islands with an abundance of surplus labour, planters turned to Europe, Madeira, Africa and China. Labourers obtained from these sources, however, proved incapable of or disinclined towards estate labour, and their immigration did not last long. Immigration from India was more important; the suitability of Indians for estate work made them clear favourites, and their recruitment continued until 1917 when it was brought to an end.

Immigration represented one movement of people in the British West Indies; emigration was another. The two movements were closely inter-related: emigration gave rise to immigration, and immigration in turn prompted further emigration. In their search for better employment opportunities, ex-slaves left the British colonies for foreign parts. The first phase, lasting until about the First World War, however, was more or less confined to the Caribbean area. Thereafter, West Indians became more attracted towards the metropolitan countries, mainly the United States and Britain.

1. Conditions giving rise to Immigration in the British West Indies

Even before full emancipation in 1838 employers anticipated a decrease in their labour force, and there was general agreement that alternative sources had to be found if economic disaster was to be averted.

The overriding consideration behind the immigration of labourers into the British West Indies after 1838 was the continuous exodus of ex-slaves from the estates thereby creating a scarcity of regular labour. A solution had to be found if cultivation was to continue and production be maintained. Immigration was seen as the answer to the problem of labour shortage.

Not only were a sufficient number of labourers required to replace the ex-slaves who left the estates, but such replacements had to be capable of performing the work they did. Also, there had to be some assurance that such labour would be cheap and that supplies would be reliable. Moreover, immigrant labourers had to be amenable to regulation and control. Before embarking on their immigration schemes, employers were satisfied that their expectations would materialize.

With the legal abolition of slavery, labourers brought into the British West Indies would assume the status of indentured immigrants to labour under contract for a fixed period of time. It was hoped that at the end of the period of indenture, the immigrants would settle in the respective colonies to which they were assigned, raise families, and so provide a permanent reservoir from which labour could be obtained whenever desired.

Planter expectation was that the existence of an alternative labour supply to the ex-slaves would generate competition for the work available and so help to keep down wages. With wages reduced, planters would then be better able to compete with foreign cane and beet sugar. Besides, the existence of a labour force larger than was necessary would enable employers to dictate the terms of employment.

The cost of immigration was high if expenses for the upkeep of recruiting agencies, transportation, wages and return passages are considered. But as Professor Douglas Hall has pointed out, immigration 'allowed the planters an advantage in a sort of dual labour–cost system.' In the long run by balancing cost and output, it would be more economical to employ immigrants than the resident ex-slaves.

Immigration was a risk which the planters were willing to take with regard to such matters as the suitability of the immigrants to perform the expected labour, the reception which would be extended to the immigrants by the resident ex-slave population, the conditions of the export market, etc. As time passed, confidence in immigration grew even when conditions did not warrant its continuation.

Initially some opposition towards immigration developed on the part of the British Government from fear of a possible revival of slavery. However, in an age of *laissez-faire* and free trade when the British Government itself was already deeply involved in large-scale organized emigration of Britons to such places as Australia and New Zealand, such opposition could not be maintained for long.

Like the British Government, the abolitionist forces that had helped to bring about the end of slavery were somewhat skeptical about immigration; nevertheless they accepted the argument of the planters that immigration was essential for the 'moral improvement' of the ex-slaves, though they kept a watchful eye on the operation of the system.

The willingness of foreign peoples to come and labour in the West Indies stemmed basically from the attractions of the labour situation here. Immigrants were dominated by their anticipation of gain and by their desire to escape from the adverse social and economic conditions of their native lands.

2. Immigration of Europeans, West Indians and Africans

A declining white population and apprehension about the effects of freedom on the labour supply led some planters to seek labourers in Europe. It was believed that Europeans would not only make industrious workers and so set an example to the ex-slaves, but also that they would eventually develop into a middle-class and help to stabilize the society.

Portuguese coming from the Azores to Trinidad in 1834 under three to five year contracts may be regarded as the first European indentured labourers to the post-emancipation West Indies. However, the following year recruiting agents operating under a government bounty were sent to Europe from Jamaica, and that island became the largest recipient of European immigrants. Between 1835 and 1845 a total of 4,087 Europeans went to Jamaica, including 2,698 from Britain and 1,038 from Germany. During the same period 381 Europeans went to Guyana, and between 1839 and 1846 several hundred British, French and German immigrants went to Trinidad.

Meanwhile, a few hundred Portuguese from Madeira had entered Trinidad and Guyana in 1835 before the Madeiran authorities prohibited the traffic the next year. With the assistance of a bounty in 1841, the immigration of Madeiran Portuguese was revived and within one year 4,312 had entered Guyana. They suffered so severely from yellow fever and malaria, and from overwork and inadequate food, that the bounty was withdrawn, and recruitment ceased in 1842.

Four years later famine in Madeira led to the renewal of Portuguese immigration and fairly large numbers were brought to Guyana and Trinidad and smaller numbers to Grenada, St. Vincent, Dominica, St. Kitts, Nevis, Antigua and Jamaica. When the famine ended in Madeira in 1847, the rate slackened considerably and immigration was confined mainly to Guyana, St. Kitts and Antigua. Between 1835 and 1881, a total of 40,971 Madeiran Portuguese entered the West Indies with the largest number of 32,216 going to Guyana.

By and large, the Europeans proved to be unsatisfactory labourers. Many of those who went to Jamaica were accustomed to a sea-faring life and found agricultural labour uncongenial. In all the colonies, employers failed to provide adequate food, shelter and medical facilities to overcome the difficult initial period of acclimatization. Immigrants fell prey to the hot climate combined (in Jamaica) with excessive rum-drinking, while the survivors, unwilling to do work previously done by slaves, drifted into the towns, emigrated to the United States, or returned to their native countries.

The Portuguese proved slightly better; those who survived malnutrition performed well enough in the fields. However, they showed their dislike for field work by moving off the estates after their contract had expired and setting themselves up as petty-shopkeepers. They quickly became successful in the retail trade.

In addition to Europeans, planters in Guyana, Trinidad and, to a lesser extent, Jamaica where the labour problem was most severe, successfully sought to attract labourers from the other more densely populated British Windward and Leeward Islands. Immigrants were influenced by geographical factors such as the contiguity and ease of travel among the colonies as well as by economic considerations. Agents despatched to the smaller islands used specious promises of little work and high wages to recruit large numbers of labourers.

Colonies losing labourers sought to limit their movement as much as possible through restrictive legislation, but such measures were discouraged by the British Government as being contrary to the principle of freedom of movement. However, the British Government moved to prevent any abuse of the system, and in 1838 two Orders-in-Council were issued invalidating all contracts made outside the colony in which the work was to be done and limiting all contracts to one year.

These regulations did not have any serious results for inter-colonial migration. By 1837 the intra-West Indian traffic had already assumed significant proportions; from year-end 1839 to year-end 1849, 10,278 West Indians were said to have emigrated to Trinidad, 7,582 to Guyana and 790 to Jamaica. Barbados was the chief loser with considerable numbers of labourers going to Trinidad and Guyana, but large numbers of Grenadians went to Trinidad also.

Generally speaking, West Indian immigrants did not live up to planter expectation; many of them became disillusioned when they did not get the high wages promised them, and they soon joined the ranks of those resident labourers leaving the estates to establish a more independent existence as urban artisans or rural peasants.

In addition to British West Indians, a number of negroes from the United States, driven by racial discrimination and depressed economic conditions there, emigrated to Trinidad. The first group of 216 arrived at Port-of-Spain in November 1839, their passage having been paid by the government of Trinidad. Thereafter, there were periodic arrivals, and by June 1847, 1,307 had come in from Delaware, Maryland, New Jersey, Pennsylvania and New York. Most of them were craftsmen and mechanics who did not envisage a future for themselves in the cane-fields. Besides, from past experience, they had become wary of white people. By 1848, only 148 could be found still working on the estates; most of the others had returned to the United States. Immigration from the United States faded out of existence, and a further recruitment drive in 1851 produced only five men and their families.

The British Government was understandably very reluctant to approve plans to recruit labourers from Africa since it was held that this must inevitably revive the slave trade. However, under pressure from colonial planters and governors, approval was granted in December 1840 to a colonial bounty on immigration from Sierra Leone. The first batch of immigrants to Guyana, Trinidad and Jamaica arrived in 1841 in merchant ships chartered by private individuals, but two years later the British Government assumed direct control. The cost, however, was borne by the colonies.

Emigration from Sierra Leone was opposed by European timber merchants there who were fearful of losing their best labourers, and by the Christian missionaries who did not want to lose prospective converts and evangelists. Besides, Africans showed little interest in emigration despite the considerable effort to induce them by offers of high wages and free return passages. The stimuli for emigration were absent here as they were in Gambia and on the Kru Coast where recruitment was pursued in 1843 and 1847 respectively. Kru men who came to the West Indies were mostly recruited in Sierra Leone.

A few hundred labourers were recruited in Liberia, but the greatest number of Africans were obtained from seizures made from foreign slave ships captured by British naval patrols in the Atlantic. Africans liberated in the western Atlantic were landed directly in the British West Indies; others intercepted off the African coast were condemned to the British by the International Courts of Mixed Commission at

Sierra Leone and at St. Helena, and later transferred to the West Indies. By 1867 Trinidad had received 8,854 liberated Africans, Guyana 14,060, and Jamaica 11,391, while 5,027 others had been distributed among Grenada, St. Vincent, St. Lucia, Dominica and St. Kitts.

The assimilation of liberated Africans into West Indian society proved difficult, moreso, since they were from various tribes. Besides, their numbers were too small to create any appreciable impact upon the labour situation, and, in any case, like the West Indians, they abandoned plantation labour for other work.

3. Chinese and East Indian Immigration

Chinese labour had been used in Cuba from the early nineteenth century, and Chinese immigration was suggested for the British West Indies as early as 1843. However, for the next decade nothing was accomplished because the Chinese would not come without contract and under the Order-in-Council of 1838 contracts could be made only in the colonies. Moreover, attention was diverted after 1844 towards immigration from India.

It was not until 1853 that Chinese immigration to the British West Indies started, and during the following year Trinidad received 988, Guyana 647, and Jamaica one shipload from the Chinese ports of Namoa and Whampoa. However, the recruitment and transportation of Chinese immigrants was expensive and the mortality high, and in 1854 the project was abandoned.

Immigration from China did not resume until 1858 when two ships with 761 Chinese were sent to Guyana. With the British occupation of Canton the following year, the trade could be better organized. From that port and from Hong Kong, 11,282 Chinese were imported into Guyana, and 1,557 into Trinidad by 1866.

Chinese immigration into the British West Indies fell off sharply after 1866 due in part to the difficulties of recruitment, the high cost of transportation, and French and Spanish competition for Chinese labour. In addition, those Chinese desirous of emigration to do agricultural work could find it nearer home in Java and the Philippines. The Chinese government also became opposed to it on learning of the brutal treatment of Chinese in Cuba and the excesses committed against them on the high seas. Of considerable importance too was the fact that British West Indian employers had found a more worthwhile alternative to the Chinese in East Indian labourers. In all a total of 17,430 Chinese came to the British West Indies between 1853 and 1884 – 13,533 to Guyana, 2,645 to Trinidad, 1,152 to Jamaica, and 100 to Antigua.

Compared with the East Indians, the Chinese proved to be unsatisfactory labourers even though they were hardworking. Many of them had little or no experience with and were not physically capable of agricultural labour particularly of the West Indian plantation type. Moreover, their expectations in terms of wages and working conditions exceeded reality. It is not surprising, therefore, that they turned to more amenable occupations such as shop-keeping, huckstering and market-gardening when their initial period of indenture ended.

Compared with the Chinese, East Indian immigration to the West Indies was more regular, more prolonged and larger. Indian immigration was begun on the initiative of John Gladstone, father of the later famous British Prime Minister William Ewart Gladstone, who held plantations in Demerara, and the first trial has been appropriately called 'the Gladstone experiment.'

The first group of 396 Indian immigrants arrived in Guyana in May 1838 on board the ships *Whitby* and *Hesperus*. They were distributed among six sugar estates to labour under contract for five years, and though their treatment was satisfactory on three of the estates, on the others belonging to Andrew Colville (Belle Vue) and John Gladstone (Vreed-en-Hoop and Vreed-estein), there was illtreatment, sickness and mortality. The suspicions of the Anti-Slavery Society were immediately aroused, and through a propaganda campaign it secured the appointment of a local Commission to investigate immigrant conditions. The upshot of the enquiry was the suspension of immigration from India for an indefinite period. Indians who survived their indenture were returned to India in 1843.

Regular Indian immigration was reopened in 1844 under government control, and in the following year two shiploads reached Guyana while one shipload each went to Trinidad and Jamaica. The performance of these labourers exceeded expectations, and in 1846 Jamaica requested an additional 5,000, Trinidad 4,000, and Guyana 10,000. However, due to the depression in the sugar industry caused by the Sugar Duties Act of 1846 and the commercial and financial crises of 1847-8, orders had to be cancelled for financial reasons.

The depression served to convince the British Government of the need to assist West Indian planters, and among other actions taken, it guaranteed a loan of £500,000 to be shared by Jamaica, Barbados, Trinidad and Guyana. With the assistance of this loan, large-scale Indian immigration was resumed in 1851, mainly to Trinidad and Guyana. Within the next decade other colonies began to import limited numbers – Grenada in 1856, St. Lucia in 1858 and St. Vincent in 1861.

Requests for Indian indentured labour for the Windward Islands were made irregularly until they finally ceased in the 1880s. Meanwhile, immigration into Jamaica was resumed in 1860; three years later it was suspended and again started in 1867. Subsequent importations were also irregular and comparatively small ranging from a few hundred to 2,135 a year. Only in Guyana and Trinidad was Indian immigration heavy and continuous.

Indian immigration to the British West Indies ceased in 1917 and until that time a total of 429,623 immigrants had entered – 238,909 in Guyana, 143,939 in Trinidad, 36,412 in Jamaica, 4,354 in St. Lucia, 3,200 in Grenada, 2,472 in St. Vincent, and 337 in St. Kitts.

Except for a brief period in the 1850s Indian immigrants were always promised a free return passage to India after a period of 5 or 10 years until 1895. In that year they were required to assist towards the cost at the rate of 25 percent for men and $16\frac{2}{3}$ percent for women, and this rate was doubled three years later. From the late 1870s, many Indians, generally the most energetic and industrious, were prepared to commute their return passage for land or cash with which they later purchased or rented lands. Those who decided to reside permanently in the West Indies numbered 163,362 in Guyana, 110,645 in Trinidad, 24,532 in Jamaica, and 6,252 in the Windward Islands.

Many of the Indians who remained in the West Indies continued to reside on and to work for the estates. A much smaller number set themselves up as peasant proprietors and, while working part-time on the estates, cultivated their lands in sugar cane, rice, ground provisions and fruits for their own consumption and for sale. These Indians were able to achieve a greater economic standing and social mobility than those who remained on the estates.

Indians proved to be the right kind of labourers for the sugar estates and it was mainly due to them that the sugar industry achieved the measure of success it did. The suitability of Indians, and moreover their availability in large numbers, removed the need for planters to seek European, West Indian, African and Chinese labourers.

4. Reasons why Indians Emigrated

(a) Emigration was closely related to crop yields and food prices in India: when food was plentiful and cheap, emigration was low; alternately, when adverse weather conditions caused distress as in 1860–1, 1868–9 and 1874 emigration was heavier.

(b) The establishment of the British factory system in India destroyed Indian domestic industries such as the home spinning of cloth, and created a mobile population subject to emigration.

(c) An increase in the Indian population dependent on the land for their livelihood was accompanied by the division of plots until these reached uneconomic levels. Indebtedness grew and cultivators lost their land. Emigration to the West Indies promised to put them in possession of land once more.

(d) Displaced workers in cottage industries and agriculture, and labourers experiencing seasonal unemployment were forced to wander in search of work; when jobs could not be obtained, they were ready to listen to the recruiters' propaganda.

(e) The promise of higher wages in the West Indies than could be obtained in India together with the possibilities of greater savings and better living was a powerful argument to leave India. In the 1850s agricultural labourers in India were paid in grain or between 1½d and 2½d a day; in Trinidad they could receive as much as 2/- and in Guyana about 1/8 a day.

(f) Some people found joint family and village community life intolerable; adventurers, village outcasts and those who had quarrelled with relatives were among those recruited.

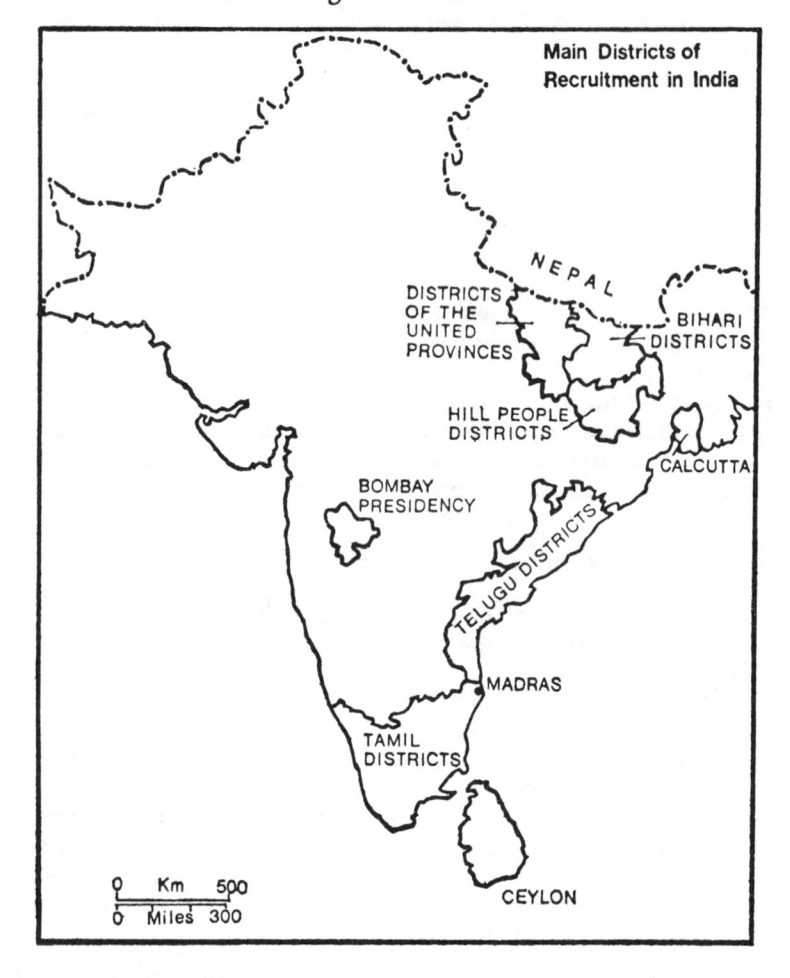

Main Districts of Recruitment in India

(g) Criminals escaping from the police and afraid to return to their villages, as well as loafers and vagrants also formed a part, though small, of the body of emigrants.
(h) Some Indians were led to emigrate in the belief that they would find opportunities for non-agricultural work such as being policemen, teachers, priests and clerks.
(i) Contacts with returning relatives and friends or because they were impressed with the money brought back or remitted by those who had emigrated led some Indians to emigrate. A few accompanied friends who were emigrating, but the great majority went alone.
(j) After emigration had been established wives accompanied their husbands, but some women who had already adopted independent lives such as widows, or women who had been deserted or were escaping from bad husbands or tyrannical mothers-in-law were willing to leave for the West Indies. Besides, emigration must have seemed an honourable alternative and promise of a fresh start to those who had fallen from social virtues.

5. Recruitment and Trans-Oceanic Transportation of Indian Immigrants

Indians recruited for the West Indies came from densely populated areas where the rate of unemployment was high, mainly in Bengal, Bihar, the United Provinces and, to a much less extent, the Madras Presidency. Experience showed that while the northern Indians gave satisfactory service, the Madrasis were less efficient and of more independent disposition.

Appointed at each port of departure – Calcutta and Madras – was an Emigration Agent for all the colonies who maintained a depot there and was chiefly responsible for recruitment. On receiving requisitions from the colonies he would contract with licensed sub-agents up-country for the supply of recruits. The system was highly commercialized, and sometimes unscrupulous and improper methods of recruitment were adopted such as intimidation and misrepresentation of West Indian conditions, especially when conditions were unfavourable.

When a sub-agent or his unlicensed assistant found a prospective emigrant, he would take him to a sub-depot where he would be fed, clothed and, if necessary, persuaded to emigrate. Then he would be medically examined and taken before the registering officer, usually a magistrate appointed under Indian Emigration Acts, to ascertain that he understood the terms offered and was willing to emigrate. Since many recruits were often too frightened or ignorant to exercise independent judgement such examinations were usually routine.

After registration the recruits were taken by train to Calcutta or Madras; some would desert on the way, but the rest would be taken to the depot where they lived until a sufficient number was collected to fill a ship. At the depot they were again medically examined, questioned by the Protector of Emigrants, an official appointed by the governments of Bengal and Madras, concerning their willingness to emigrate, and finally embarked on board ship for the West Indies.

The number of recruits registered was always much greater than the number of actual emigrants, since apart from deserters, others were rejected as unfit or else discharged at their own request. Recruits were accepted generally because of their potential for agriculture and between the preferred ages of 16 and 25 years; but when the demand was high and the supply limited due to competition for labour in India, less likely candidates were recruited. One study showed that 13.6 percent belonged to the higher castes, 30.1 percent came from agricultural castes, 8.7 percent from artisan castes, and 31.1 percent from menial castes though these also were probably agricultural workers. Of the total, 83.6 percent were Hindus and 16.3 percent Muslims.

The need to have a relatively large number of women was recognized from a moral viewpoint; the proportion was legally fixed and ranged from 25 to 40 women for every 100 men. However, it was often difficult to obtain the required number since women were less inclined to emigrate than men, and men were known to have been refused because enough women could not be obtained.

Emigrant ships from Calcutta and Madras crossed the Indian Ocean, rounded the Cape of Good Hope after stopping at Cape Town for supplies, thence across the Atlantic Ocean in a northwesterly direction bound for Guyana, Trinidad, Jamaica and the other British West Indian islands. For sailing ships the journey was long, lasting from three to four months depending on weather conditions, but steam ships used intermittently in the nineteenth century and more regularly in the twentieth century, took less time. Cargoes were large and increased with the size of the immigrant vessels as emigration continued. Space was limited and congestion common, but greater discomfort was experienced from the monotonous conditions of life on board.

Emigrants were not confined to any part of the ship, but male and female quarters were kept separate in order to maintain discipline. The entire batch was divided into groups each under the control of Indian supervisors who were responsible for their good conduct and well-being. Meals were served twice a day, emigrants were allowed a bath each day, and music and singing were allowed.

Despite the presence of a surgeon on board ship the death rate was high, that on Calcutta ships between 1860 and 1868, for example, being calculated at 5.45 percent. After conditions were improved during the

1870s, the rate dropped to less than 3 percent. Mortality was due to diseases such as cholera, dysentery and diarrhoea compounded by such factors as impure water, poor ventilation and insanitary conditions. Many of the emigrants were in a bad physical state prior to departure and the deficient diet on board led to greater debility.

Upon arrival at the West Indian port of destination, the Indians were put under the supervision of the Protector of Immigrants (sometimes called the Agent-General of Immigration) who informed them of the terms of indenture. Except those who were sick and had to be hospitalized, the immigrants were kept in the depot until they were distributed by the Protector among those who had made application for them. The vast majority were 'bound' to specified estates to perform manual labour while a few were assigned to domestic and other types of service. Husbands and wives and their young children were indentured to the same estate to prevent the break-up of families.

Employers receiving immigrants had to sign the indenture certificate before the proper authority and to give a written guarantee that the estate would provide regular medical services and housing. On their arrival at the estates the Indians were immediately put to work or allowed a period of familiarization, depending on the demand for their services.

6. Working and Living Conditions of Immigrants

Except for Sundays and certain public holidays such as at Christmas and Easter time, the immigrants were required to labour on the estates at certain specified tasks. Field work employed the largest number with men performing the more strenuous tasks of digging, planting, reaping and transporting, while women and children did the weeding and manuring.

Wages were naturally higher for able-bodied men than for women and children, and variations existed among the various colonies. The highest wages were offered in Trinidad and Guyana. In the former, wages in the 1840s were about 2/1 a day, sometimes more, but they fell thereafter. A similar pattern developed in Guyana where wages ranged between 1/4 and 2/- in the 1840s. In the 1870s Guyana and Trinidad fixed a legal minimum wage of 1/0½ a task, that is, the estimated amount of work which an able-bodied workman could do in a day, and this remained constant until the end of indenture. However, while a few workers could earn from 1/3 to 1/8 a day, the majority earned below the minimum wage. The situation worsened because of the tendency of planters to increase the size of the task. In 1895-6 it was shown that a significant proportion of the indentured immigrants in Trinidad were earning less than 6d a day.

Harsh as the system was it seems that the most enterprising Indians found time, in addition to their work commitments on the estates, to engage in some form of business or trade, small-scale agriculture, or livestock-rearing, and so were able to earn additional money.

The low wages earned by the immigrants produced a number of unfortunate results probably the most serious being the low quality of their diet which helped to undermine their health. In a mutual cause-effect relationship, this in turn reduced their capacity to work. Employers successfully sought to reduce the high rate of sickness and mortality by issuing food to new arrivals for a period of time varying among the various colonies from a few months to a couple of years. Since the cost of such rations was deducted from the immigrants' wages, the system was unpopular among them.

In addition, free medical treatment was given to the immigrants by the estate authorities, and in keeping with colonial government requirements, estates in Guyana, Trinidad and, for a time, Jamaica maintained estate hospitals. In the smaller colonies, and in Jamaica after 1879, immigrants were treated in the public hospitals. Not all the hospitals were models of efficiency, but they provided services which were for long denied to the general population until the medical facilities were extended to them.

Despite these services, however, the health standards of the immigrants remained very low. Especially in the later decades of immigration, diseases such as malaria and hookworm were prevalent, and the immigrants also suffered from typhoid, yellow fever and dysentery. The spread of disease was aided by the poor state of sanitation, of waste disposal, of water supply (usually creek and trench water), and of housing on the estates as well as the practice of workers going about bare-footed.

The most common dwellings of the immigrants were simple, uncomfortable, wooden, barrack-like structures called 'lodgies' or 'ranges'. They were either single ranged, or were broad enough to be divided lengthwise by a thin partition into a double range. Each range had a narrow gallery or verandah running the entire length, and it was subdivided to accommodate several individual families. Cooking and eating took place on the verandah while the main body was divided into two by a half-wall to serve as bedroom and living-room. The entire range might have a mud floor or the sleeping and living quarters might have a raised board floor. Poor ventilation, heavy overcrowding generally, and an absolute lack of privacy were the main features of such dwellings.

Indenture virtually excluded any form of individual or collective bargaining, but though employers sought to bind the immigrants as closely as possible to the estates, the labourers were not powerless. One

response of Indians to unsatisfactory working and living conditions was riots and strikes which were prevalent in Guyana and Trinidad from the 1860s, sometimes involving loss of life. In other instances, they were content merely to refuse to work, to absent themselves from work without leave, and to desert the estate in violation of other regulations requiring passes to leave the estate.

Probably the most serious indentured Indian uprising was the one which occurred on the Leonora Estate in Guyana in August 1869 which led soon after to the famous letter to Lord Granville, Secretary of State for the Colonies, from George William Des Voeux, previously a magistrate in Guyana but at that time serving as Administrator of St. Lucia. Des Voeux identified several areas of immigrant grievance including the miscarriage of justice since the magistrates were indirectly 'subject to the planting interest' and that their decisions were 'the chief cause of the prevailing discontent.' In 1870 a Commission to Enquire into the Treatment of Immigrants in British Guiana was appointed with Sir George Young as chairman, and W. E. Frere, an Indian Government civil servant, and Charles Mitchell, a former Trinidad magistrate, as members. Hearings began in Georgetown on 26 August 1870, and thereafter 46 witnesses were examined and 56 estates visited. The Commission found that Dés Voeux's general allegations could not be substantiated, but in contradiction, its report showed that indenture was subject to a variety of serious abuses: judicial bias in favour of employers leading to too long jail terms and too high fines for immigrants; high cost of proper legal counsel for immigrants and high-handed and arbitrary rule by estate management. Other evidence indicated the unsatisfactory conditions pertaining to immigrants: longer hours of work and lower wages than the legal stipulations; unjustified deductions from wages; abuse of vagrancy laws and the pass clause; deficient medical facilities and services and inadequate supervision by the government medical inspector; and the poor quality of housing and water supply.

Following the recommendations of the Commission slight modifications were made in the indenture system, but the immigrants were left bound in every important aspect, physically by the pass system, legally by contract, and economically by their inability to bargain freely for wages. After 1870, estate housing seems to have been extensively reconstructed and on some estates serious attention was given to improving the supply of drinking water, but it is doubtful if the overall material condition of labourers really improved especially in the face of falling wages.

Breach of contract was treated as a criminal offence and all too often employers took legal action against Indians in order to punish them, maintain labour discipline, and secure docility. Since an immigrant could not give evidence on his own behalf, and friends were too afraid of reprisal by their employers to do so, the result was a foregone conclusion since magistrates all too often sided with the employers. Punishment of immigrants took the form, separately or in combination, of fines, imprisonment, or an extension of the indenture period.

Immigrants also sought redress in court against their employers, but the system was expensive, complex and too weighted against them to make it popular among them. And though their unauthorized departure from the estate made them subject to charges of vagrancy, immigrants laid their grievances before the Protector of Immigrants (or Agent-General). The office of Protector had been created as early as 1838 in Guyana, and extended to other immigrant colonies later on. In addition to receiving new immigrants, examining their condition, registering them, and allotting them to various estates, the Protector was responsible for ensuring that their living and working conditions met the terms of the statutes governing indentured labour. Finally, he was expected to receive and investigate any complaints that immigrants might make concerning their treatment. Dr. Charles Mitchell of Trinidad and James Crosby of Guyana were noted for their dedication to the immigrants' welfare. It was said of Mitchell that 'he never lost an opportunity when he saw it of turning the scale in favour of the immigrants.' The same could be said of Crosby, beloved by immigrants, so much so that his successors in office were referred to as 'Crosbys'. However, his efforts to assist the immigrants were successfully frustrated during the governorship of Sir Francis Hincks who in effect assumed control of the Immigration Department.

Detailed regulations were adopted governing immigrant housing, medical treatment, sanitation and conditions of work, and though some estates sought to care for the immigrants accordingly, many others were negligent of their responsibilities. The system of government supervision was inadequate especially in the smaller islands, or on remote estates difficult of access in the larger colonies. Besides, some officials were either indolent or unmindful of the workers' interests and added to the difficulties they experienced; too many offending employers were allowed to escape punishment too often.

Indians were desired for their labour, and they were allowed to retain the essential forms of their culture – food, clothing, language and religion and to make whatever adjustments they thought necessary in their new environment. Generally, the Christian denominations left them alone until the Canadian Presbyterian Mission arrived in 1868 to begin serious evangelical work among them. Even so pride in their ancient religious heritage of Hinduism and Mohammedanism made the Indians resistant to efforts to convert them, and only a small percentage of them became Christians. However, they had a wider appreciation of western education and pursued it wherever possible. Planters themselves recognized the value of education in making the Indians adjust more readily to their new society, but higher education was discouraged on the ground that immigrants who received it would forsake plantation labour.

7. The Termination of Indian Indentured Labour

In the Windward Islands where the sugar industry was declining steadily and giving way to other economic crops, Indian immigration was discontinued in St. Vincent in 1880, in Grenada in 1885 and in St. Lucia in 1893. However, it continued elsewhere and the system itself remained in effect until 1917 when it was terminated.

Indian immigration involved a conflict of interest between those who supported it and those who opposed it, and its final termination represented a victory for the latter.

Sugar planters were the main beneficiaries of Indian indentured labour, and they naturally supported the system. They were motivated by the conviction that Indian immigrants were essential to their survival; they could not foresee the sugar industry operating on a less dependable and less obedient labour force.

The planter position was supported by the Colonial Office which had grown accustomed to doing so by the beginning of the twentieth century. The depression in the sugar industry around that time led to the view that the termination of immigration would be detrimental to the industry.

The attitude of the Colonial Office was further supported by an official Committee of Enquiry appointed in 1909 to investigate continued Indian indentured labour in response to opposition against government subsidized immigration. The Committee was led by Lord Sanderson and its members were drawn from the Colonial and Indian Offices. It came out in favour of government-aided immigration to maintain West Indian sugar production.

The Sanderson Committee rejected the view that immigration had caused unemployment or a decrease in wages except in times of crisis. These charges had been made continuously by West Indian creoles in their opposition to Indian immigration from the 1870s. In addition, the creoles complained that they were being asked to subsidize a project from which they received no direct benefit. They were afraid that continued Indian immigration would reduce their numerical preponderance in those places where it existed.

In addition to the creoles, Indian immigration was opposed by abolitionists in the Anti-Slavery Society, missionaries and other humanitarians who saw in it the reflection of slavery. The voice of humanitarianism was an ever weakening one, but in the twentieth century two British missionaries, C. F. Andrews and W. W. Pearson, spoke out strongly against the immorality of the system stemming mainly from the disproportion of the sexes.

More important and decisive than the objections of the creoles and the humanitarians was the opposition of Indian nationalists to continued Indian emigration overseas. The Indian National Congress established in 1885 to work for greater Indian self-government had as one of its objectives the prohibition of indentured emigration, and it applied constant pressure upon the Indian Government in and out of the Indian Legislative Council to bring it about. Injustice against Indians in Fiji and South Africa was the primary target, but the West Indies became involved as a recipient of Indian indentured labourers also. The most powerful argument of the Congress expressed by its leader Gopal Krishna Gokhale was that the system was 'degrading to the people of India from a national point of view.'

Because of the prevailing dislike of continued Indian emigration, great impatience was shown by the Congress Party at the Report of a Committee of Enquiry comprising of James McNeill and Chimman Lal submitted in June 1914 which presented a generally favourable picture of Indian immigrants in the West Indies.

The outbreak of the First World War interrupted the recruiting and transportation of Indian emigrants, and in 1916 the Indian Government legislated that emigration would end in five years. Shortly after, however, in March 1917, under further pressure from India, the British Government officially ended Indian indentured immigration.

8. Overall Impact of Immigration

Immigration, and in particular Indian immigration because it was large and continuous, affected the West Indies in various ways. The impact was most noticeable in Trinidad and Guyana which received the largest number of immigrants.

(a) Immigration undoubtedly helped to perpetuate the inefficient use of labour. Nevertheless, in the first two or three decades immigration halted the economic decline of the colonies and brought them substantial prosperity. Partly as a result of immigrant labour, between 1839 and 1903 sugar production increased from 17,214 to 45,000 tons in Trinidad, and from 28,343 to 100,000 tons in Guyana.

(b) The importation of immigrants stimulated the expansion of social services, especially medical facilities which were applied first to the immigrants and then extended to the population at large. Similarly, the increase in population led to the development of a larger and more efficient police force.

(c) The stimulus which immigration gave to sugar production might have militated against the diversification of the West Indian economy initially. However, immigrants swelled the ranks of shop-keepers and hucksters, while many more engaged in peasant farming on land acquired by grant or purchase. In order to avoid repatriation and immigration expenses, planters and legislatures made grants of land to Indians in commutation of return passages. Indians in Guyana received free land grants of 32,000 acres between 1891 and 1913, while in Trinidad they were sold 23,000 acres between 1885 and 1895, and a further 31,766 acres between 1902 and 1912. Some immigrants also possessed special skills such as metal and leather working which they utilized to the benefit of their adopted country.

(d) The employment of immigrants in manual field labour opened up a wider range of employment for resident negroes as artisans, factory workers and policemen.

(e) The growth of the rice industry in Guyana and Trinidad was due to the East Indians. By the 1890s rice growing in Guyana had reached significant proportions, and by 1903 an estimated 23,853 acres of rice were under cultivation for the domestic as well as for an export market.

(f) To the Indians can also be attributed the introduction into the West Indies of the age-old traditional Indian skill in irrigation, first in connection with rice-growing, but with implications for the sugar industry also.

(g) The vast majority of East Indian immigrants were tied to plantation agriculture and continued to experience the low standard of living and destitution common to the West Indian working-class generally. Nevertheless, a number of them who had divorced themselves from the estates, through industry and thrift, were able to acquire some wealth which was used to educate their children in the professions – medicine, law and teaching – and to become community leaders.

(h) The entry of the various immigrant groups into the West Indies led to the emergence of a plural society where the races mixed but did not combine. Friction, both latent and manifest, existed among the different occupational groups. For example, in February 1856 the notorious 'Angel Gabriel' Riots fomented by the apocalyptic negro preacher, James Sayers Orr, resulted in the widespread destruction of Portuguese shops in Guyana by negroes suffering from a sense of oppression and competition from Portuguese businessmen. Among the field workers also some hostility did develop as time passed since immigration had a tendency to lower wages. By and large, however, the governing class failed to develop measures to effect a harmonious integration of the races.

THE RACIAL COMPOSITION OF CERTAIN CARIBBEAN TERRITORIES AT DIFFERENT PERIODS

Country	Year	Negroes	East Indians	Whites	Chinese	Portuguese	Mixed	American Indians
Barbados	1946	148,923	—	9,839	—	—	33,828	—
	1960	207,156	ca. 500	10,083	—	—	13,993	—
	1970	215,204	675	9,354	—	158	9,305	—
Grenada	1921	51,032	2,692	905	—	—	11,673	—
	1946	53,265	3,478	635	16	—	14,769	113
	1960	46,690	3,767	699	—	—	37,393	9
Guyana	1921	117,169	124,938	3,291	2,722	9,175	30,587	18,850
	1946	143,385	163,434	2,480	3,567	8,543	37,685	16,322
	1960	190,380	279,460	5,230	3,550	7,610	66,180	22,860
	1970	227,091	377,256	4,056	4,678	9,668	84,077	32,794
Jamaica	1881	441,200	11,000	14,400	100	—	110,000	—
	1921	660,420	18,610	14,476	3,696	—	157,223	—
	1943	965,960	26,507	13,809	12,394	—	216,384	—
	1960	1,236,706	27,912	12,428	10,267	—	271,520	—
Leeward Islands	1921	69,038	—	2,281	—	—	13,864	—
	1946	94,388	99	1,726	4	—	12,156	—
St. Lucia	1946	40,616	2,635	343	—	—	26,326	13
St. Vincent	1931	33,257	653	2,173	—	—	11,292	—
	1946	45,042	1,817	1,906	—	—	12,631	242
	1960	57,207	2,444	1,804	—	—	17,444	1,265
Trinidad & Tobago	1946	261,485	195,747	15,283	5,641	—	78,775	26
	1960	358,588	301,946	15,718	8,361	—	134,749	—
	1970	398,765	373,538	11,383	7,962	—	131,904	—

9. Emigration from the British West Indies

Nineteenth and early twentieth century emigration from the British West Indies was partly the result and partly the cause of immigration into the region. It stemmed mainly from the depression in the sugar industry, the inducements of higher wages and continuous labour abroad, and the growing facilities for travel. The main recipients of British West Indian emigrants were Panama, Costa Rica and Cuba.

Emigration to Panama was conspicuous in the 1850s with workers seeking employment in railway construction there. With the end of the project emigration slumped, but it revived in 1880 when the French began work on the Panama Canal. That project also ceased a few years later due to the outbreak of yellow fever, and many West Indians returned home. With the resumption of work on the Canal by the United States in 1904 fresh impetus was given to West Indian emigration which continued high until 1914 when the project was completed.

Serious emigration to Costa Rica began around 1885 when railway construction work was started in that country, and when it was completed labourers sought employment in banana planting from 1904. However, the outbreak of Panama Disease in the banana walks reduced the demand for West Indian labour.

The abolition of slavery in Cuba in 1886 was a signal for British West Indians to emigrate there, and the trend gathered momentum with the boom in the sugar industry after the First World War. The men were employed in agricultural and construction work and the women in domestic service, dress-making and laundering. However, emigration to Cuba received a severe set-back with the fall in sugar prices in 1920.

In addition to the three countries mentioned above, emigrants also went to Haiti, the Dominican Republic, Colombia, Honduras, Brazil, Venezuela, the United States and the Danish West Indies, though in smaller numbers, more or less to engage in manual work. Most of the emigrants were Jamaicans because of the shorter distance of travel involved to some of the countries, but other West Indians also went in significant numbers. Available statistics show that net departures from Jamaica totalled 144,300 between 1881 and 1920, while Barbados experienced a net loss of about 74,000 people between 1891 and 1921.

With the depression in the sugar industry in the 1920s culminating in the general world economic depression of 1929-32, the emigration of agricultural labourers was severely curtailed. Besides, in the 1920s the United States Congress adopted measures to limit the entry of foreign nationals into that country thereby denying West Indians an important outlet. In 1928 emigration to Venezuela was forbidden, and in the early

1930s restrictive legislation in Central American countries ended the flow of West Indians to the banana plantations there. In 1930 bad working conditions in Cuba led to the repatriation of more than 2,000 Jamaicans. West Indians were not only forced to remain at home, but seasonal and permanent residents abroad returned and swelled the ranks of the unemployed. This situation contributed to the labour unrest of the mid-1930s.

Large-scale emigration began again during the Second World War when British West Indian workers sought gainful employment on the United States naval and air bases being constructed in Guyana, Trinidad, Antigua, the Bahamas, St. Lucia and the United States Virgin Islands, and in the oil refineries of Curacao and Aruba which were being expanded to meet wartime demands. In addition to West Indians joining the British military forces and serving overseas, others filled jobs in the United States created by American men leaving to join the services. After the war, however, the labour situation in the British West Indies again became acute with the repatriation of workers following the stoppage of work on the military establishments and the disbandment of military personnel.

The last phase of emigration involving not only unskilled but, moreso, skilled workers, took place after the Second World War due to a variety of reasons including (1) population pressures resulting from high rates of natural increase, (2) high levels of unemployment and underemployment due to the limited economic development in the region, (3) widespread poverty and low standards of living, (4) extreme difficulty in finding worthwhile outlets for talent in the West Indies, (5) the discriminatory operation of West Indian political systems against those in opposition to ruling political parties, and (6) the more favourable conditions of employment and higher wages in the recipient countries.

Britain was the largest recipient of West Indian emigrants most of whom entered as British subjects before 1961 when Britain passed the Commonwealth Immigration Acts imposing severe restrictions on future entry. In 1966, there were about 330,000 West Indian-born persons in Britain. Large numbers of West Indians also went to the United States and, more recently, to Canada, beginning in the former with farm workers and in the latter with an annual quota of women domestics, but developing in both into a more regular flow of skilled people. A fairly large number of British West Indians also emigrated to the United States Virgin Islands as bonded aliens or permanent residents to find employment in tourist-oriented services and construction. In addition, smaller numbers have emigrated to other Caribbean lands and other parts of the world in search of a better livelihood.

10. The Impact of Emigration on the West Indies

The emigration of West Indians has had certain important and far-reaching consequences of which the following can be mentioned:

(a) The emigration of resident creoles in the nineteenth century created a labour shortage which made it necessary for planters to import African and Asian indentured labourers to work on the estates.

(b) Whenever emigration was permitted it tended to offset the high rate of population growth resulting from rising birth-rates and falling death-rates. Accordingly, in an area with very limited potential for economic development, emigration has served to ease the heavy unemployment and under-employment which would otherwise have existed. On the other hand, whenever emigration was stifled as in the 1930s it led to social unrest and conflict.

(c) Especially after the First and Second World Wars, West Indian emigrants returning home brought back with them new experiences and ideals, such as for example, ideas of trade unionism and self-government, which they sought to introduce into their own country.

(d) Emigration also eased the strain on limited social services – education, health and housing – which West Indian governments provided from extremely meagre budgets.

(e) Emigrant West Indians who left relatives behind remitted or returned with much needed money which they used to improve economic and social conditions by purchasing land for peasant farming, by starting small businesses, by building better homes, and by educating their children. In 1960, Montserratians abroad sent back nearly one quarter of the island's revenues; in 1966–7 West Indian emigrants in Britain remitted £8.6 million in money and postal orders; and Jamaica alone netted £8.1 million in 1963 and £6.5 million in 1968.

(f) The emigration, seasonal and permanent, of ambitious and progressive, industrious and enterprising young people leaving a greater proportion of dependants and less able-bodied behind, constituted a severe constraint on the economic development of their homelands. As the labour force dwindled the economy progressively deteriorated: plantation staples gave way to cattle, and pasture to woodland.

(g) The emigration of skilled people such as technicians, mechanics, civil servants and professionals (teachers, doctors, nurses, and engineers) though of immeasurable benefit to the countries to which they went, was a loss which their homelands could ill-afford. The 'brain-drain' has continued to be a serious problem with which West Indian governments have to contend and for which there seems to be no adequate solution. High turnover in governmental, educational and commercial personnel has caused administrative chaos.

(h) Most of the seasonal workers have been male; their departure has disrupted family organization and has placed the burden of domestic control on the women as remaining heads of households thereby leading to a weakening of parental control over children with attendant social ills.
(i) The scarcity of the able-bodied made it difficult, if not impossible, to cultivate family farms, and to support community organizations.
(j) The emigration of educated and prosperous middle-class people because of their better knowledge of opportunities elsewhere and their financial ability to move, has created a fluid social structure in the West Indies.
(k) For the emigrants themselves, better conditions of employment, higher living standards, an environment free of political anxieties, the intellectual and spiritual rejuvenation, and the scope to utilize their talents more extensively and beneficially, have been gains which have outweighed the nostalgia for friends and relatives and more familiar surroundings left behind, and even the racial discrimination experienced in their adopted country. Overseas opportunities have been used as the avenues to success and greater social status.

Conclusion

The immigration of Portuguese, Chinese and East Indians to the West Indies introduced new elements of race and class into a society traditionally composed of people of European and African origin dependent for their social position on a combination of colour, wealth and education. Except possibly for the Portuguese, the new immigrant groups were neither white nor black and they held a balance between those two: though they could be classed as white, the Portuguese were not regarded as such, and they occupied a lower rung on the social ladder than the other people of European descent.

Like the negro creole population, the immigrants who remained in the West Indies after their indentureship realized the value of wealth and education to give them a higher status, and they sought to achieve these attributes whenever possible. In terms of wealth, the Portuguese and Chinese were more successful; no sooner had their indenture ended than they set themselves up as petty shop-keepers. Only a comparatively few East Indians followed their example since preference was given instead to peasant farming.

Wherever their means allowed, the Portuguese, Chinese and East Indians secured higher education for their children, mainly in professions such as medicine, law and land-surveying. The negro population sought employment mainly in teaching and the public service. More recently, their example has been followed by the other racial groups, especially the East Indians.

In the territories of high immigrant concentration such as Trinidad and Guyana, the competition for jobs has created a critical situation among the races. Because of slow economic development and expansion, governments have found themselves unable to provide employment within the public sector for all those who qualify. Consequently, they have resorted to patronage based largely on political party affiliation. Since political parties in Trinidad and Guyana have been organized essentially along racial lines, the situation became explosive, and racial animosity flared into open conflict in those territories in the 1950s and 1960s. Though not confined to it, tension heightens at the time of general elections for the national legislatures as the races seek political control to secure the spoils of office which victory would bring.

Inter-racial friction has been yet another factor leading West Indians to emigrate in search of a more peaceful and congenial environment in which to live and work. Their departure both worsens and relieves racial tension. Since they are mainly people with some skill or talent their emigration restricts development which would create new jobs to ease the unemployment situation and the pressures on existing jobs. At the same time, emigration drains away people with grievances leaving behind those more tolerant of the existing situation and is thereby conducive to peace.

Revision Questions

1. What territories in the West Indies had the most difficult labour problems after emancipation and for what reasons?
2. What were the main sources of immigrant labour for the West Indies? To what extent did the various groups of immigrants prove successful workers?
3. What conditions led East Indians to emigrate to the West Indies? What problems did the recruiters encounter?
4. Show the consequences for the West Indies of the importation of immigrant labour in the nineteenth century.
5. Why did West Indians emigrate in the twentieth century?
6. What problems have developed in the West Indies and in recipient countries through the emigration of West Indians?

3. The Public Welfare

Before emancipation, slaves had been dependent upon their masters for their welfare supplied essentially in the form of food, clothing, housing and medical care. Where religious instruction and education were received it was also with the masters' permission. The free population provided for their own welfare, or in extreme cases of destitution looked to the colonial legislature for assistance. Even so, the legislatures were in the practice of shifting the responsibility elsewhere – mainly on to the religious bodies.

After emancipation when their responsibility for providing social services had considerably increased, the legislatures sought to evade it through neglect or expected employers to continue to provide such amenities as housing and medical care, and the religious societies to provide education. Generally the labouring class had to provide its own food and clothing. Those who set themselves up independently as peasants or artisans had to provide for their entire material and spiritual welfare. Only in a limited way did the legislatures make provision for poor relief, aid to the aged and infirm and the care of lunatics, and even then they did so in co-operation with voluntary and charitable organizations. Prisoners alone received their full attention and even so it was mainly in terms of imprisonment.

Co-operation between government and private charity continued throughout the post-emancipation period. During the second half of the nineteenth century legislatures gradually broadened their functions but up to the time of the Moyne Commission in 1938 social welfare was of poor quality and barely touched the lives of West Indians. Since then, with the coming of internal self-government and political democracy, governments have come to provide welfare services to a greater degree of satisfaction.

1. Establishing Education, 1834-45: The Negro Education Grant and the Mico Charity

According to Shirley C. Gordon, 'to give an account of education before emancipation is to catalogue partial educational activities.' During slavery the education of the children of well-to-do white parents was conducted by private tutors, and later on the boys were usually sent abroad to England or North America to finish their education in grammar schools and universities while the girls remained in the colonies to finish their studies under private tuition. Parents who could not afford private tutors found their children growing up without formal learning because colonial legislatures neglected to make provision for education. Private tuition was sometimes supplemented by endowed schools such as Harrison's Free School and Codrington School in Barbados and Wolmer's School in Jamaica which offered an English grammar school type of education in the classics for fees or a general elementary school education without fees.

Before the middle of the eighteenth century almost no attention was paid to the formal education, or even the religious instruction, of negroes in the British West Indies. Slave-owners were afraid that teaching might unsettle the minds of the slaves and make them contemplate alternatives to slave labour. Consequently they expressed resentment at the efforts of the various missionary societies which sought to teach the blacks, for example the Moravians who became active in 1754 and the Methodists and Baptists later on. The education offered by the missionaries was essentially of a religious nature and opposition lessened when it became obvious that such teaching was making slaves more obedient and reliable workers. Supplementing the work of the mission schools was a fairly large number of private schools operated by interested individuals as well as those conducted by the Anglican clergy or Catholic priests according to the religious persuasion of the colony. These schools catered essentially to the free blacks and free coloured community which was very conscious of the social value of education.

After emancipation a more vigorous attempt was made to introduce a more universal system of education through co-operation between the religious bodies and the British Government. Since the missionary societies did not have adequate finances to enable them to meet the anticipated demand for education after emancipation, the British Government voted £25,000 a year in 1835 and 1836, and £30,000 a year thereafter until 1841 to assist their educational efforts. The so-called Negro Education Grant was distributed among the various religious groups to be used to construct schools and, after 1837, to assist in paying teachers. Among the societies in receipt of grants were the Moravian Society, the Wesleyan Missionary Society, the Baptist Missionary Society, the London Missionary Society, the Society for the Propagation of the Gospel, the Church Missionary Society and the Ladies Negro Education Society. In addition to elementary schools, 'normal' schools were to be established to train local teachers, since before this time teachers had more often been brought from England.

Through the Negro Education Grant considerable progress was made in education; 38 new elementary schools were erected in 1835 and 52 in 1836 while normal schools were established in Jamaica, the Bahamas and Antigua. Inspection was provided for by the British Government, and in 1837 Charles Latrobe was sent out to report on the first two years' work under the grant. Progress was retarded only because of the difficulty of acquiring land sites with satisfactory titles and because the religious bodies began to find it increasingly difficult to meet their financial obligations. The problems worsened after 1841 when the British Government began a phased withdrawal of the Negro Education Grant which ceased completely in 1845. Since local legislatures were not yet prepared to make adequate financial provision for education, many schools had to be closed. However, when the grant was withdrawn the hope was expressed that the colonial legislatures would raise the funds necessary for public education and that the labouring population would assist in providing for their own instruction.

In addition to the Negro Education Grant, assistance was given by the Mico Charity which the British Government was instrumental in applying in part to British West Indian education. Lady Jane Mico, widow of Sir Samuel Mico, willed £1,000 in 1666 to her nephew Samuel on condition that he married one of his six cousins; if not, the money was to be used to redeem Englishmen enslaved by Barbary pirates. The terms of the will could not be implemented since Samuel did not marry a cousin and the Barbary pirates had been suppressed; accordingly, the Court of Chancery decided in 1690 that the £1,000 should be invested. By the time of emancipation the sum had grown to £120,000, and in 1835 the trust was reorganized so that the money could be applied to 'the religious and moral instruction of the Negro and Coloured Population of the British Colonies.'

Administered by a Board of Trustees, the Mico Charity was put to use even before the parliamentary Negro Education Grant and was subsequently supplemented by it. The money was used to build elementary schools where the religious bodies did not, such as in isolated areas and in Catholic colonies like St. Lucia and Trinidad. By 1841 the Mico Charity was operating as many as 196 schools with some 15,000 pupils throughout the British West Indies. In addition, normal schools had been started in Jamaica, Antigua, Trinidad and Guyana, though those in the last two were closed in 1840.

The early attempts at public education suffered from a number of weaknesses including a heavy emphasis on religion, insufficient and poorly trained teachers, a scarcity of teaching equipment, inadequate supervision, and a shortage of funds for steady and continued expansion. Nevertheless, through the application of the Negro Education Grant and the Mico Charity, a firm foundation was laid for future consolidation and expansion.

2. Developments in Education, 1845-1900

Despite the termination of the Negro Education Grant in 1845, the educational process of the British West Indies continued to expand. The religious denominations continued to participate and their efforts were supplemented by colonial legislatures even though their contribution fell below expectation and requirement due to low revenues as well as to inherent reluctance to educate the negro. With the adoption of Crown Colony Government, grants were substantially increased. Governments paid the teachers' salaries and in some colonies provided as much as 50 percent of building costs and repairs.

A conscious effort was made to break away from the bible-oriented education of earlier years and to introduce a more secular system. Religious instruction was not abolished since it was considered necessary for the moral improvement of students, but it was de-emphasized and religion assumed a less prominent place in the various subjects on school curricula. Besides, while emphasis was placed on reading, writing and arithmetic, some attempt was made to introduce such subjects as history, geography and science.

Government financial contribution to education together with the shortage of funds, made control somewhat imperative. Accordingly, Boards of Education or Education Committees were set up to supervise education grants and to formulate policies relative to education. Besides, while ministers of religion continued to supervise church schools, governments appointed inspectors of schools to ensure that their contribution was spent in conformity with policy. Individual colonies generally had their own inspectors, but with the formation of the Leeward Islands Federation of 1871, one Inspector-General was appointed for all the units.

Inspectors were responsible for examining grant-in-aid schools at periodic intervals to ensure that minimum standards were achieved and maintained. According to the results schools were placed in one of three classes – first, second and third – and for the sake of efficiency grants were awarded to the various schools according to their class. The system was known as 'payment by results.' First started in Barbados in 1866, it later spread to the other colonies, and it continued to influence educational policy well into the twentieth century.

While emphasis continued to be placed on elementary education some attempt was made to introduce secondary education. In this respect, both the religious denominations and governments were active, but a number of private secondary schools were established also. In some instances where the initiative was taken by the religious denominations, legislative support was soon forthcoming as in the case of Queen's College founded by the Anglicans in Guyana in 1842. In other instances government initiative stimulated denominational action; the founding of the Queen's Collegiate School (later Queen's Royal College) by the Trinidad government in 1859 was soon followed by the establishment of Catholic Colleges in the island. In Barbados, the Codrington Grammar School was kept in existence with governmental assistance while in the Leeward and Windward Islands and in Jamaica government also deployed resources to assist in the development of secondary education later in the nineteenth century. Students were often recruited on the basis of competitive examinations and many of them were assisted by exhibitions and scholarships.

To some extent secondary education was developed because of the need for teachers generally. To produce better teachers, teacher training centres were also established. In the main, however, because of considerations of economy, greater reliance was placed on the pupil teacher system by which young capable students were recruited into the teaching profession after completing the highest classes in the elementary school and passing additional competitive examinations. The system was reinforced by a series of teachers' examinations designed to stimulate and test teachers' professional and academic competence.

An attempt was made to introduce industrial education to develop skills and talents among students ill-equipped for formal academic studies. However, parents were opposed to any plan which threatened to turn their children into manual labourers, and they favoured education which promised them a higher social status and prestige through 'white collar' jobs. Because of parental resistance, therefore, industrial education was confined to orphanages and reformatories which were established to deal with destitute and refractory children respectively. The association of industrial education with poverty and destitution lowered its status still further in the eyes of West Indian parents.

The education of East Indian children in Trinidad and Guyana created special problems which required special attention. East Indian parents were unwilling to send their children to schools attended by negro children, but to prevent them from growing up illiterate, governments established estate schools in which the regulations pertaining to 'payment by results' were not rigidly enforced. In addition, the governments supported the Canadian Presbyterian Mission on the same terms as other religious denominations to enable it to establish schools on the estates or in nearby villages for the education of East Indian children.

3. Developments in Education in the twentieth century

The twentieth century was concerned with the expansion of those educational services begun in the nineteenth century and with the improvement of the quality of education.

The religious denominations continued to be very influential in education as witnessed by the continuation of the dual control of education between church and state in some places and by the presence of parochial schools in many others. However, under the impetus of the theory of the welfare state, West Indian governments began to assume an even greater responsibility to provide education, especially after the introduction of self-government and independence. Elementary and secondary schools have been increased in number and expanded, and the general tendency has been to offer education free of charge at least to the secondary school level.

Teacher training in the nineteenth century had been a haphazard affair and in the last decade of that century many of the training centres had been closed. However, teacher training was revived and systematized in the twentieth century. Government Training Colleges were established in Jamaica, Trinidad and Guyana, and in the 1930s there were ten training centres both government and denominational, four in Jamaica, three in Trinidad, and one each in Antigua, Barbados and Guyana. Teacher training has become an essential part of the preparation of young people for the teaching profession, and an attempt is being made to relate it more closely to the Universities where also Diploma courses in education are being offered.

After the First World War, teachers in most territories began to receive fixed salaries, and pension schemes were introduced. The system of 'payment by results' was abolished, and in order to encourage teachers to become better qualified a financial incentive was offered for training and certification. In addition, as revenues permitted, teachers were given overall salary increases as well as annual increments for merit in an effort to attract talented and dedicated teachers.

Because of the financial stringency under which governments operated most of the time, it was necessary to administer budgetary appropriations for education more efficiently. Accordingly, after the First World War, Boards (or Committees) of Education were replaced by Departments of Education under Directors responsible directly to the governors. Many of the Directors of Education were capable men and with the assistance of an expanded body of school inspectors (also called education officers) did much to improve the quality of education in the colonies. With the introduction of internal self-government, Departments became Ministries, and education policies were integrated into the general scheme for national development.

Very slowly during the twentieth century more realistic curricula have been introduced into the school system and syllabuses have included more general science, commercial subjects, domestic science for girls and handicraft for boys. Technical institutes, previously just handicraft centres, have been established to give technical education, and more and more the emphasis has been placed on vocational training to provide skilled workers in an attempt to beat the growing problem of adolescent unemployment.

An important development in education for nation-building has been the integration of East Indians into the mainstream of the education system in areas of heavy East Indian population density, like Trinidad and Guyana. Many East Indians have become teachers at all levels of education from elementary to university, while others have become doctors, lawyers and technicians.

Beginning with the establishment of the West Indian Department of Agriculture in 1898 and culminating in the creation of the Imperial College of Tropical Agriculture (ICTA) in 1922, an attempt was made to improve agricultural education in the British West Indies generally. The educational programmes were designed to educate not only administrative personnel but also local peasant farmers in the methods and techniques of scientific agriculture. ICTA was eventually incorporated into the University (College) of the West Indies as its Faculty of Agriculture.

The most outstanding advancement in the field of higher education was taken in 1948 with the establishment of the University College of the West Indies located in Jamaica. Henceforth higher education would be available to many more than just the few students who had previously gone to universities in other countries, mainly on government scholarship. At first the institution was an adjunct of the University of London, but it became a full-fledged university in 1962. Shortly afterwards, campuses of the university were opened in Trinidad and Barbados. Originally, Guyana had been a participant in the University College, but the University of Guyana was founded in 1962 as an autonomous institution. In both universities, the education offered has been directed towards the needs of the area; courses have been offered in the traditional subjects in the arts and sciences but, in addition, the University of the West Indies teaches medicine, law, agriculture, international relations and theology. To make university education more easily available to students, governments have subsidized it heavily, and in addition they have provided scholarships, bursaries and loans to an increasing number of students.

The University of the West Indies has served to provide uniform standards of education for students drawn from all parts of the Caribbean. However, students have matriculated by passing examinations set by British universities, mainly Cambridge and London. In their search for a type of education more relevant to local conditions West Indian governments created in 1972 a Caribbean Educations Council which would be responsible, among other things, for preparing textbooks, and conducting school and university entrance examinations based on mutually agreed syllabuses.

4. Problems of Education since Emancipation

For too long education was dominated by religion despite the valuable role which the church played in establishing education. Progress was slow since ministers of the gospel who served variously as teachers, supervisors and managers were not trained educators, and there was little inclination to offer more comprehensive syllabuses. The prevalence of dual control in education between religious denominations and governments left the administration of education confused.

There has never been a fully trained teaching profession in the British West Indies since the normal schools and training colleges were too few and sometimes ill-equipped to train all the teachers. On occasion some of the training centres were closed in the interest of economy. There was no lack of teachers since teaching has always been attractive for its high social value, but the number of teachers trained has always remained a small fraction of the whole. Indeed, reliance was put on methods which placed the responsibility for professional achievement and improvement on the teachers themselves such as the system of 'payment by results' and teachers' examinations which were both wasteful of talent and energy. Within more recent times 'refresher' courses have been offered to teachers to improve their efficiency, but such courses pre-supposed the existence of an educational base which did not in fact exist.

Because of the low state of British West Indian economies since emancipation there has never been enough money to provide adequate social services, education included, especially in face of the high rate of population increase. Consequently, conditions in the schools were far below even modest modern standards: buildings were too few and generally in poor condition, class-rooms were badly overcrowded, teachers were burdened with overlarge classes, and equipment was scanty and out-of-date. Only since the Second World War have school health and school feeding programmes been introduced through international agencies such as the World Health Organization, UNESCO and UNICEF.

The economic weakness of governments meant that teachers' salaries have always been low; even so occasionally they have been reduced, and sometimes teachers have not been paid. Such a situation was unlikely to attract the best minds or to retain them for long. Many teachers have consequently left the profession to seek alternative employment in the local public service, or they have emigrated to seek more favourable opportunities in other countries.

The inability of governments to meet the financial needs of education was not corrected by parents' ability to do so. For the majority of West Indians during the post-emancipation period, there was little means of livelihood beyond subsistence farming. Unemployment was high everywhere, earnings were extremely low, and the destitute condition of the people did not favour educational progress.

West Indian education has been persistently alien to the people for whom it catered. For the most part the system introduced was based on the British model though it was a pale imitation at best. Its content was divorced from the needs of the West Indian people and from the reality of the West Indian situation. Emphasis was placed on the humanities (classics and arts) at the expense of the scientific and technical knowledge necessary to develop the area, socially and economically. There was seldom a coherent idea of what public education was intended for, beyond the establishment of a limited personal status for a minority of West Indians.

5. Transportation and Communication

When speaking of transportation and communication facilities in the British West Indies three levels should be recognized, namely, territorial, regional and international.

For a very long time the internal means of communication and transportation in the West Indian territories were bad, and in some of them that condition has persisted. Traditionally, such roads as there were linked colonial plantations with the capital city and port, and the means of conveyance was the horse-drawn coach or ox or donkey-cart. Little or no consideration was given to the small producers. Peasants who established themselves in separate villages did so along traditional lanes of transportation; otherwise they suffered extreme difficulty in getting their produce to market.

Early roads were merely dirt-tracks which became impassable during rainy seasons. The European technique of building durable hard-surfaced roads, developed around the turn of the nineteenth century, was not introduced into the West Indies until much later and, even so, was at first confined to the towns. With the introduction of motor vehicles in the twentieth century, more extensively after the Second World War, oil-surfaced or pitched roads were introduced. In this respect Trinidad was most fortunate by virtue of its pitch lake; in most of the territories much still needs to be done to achieve modern standards.

Because of the bad roadways, wherever possible in the several colonies the sea was utilized to transport produce and supplies between plantations and capital ports. The many rivers of Guyana have also been used for transportation between the coast and the hinterland where logging and mining have been undertaken.

Beginning during the early post-emancipation period, railways were constructed in colonies like Jamaica, Barbados, Trinidad and Guyana, linking centres of production, usually the plantations, with seaside ports. Since railways were usually built along public roadways they suffered from competition from road transport. Consequently, all of them operated at a deficit and had to be subsidized by government. Recent increases in the speed and number of motor vehicles have resulted in the displacement of trains from passenger and goods transportation.

Under the doctrine of mercantilism, colonies had been founded to form the economic complement of the mother-country. This meant in effect that colonies would produce such goods as the mother-country could not and buy surplus imperial manufactures. Accordingly, the essential link has been between the mother-country and individual colonies rather than among the colonies themselves. Besides, since the colonies produced very nearly the same staples, such as sugar, cotton and tobacco, there was little need for them to trade with each other.

The seagoing vessels which called at the various colonies were usually those from metropolitan countries. But for these visits a colony could be out of touch with the others. This gave rise to a situation where it was possible to travel faster between a metropolitan country and a colony than between two colonies, depending on their location. In explaining the poor transportation which existed in the West Indies in 1922, Major Wood reported that his mission was made possible only because a British warship had been detailed for his use, that a letter from Trinidad to Jamaica had taken five and a half months to arrive, and that Jamaican letters to Barbados, Trinidad and Guyana were usually sent via New York, Halifax and England.

West Indian colonies have existed more or less in isolation from each other, a condition which has bred particularism among the island communities separated by wide expanse of sea. Economic diversification during the late nineteenth and twentieth centuries made some trade possible among Caribbean territories, culminating in the formation of CARIFTA and thereby requiring better means of inter-territorial transportation. In the main, however, these have continued to be sloops and schooners which are awkward and slow. With the formation of the federation of the West Indies in 1958, the Canadian government presented two steamships, the *Federal Palm* and the *Federal Maple* to the federation for transportation of passengers and goods among the constituent units at fortnightly intervals, but the service was far from satisfactory and the *Federal Palm* has since been sold. In any case, people have preferred to travel by aeroplane.

Until the later nineteenth century, sailing ships dominated transportation and communication between the West Indies and metropolitan countries. Such vessels were of very limited capacity and depended for their movement on the direction and velocity of winds and ocean currents. By the middle of the nineteenth century, however, steamships had appeared, and gradually they replaced sailing ships in transatlantic navigation. Metropolitan and colonial markets were drawn closer together and larger amounts of goods could be transported as steamships became larger.

Steamships revolutionized international transportation especially with the development and application to international trade of the cable, and later wireless telegraph, and refrigeration. Cable and wireless brought producers in almost instant touch with market conditions. Refrigeration enabled perishable cargoes like fruit and vegetables produced in the West Indies to reach metropolitan markets without spoiling. It was the beginning, for example, of the banana industry of Jamaica.

During the twentieth century and more obviously after the Second World War, territorial, regional, and international transportation and communication have been considerably affected by the development of air transport. National and international airlines have been organized and a major value of these has been to cater to the growing Caribbean tourist trade. Aeroplanes have also promoted West Indian awareness and consciousness of each other and have stimulated the desire for closer association and co-operation.

The introduction of radio and television communication has been important as much for its entertainment value as for instilling among West Indians new concepts and values as well as the high standards of living of other societies which they were to desire for themselves. The consequent 'revolution of rising expectations' was to have profound impact on West Indian social, economic and political aspirations during the twentieth century.

Much has been achieved in the areas of transportation and communication in the West Indies since emancipation. Progress has been limited essentially only by lack of finance, inadequate planning, and the inability of West Indians to co-operate fully among themselves.

6. Health and Medical Services

Despite their equable temperature, abundance of fresh sea-breeze and plenty of sunshine, the West Indies have had an unenviable reputation for the prevalence of epidemic diseases from the early years of colonization. Diseases like malaria, yellow fever, smallpox and cholera, the exact origin of which is uncertain, took a heavy toll of human life both slave and free during the colonial period, as did other diseases such as yaws, leprosy, hookworm, typhoid, dysentery, diarrhoea, syphilis and tuberculosis.

The prevalence of diseases called for medical attention and doctors in private practice quickly made their appearance. In addition, some resident doctors were attached to estate hospitals where the number of slaves and the wealth of the estates permitted this arrangement. More often, however, private doctors under contract were paid a fixed fee for each slave, sick or well, on the estate, or else they were paid for each slave they attended to on an individual basis. With the collapse of plantation agriculture after emancipation the number of doctors declined and those who remained tended to live in the towns since the rural peasantry was too poor to pay for medical services.

After emancipation planters continued to provide limited medical care to those ex-slaves who continued to live and work for them, in an attempt to retain their services. They were not, however, responsible for those who left to take up other employment. As an increasing number of ex-slaves set themselves up as peasant farmers, therefore, a large number of people had to provide medical help for themselves or look to the government to do so. At government insistence, estates in Guyana and Trinidad established hospitals for their immigrant workers, but their services were also to be available to the general population.

Because of financial backwardness governments tried to limit medical expenditure by resorting to preventive measures though these were of partial application. Quarantine regulations were adopted governing incoming ships and passengers, but they were invariably confined to capital ports; the freedom of outports from similar restrictions consequently allowed infected persons to enter undetected. To quarantine was added during the second half of the nineteenth century such measures as vaccinations against smallpox not, however, compulsory, as well as regulations governing the disposal of refuse.

Boards of Health were usually established and charged with the responsibility of keeping streets and markets clean and of supervising the sanitation of abattoirs. Flush toilets and a modern sewage system, paved streets and covered drains were also gradually introduced to improve environmental sanitation. At first, however, such measures were confined to the main towns of the larger colonies. A number of sanitary inspectors were employed to enforce the observance of health regulations but initially their inspection also was more or less confined to the towns. When, later on, sanitary inspectors were appointed to the rural areas their inspection was too infrequent, cursory and tolerant to be beneficial.

In an attempt to escape from reliance on an uncertain supply of water from rainfall and shallow wells, from 1850 onwards governments began to install waterworks and piped supplies in the towns. In some colonies artesian wells were drilled in the rural areas and water was available from roadside stand-pipes. In Barbados and Grenada such water supplies seem to have catered to the majority of the people, but in the larger colonies such as Jamaica and Guyana only a small percentage of the rural population had piped supplies. Reliance was still on rainfall collected in discarded oil drums and on trench water. Since such water was invariably polluted and impure the dangers to health were manifold.

During the second half of the nineteenth century, colonial governments sought to introduce colony-wide medical services. General hospitals were established in the larger towns, while district medical officers, dispensers and dispensaries were provided for the rural areas wherever the size of the colony and the density of the population made them necessary. Generally, government doctors were allowed private practice but they were required to treat patients under a government-devised scheme. Nominal fees were charged at the dispensaries, but doctors had a tendency to overcharge their patients, most of whom had very modest incomes. However, the net effect of the medical services provided was to reduce drastically the incidence of sickness and ill-health.

Epidemic diseases continued into the twentieth century but the development of scientific medicine has practically eliminated them from serious consideration as killer diseases. Malaria and yellow fever have been effectively brought under control as much through medicine as by the use of insecticides, chiefly DDT, to eradicate the germ-carrying anopheles and aedes aegypti mosquitoes. The possibility of infection through contact, particularly by air travel, with areas in Africa and South America where the diseases still exist, has to be considered, though the possibility of epidemic outbreaks is probably unlikely.

To deal with some of the other diseases special V.D. clinics, tuberculosis sanatoriums, leper asylums and mobile anti-yaws clinics were set up before antibiotics and vaccines were developed to assist in their control. The greater emphasis on pure water supplies, nutrition, improved sanitation, slum clearance and better housing, and health education for the people has served to ensure a generally higher standard of health for West Indians within recent times.

From 1940 the efforts of West Indian governments were assisted by financial grants under the Colonial Development and Welfare Act, and after the Second World War assistance was also received from such international agencies as WHO, UNESCO and UNICEF. An important aspect of the assistance received was limited provision of free milk and biscuits and of free medical and dental care for school children. Besides, such external assistance enabled local resources to be utilized for the development of other health services such as the construction of rural health clinics, the expansion of medical staffs and the adoption of preventive controls.

West Indian doctors have been either in government employment or in private practice. In proportion to population there has always been a shortage of doctors especially in the smaller colonies suffering from economic depression. In the early post-emancipation period, West Indian doctors were invariably Englishmen in the colonial overseas service. But with the rise of West Indians of affluence, their children were educated in medicine and dentistry, among other professions. However, initially such training was obtained in British and North American universities.

An important development, therefore, has been the establishment of the University (College) Hospital in conjunction with the University (College) of the West Indies in Jamaica where West Indians could be trained as doctors under conditions in which they would practise later on. In addition, nurses were educated there both in theory and practice, though most West Indian nurses have continued to be given in-service training to develop their proficiency.

Several important advances were made in reducing the incidence of death and disease in the West Indies during the post-emancipation period. Nevertheless a number of conditions retarded progress. High birth-rates combined with falling death and infantile mortality rates led to a high rate of population increase which taxed existing facilities beyond capacity. The poverty of the people generally made it impossible for them to provide themselves with a proper diet when well or with medical care when sick. The problem was aggravated by the high rate of illegitimacy, the practice of having large families, parental irresponsibility and neglect. Deplorable housing accommodation, poor sanitation, ill-balanced diet and malnutrition were also serious defects which lowered health standards. Inadequate revenues made governments unable to provide sufficient facilities in terms of buildings and equipment and to hire sufficient staff especially for the rural areas. In addition to the too few doctors, there has been a chronic shortage of specialists as well as insufficient trained nurses and subordinate medical staff in proportion to doctors. For too long was the emphasis on curative rather than on preventive medicine, and insufficient attention was given to research into the causes, distribution and control of diseases. Lastly, there was a need to co-ordinate health and medical programmes with other aspects of governmental social and economic planning.

7. Current Health Problems

The health problems of the British and Commonwealth Caribbean can be conveniently divided into two main classes: those which result in sickness and possibly death; and those related to governmental and community action. Because of the recognized responsibility of governments to safeguard the health of their people, it is difficult to separate the two. The following are among the most outstanding of the current health problems of the West Indies:

(a) Diseases for which effective immunization or treatment exist such as polio, tuberculosis, smallpox and venereal diseases, to mention only a few. Indeed, venereal diseases have been recognized as the most frequently notified of the communicable diseases while tuberculosis is still a major problem in many islands. Inadequate measures are being adopted to deal with these diseases.

(b) Dental caries and periodontal disease are universal, but in too many places the only dental programme seems to be mass extraction; much remains to be achieved to prevent or treat tooth decay.

(c) Malnutrition is still widespread in the area due mainly to the neglect of agriculture and a fall in local production. Deficiencies in proteins, iron and vitamins in diets have led to anemia, dental caries and mental retardation among other ill-effects. The need exists for more milk and milk products, meat, eggs, fish and legumes.

(d) A major problem is the low quality and quantity of the pure water supply because of the considerable expense involved in installing the necessary machinery. Mainly cities and towns are provided for but there is still heavy reliance on rainfall, and fluoridation is practically non-existent.

(e) Sewage and garbage disposal is more or less confined to the urban areas; in the rural areas the lack of facilities leads to environmental pollution and insanitary surroundings which provide a favourable breeding ground for pests and diseases.

(f) Effective insecticides are available for the eradication of disease-carrying mosquitoes and the housefly, but the current situation is far

from satisfactory. Malaria and yellow fever germs are still prevalent in mainland territories, and the speed and ease of modern travel make them a threat to the Caribbean islands.
(g) The tremendous population growth due to the high birth-rates and falling death-rates has aggravated problems of unemployment and planning especially in view of the limited financial resources and space for development and expansion in most places. Increasing population, therefore, presses uncomfortably on available hospitals, clinics, social welfare facilities and housing.
(h) There is a marked lack of co-operation between governments and voluntary organizations such as the Red Cross, the St. John Ambulance Brigade and other civic and religious groups. The result is competition and, more importantly, unnecessary duplication of effort and expense.
(i) The lack of qualified personnel in the various areas of health make it impossible to give adequate service. The problem has been caused by the training of an insufficient number of people in the first place, and even so the situation has been aggravated by the emigration of some of those who have been trained, to seek better job opportunities in other countries. Health services consequently suffer from technical and administrative incompetence.
(j) Central planning, such as it is, suffers from the lack of specified long-term objectives and goals and from insufficient knowledge of the true nature and extent of the problems involved. Moreover, it suffers from inadequate finances and from failure to mobilize public support through appropriate educational programmes.

8. Social Welfare

As defined by the Moyne Commission social welfare seeks to 'understand from within the problems of the poor, the maladjusted and the unfortunate, and to help in the solution of those problems.' Rightly speaking, the term should embrace all aspects of the social life of a people including education, communication and transportation, and health and medical services, but more properly it can be limited to the relief of the poor, the aged and infirm, the care of criminal offenders and lunatics, and the provision of housing.

In the early post-emancipation period governments gave modest support to social welfare because of low finances and the operation of the *laissez-faire* theory which stressed private rather than public involvement. Financial provision was minimal and directed more or less towards assisting the efforts of charitable organizations, mainly denominational and missionary societies.

Examples of co-operative enterprise were to be found in all the colonies. In Antigua, poor relief was granted on a parochial basis and financed by a legislative appropriation to the parish vestries of 2½ percent of the customs duties plus the receipt of a small land tax levied by the vestries themselves. In Montserrat, the legislature provided £400 a year for poor relief while in Nevis small government contributions assisted voluntary subscriptions to provide aid for widows, orphans and deserted women and children. While some colonies made institutional provision for the care of the poor and lunatics, in others the poor were given meagre out-door relief while lunatics were housed in the colonial hospital or jail.

In keeping with the *laissez-faire* theory West Indians took an active part in providing social welfare benefits for themselves. In several places they formed Friendly Societies which provided a wide range of benefits including sickness payments and burial expenses, and they often catered for the recreational needs of members through organized dances and outings. Unfortunately, Friendly Societies did not succeed in some places because the newly-emancipated people could not fully understand the advantages of a system calling for a regular financial outlay but promising only a prospective and indefinite relief. Beginning in the later nineteenth century further social welfare assistance was obtained from other voluntary organizations. The Salvation Army engaged in work to prevent crime and rehabilitate criminals, but moreso it established institutions for the blind and hostels and depots for the relief of the destitute and infirm. The Y.M.C.A. and Y.W.C.A. sought to offer recreation to young men and women while in certain colonies Women's Societies maintained child welfare centres and crèches and provided meals for needy children.

Two organizations formed by the East Indian community in Guyana after the First World War are worthy of mention, namely, the Dharamsala and the Balak Sahaita Mandalee. The Dharamsala, or home for the indigent poor, was founded by the Hindu Society and opened in 1929 to provide free lodging and food for over 250 needy people a day. While it was established principally to serve East Indians, no poor person of any race was refused assistance. Funds were obtained mainly from voluntary contributions but later on government assisted with a small grant. The Balak Sahaita Mandalee, or child welfare society, was founded in 1936 and one of its main functions was the education of East Indian mothers in child care.

Two other outstanding examples of social welfare enterprise should be discussed, one in the early and the other in the later post-emancipation period, namely, the Daily Meal Society of Antigua and Jamaica Welfare Ltd. The Daily Meal Society was founded in St. John, Antigua, in 1828, and it was supported by voluntary subscriptions of money and gifts, occasional church offerings and legislative grants, and parochial donations of 2/- a week for every person sent by the parish for care by the Society. Managed by a committee elected from among the subscribers, the Society operated a seaman's hospital, a leper asylum and an orphanage for girls. Besides, it offered food, clothing, shelter and medical care for the island's poor. However, during the economic depression of the 1840s subscriptions fell off and as a consequence the Society surrendered the care of its paupers to the island's poor house in 1852, and its hospital and asylum to the government in 1855 when it went out of operation.

Jamaica Welfare Ltd. was incorporated in 1937 as a non-profit making concern financed under an agreement between Norman Manley representing the All Island Banana Growers' Association and Samuel Zemurray on behalf of the United Fruit Company whereby ½d. on every bunch of bananas exported was to be made available to promote the social and economic betterment of the Jamaican working class. Not until 1942 when enemy submarine activities curtailed banana exports and revenues did the Jamaican government move in to give financial assistance. Operated by a Board of Directors, the new Company set up co-operative groups which organized the saving of money among its members, ran consumers' stores, erected houses, and to a small extent engaged in agricultural operations. These efforts were fairly successful; less so were the community and adult education activities offered by the two community centres which had been established at a cost of about £3,000 each. Consequently, the Company adopted the so-called 'Better Villages' policy which required community association before any project could be started. The work of the Company thus shifted from providing physical amenities and services in community centres to personal service given towards the development of locally controlled institutions and enterprises. The pattern of Community Association or Community Council thus developed was later imitated by other West Indian colonies like Barbados and Trinidad.

The area of social welfare which was almost completely neglected was housing, the people being left to provide this as best they could. The Moyne Commission reported in 1939 that housing in both town and country throughout the West Indies was deplorable and left much to be desired. A majority of the houses were made of rusty corrugated iron and unsound boards. Many lacked floors and had leaky roofs, and all were insanitary, overcrowded, poorly ventilated, and parasite infested. Urban slums were growing because of greater urbanization. Estates provided housing for their workers but it was only slightly better than ordinary working class dwellings. Many of the ranges or lodgies were dilapidated and they lacked privacy and essential amenities. Only in some areas was an attempt being made to build detached and semi-detached workers' cottages.

The brightest spot of legislative participation in social welfare was the provision of jails to house criminal offenders, but even so conditions fell far below desirable standards. For example, in too many instances were first offenders lodged with hardened criminals and no provision was made for the rehabilitation of prisoners. Besides, the special reformatories or industrial schools established for juvenile offenders were too few, and they gave an inadequate training for life later on.

The Moyne Commission was highly critical not only of housing and prisons but of social welfare in general. Existing facilities were confined to the towns with little or nothing being done for the rural areas. Government subsidies were granted to many of the charitable and voluntary organizations, but each year they operated at a deficit since fund raising was difficult. Active public involvement was either non-existent or unorganized, and people of leisure showed little interest in social welfare. Moreover, the work of the religious and civic organizations suffered from lack of collaboration. The major factors which inhibited progress, however, were an absence of family life, illegitimate childbirth due to promiscuity, and the refusal of fathers to maintain their children.

Following the recommendations of the Moyne Commission, a more systematic attempt was made to improve social welfare in the West Indies. While voluntary and charitable organizations continued their efforts, technical advice and financial assistance were obtained under the Colonial Development and Welfare Act, and governments recognized a greater responsibility to provide social amenities. In addition, other forces began to work to bring about change, notably trade unions and political parties.

Only some of the most important developments since 1940 need to be mentioned to indicate the progress achieved in social welfare; in many other areas, services were expanded and improved. After 1940 trained Social Welfare Officers were appointed to work out co-ordinated programmes in which government departments co-operated with the voluntary agencies. Community centres were established throughout the West Indies to provide recreation and adult education. Family planning was introduced to promote stable family life and limit population growth and to advise on child-rearing. Old-age pensions were introduced, and more recently in the independent territories national insurance schemes were enacted. Urban slum clearance was begun, and improved housing was encouraged through the provision of loans or by the construction by government of lower and middle-income housing which was sold or rented to the people. Estates followed the government example and promoted nuclear housing projects on previously abandoned estate lands. Though much remains to be accomplished, a breakthrough has been made.

Conclusion

The provision of public welfare services during the post-emancipation period was the combined effort of colonial governments and several voluntary and charitable organizations. At times the British Government gave financial assistance but, moreso, it contributed invaluable technical services and advice. Important advances were made in the fields of education, public health and medical services, communication and transportation, and in the care of the poor, the aged and infirm, the mentally afflicted and prisoners.

Progress was retarded by the philosophy under which society operated, namely, *laissez-faire* which placed upon the people themselves the responsibility for providing for their own welfare with a minimum of government involvement. However, other factors were responsible such as the financial backwardness of colonial legislatures due to the weak economies of the colonies, and the high rate of population increase among the labouring class. The fact that the people lived in isolated communities inadequately linked by passable roads made it difficult to administer regulations or to provide services for them.

Poor social services were largely responsible for the labour disturbances of the 1930s leading to the appointment of the Moyne Commission in 1938. The findings of the Commission, aided by the introduction of representative government in the colonies, led to a more systematic approach to social welfare. Despite the accomplishments, however, much is left to be achieved. The need to make education relevant to the West Indian situation and to make it more easily available at all levels through more schools and scholarships is clearly evident. Free school-lunch programmes and bus transportation for all school children are also necessary but seem a far way off. So too is proper remedial education. Health and medical services suffer from a number of defects which need correction, the most pressing needs being public education and cheap treatment in a larger number of clinics and hospitals. As far as transportation and communication are concerned, better roads are needed in already settled areas and more roads are required to open up new areas of production. A cheaper and more regular system of communication among West Indian territories is necessary to break down further the isolation and insularity among them. Lastly, in social welfare generally, the interest of the leisured class in the welfare of the poor, the needy and the social delinquent needs to be developed as should the economic opportunities and education of the people to enable them to avoid dependence upon charity.

Revision Questions

1. What efforts were made by the British to improve the social conditions of ex-slaves immediately after emancipation?
2. What agencies were responsible for providing educational services to West Indians? Explain their respective roles and the conditions which limited their efforts.
3. What were the main detriments to health which existed in the West Indies in the nineteenth and twentieth centuries?
4. What have been the major influences operating to bring about social reforms in the West Indies since emancipation?
5. What advances in the means of transportation and communication have taken place in the twentieth century?
6. Do you think that the West Indies are near to or far from achieving adequate social services? Why?

4. Organization for Development

During the first century of the post-emancipation period the West Indian working class suffered from extreme poverty and neglect. Under the old representative system while it lasted, as well as under crown colony government, West Indian legislatures operated mainly in favour of the plantocracy and other vested interests. Minimal attention was given to the economic and social well-being of the workers who were, in addition, excluded from the political process. The feeling developed among the downtrodden that organization was needed if changes were to be effected and progress achieved.

The early response of the working class to their low wages and bad conditions of employment was work stoppages or strikes as a means of bringing their grievances to their employers' attention. To the same end they resorted to sabotage by burning fields, destroying estate equipment and buildings, and maiming work animals. Occasionally they rioted. By and large, however, their actions were spontaneous and unorganized and ineffective.

Following the British example, some tentative attempts were made to form trade unions during the two or three decades immediately preceding the First World War. The return of West Indian servicemen from the war with knowledge of better conditions in more developed countries led to a more organized approach to working class problems, but the working class itself only became more directly involved following the labour disturbances of the 1930s. The result of the movement was the emergence of trade unions and political parties initially under middle class leadership but with working class support. Trade unions and political parties were formed to advance working class interests, hence the close relationship between them.

A. TRADE UNIONS

1. Early Beginnings

Early trade unionism in the British West Indies stemmed from working class consciousness of its deplorable working and living conditions – low wages, irregular employment, long hours of labour, poor housing and sanitation, deficient water supplies, inadequate medical services, and lack of educational opportunities – decades after emancipation. There was a growing consciousness that only by concerted effort could concessions be extracted from unwilling employers. Trade unions, however, were slow to take root, and when they did they were more or less confined to the larger colonies.

Among the earliest trade unions was the Carpenters, Bricklayers and Painters Union – commonly called the Artisans' Union – organized in Jamaica in 1898. This union apparently disintegrated shortly after 1901 as a result of depressed economic conditions and internal dissension over the auditing of accounts. It was followed by other craft unions including a Painters' Union around 1907 with Marcus Garvey as a member, the Tobacco Workers' Union, and the Jamaica Trades and Labour Union, No. 12575 (later No. 16203) of the American Federation of Labour. These organizations produced few tangible benefits for the working man despite some strike action taken.

A significant development in Jamaican trade unionism was the formation among dock workers in 1919 of the Longshoremen's Union whose leader Bain Alves agitated for legal recognition for trade unions in the island. The governor, Sir Leslie Probyn, was sympathetic towards the workers' cause and in October 1919 a Trade Union Ordinance was enacted freeing trade unions from the possibility of criminal charges of conspiracy to which they were subject until then. However, the Ordinance did not protect unions against liability for damage resulting from strikes, nor did it legalize peaceful picketing. The two branches (No. 1 and No. 2) of the Longshoremen's Union alone registered under it, but they remained inactive.

A Workingmen's Association was founded in Trinidad by Alfred Richards in 1894, but there is no record of achievements in spite of protest demonstrations, and it collapsed after a serious waterfront strike in 1902. However, the Association was revived in 1919 as a forceful bargaining agent under the leadership of Captain Arthur Cipriani, an ex-soldier who had served during the First World War and who was an unofficial member of the Legislative Council of Trinidad. More of the nature of a political party than of a trade union – only one branch made up of stevedores and railroad employees operated as a labour union – it secured for workers an eight hour day, a Workmen's Compensation Law, the establishment of an Agricultural Bank, and several other improvements in working conditions. The organization collapsed in 1933 without taking advantage of a Trade Union Ordinance passed the previous year giving the legal right to form trade unions. That Ordinance, however, did not permit peaceful picketing, and it allowed unions to be sued.

During the first decade of the twentieth century strikes were called in Guyana by Hubert Nathaniel Critchlow, a dockworker, and others even though there was no organizational machinery. The earliest attempt to form a trade union was made in 1910 among river captains and bowmen of Georgetown who were finding it extremely difficult to secure their wages from the diamond, gold and balata companies by whom they were indirectly employed. However, the effort was short-lived due to lack of unity among the captains and the general unemployment situation. Seven years later another attempt was made by the Rev. R. T. Frank to form a union among the labourers and tradesmen of New Amsterdam, but it disintegrated after some months due to the lack of financial support and employers' opposition. A carpenters' union and other combinations of tradesmen formed at about the same time also failed to develop into permanent trade unions.

More successful was the British Guiana Labour Union organized in January 1919 by Hubert Critchlow. It was undoubtedly helped by the Trade Union Ordinance of 1921 which gave it protection against actions for damages consequent upon strikes. Though it had continuous existence, middle class leadership during the 1920s sacrificed its trade union aims to political expediency, and its only major industrial achievement until the mid-1930s was a shorter working day for workers. Another organization, the British Guiana Workers' League, formed in 1931 among a small group of negro sugar-mill workers, was never aggressive and militant during its twenty years of existence.

There were apparently no trade unions in the smaller British Caribbean colonies until the mid-1930s. A Trade Union Ordinance was passed in St. Vincent in 1933 as a result of mass agitation and of leadership advice from Captain Cipriani, and in the following year a St. Vincent Workingmen's Association was formed. It was more middle class oriented and made no attempt to secure bargaining status from employers, but it concentrated instead on securing social reform through political action. The role of trade unions in St. Kitts and Barbados was taken by quasi-political parties founded before the mid-1930s – the St. Kitts Labour League and the Barbados Democratic League. Both were oriented towards influencing the very limited middle class electorate.

From as early as 1926 an annual Labour Conference was held by the British Guiana Labour Union and attended by delegates from other Caribbean territories in order to give a regional approach to trade unionism. However, its significance as a regional trade union organization was very limited since trade unions were non-existent in most of the colonies. It was less a conference of trade unionists than an annual meeting of political and nationalist leaders.

Trade unions before and after the First World War made a slow start for a number of reasons including the total absence or inadequacy of laws legalizing their activities and the large unemployment situation which encouraged employers' opposition. Continuous migration of labourers, both seasonal and permanent, seeking better employment opportunities elsewhere, made organization difficult. The failure of leadership to emerge from the masses, and the association of the movement with middle class leaders who were more interested in national and political rather than with working class objectives caused trade unions to be weak.

2. Later Developments and Influences

(a) The growth of trade unions in the British West Indies after the mid-1930s was due mainly to the labour disturbances of that decade which provided an impetus towards mass solidarity and produced interested leaders from both the middle class and the working class.

(b) A marked change in British colonial policy developed from the riots as well as from the reports of the Moyne Commission and of Major Orde Brown on labour conditions. As a result an active programme was adopted to encourage trade unionism.

(c) The passing of Trade Union Ordinances in Barbados and the Leeward Islands in 1939 and the relaxation of limitations contained in the Vincentian and Jamaican Ordinances were also very helpful. The legality of trade unions was fully established in all the colonies by 1943 except in St. Lucia which achieved it in 1948. The foundations laid and the machinery created by such legislation enabled trade unions to develop.

(d) Measures for the economic development of the islands such as the introduction of light manufacturing and food processing industries, provided a more stable and prosperous clientele for trade unions by creating greater employment and reducing the tendency of workers to emigrate. Similarly, the implementation of plans for social reform as well as the adoption of the policy to introduce measures of self-government, created an environment that was more conducive to trade union organization.

(e) Association with political parties and assistance from middle class leaders were particularly helpful to unions since they obtained legislative backing as well as an aura of respect and dignity.

(f) The advisory and paternal role played by Sir Walter Citrine secretary of the British Trade Union Congress, as a member of the Moyne Commission of 1938, was invaluable. He publicly exhorted workers to form trade unions and privately advised several potential leaders on the methods and techniques of forming such unions. Citrine's association with the Caribbean labour movement was largely responsible for the active interest and assistance it received from the British T.U.C. during the postwar period in the form of financial support, scholarships and training courses for trade unionists.

(g) Between 1940 and 1944 ordinances were passed in all the colonies creating Labour Departments which served to collect and collate statistical information relating to labour relations and to advise governments, trade unions and employers on proper industrial relations policies. Most of the Labour Advisers were themselves trade unionists and they assisted greatly in protecting and guiding local trade unions.

(h) Migrant West Indian workers returning from foreign countries, especially after the Second World War brought back new ideas and practices relating to trade union development. Many of them became the nuclei of new working-men's combinations and used their experience to promote trade unionism.

(i) Assistance came also from the University of the West Indies in the form of training in adult education, in trade unionism and in industrial relations, by a staff tutor in collaboration with local Labour Departments.

(j) The United States A.F.L.-C.I.O. also provided training and financial assistance to West Indian trade unionists. From time to time two of its Latin American representatives operated in the Caribbean region and helped to organize unions.

(k) Substantial external assistance came from the international level. Pressures were applied by the British T.U.C. and the A.F.L.-C.I.O. on Caribbean trade unions for them to dissociate from the World Federation of Trade Unions and to align with the International Confederation of Free Trade Unions. The I.C.F.T.U. established a Caribbean Area Division of its Regional Latin American Organization (C.A.D.O.R.I.T.) which helped to contain the trend of trade unions towards fragmentation by promoting amalgamation and by intervening to settle jurisdictional issues among its affiliates.

3. Growth of Trade Unions

Following the riots of the 1930s there was a rapid growth of trade unions in most of the colonies, even where there were no laws legalizing them or where picketing was illegal and unions could be sued for damages.

Until the 1937 disturbances the only unions in **Jamaica** were the two Longshoremen's Unions (No. 1 and No. 2), the Jamaica Workers' Trade Union and a few other insignificant ones. All these were eclipsed in importance by the Bustamante Industrial Trade Union formed in 1938 under the leadership of Alexander Bustamante. It was a blanket union, that is, a union with members drawn from among workers in different areas of employment, in the case of the B.I.T.U. from among clerks, factory workers, dockworkers and field labourers. Within six years membership had increased from an estimated 6,500 in 1939 to 46,538 in 1945. In addition, other unions making a total membership of 298,400, had been formed; these included the Jamaica United Workers' Union (defunct by 1945), the Postal and Telegraph Workers Union, the Governor Auxiliary Workers Union, the Public Works Union, and the Railway Employees Union.

The last four named unions and ten others eventually merged in 1949 into the Trade Union Congress which had evolved from the Trade Union Advisory Council formed by Norman Manley as early as 1939. By the mid-1950s the Trade Union Congress had been superseded by the National Workers' Union. By that time, also, the Jamaican trade union movement had crystallized solidly around the two major political parties – the B.I.T.U. with the Jamaica Labour Party under Bustamante and the N.W.U. with the People's National Party under Norman Manley.

In **Trinidad** most of the unions which later became major unions came into existence in 1937. Among these were the Oilfield Workers' Trade Union, the All-Trinidad Sugar Estates and Factories Workers' Trade Union, the Seamen and Waterfront Workers' Trade Union and the Federated Workers' Trade Union of public works and railroad employees. Within a year several other unions had been formed including the Public Works and Public Service Workers' Union, a Printers' Union, a Transport and General Workers Union, and a Shop Assistant and Clerks Union. In addition, a co-ordinating committee known as the Committee for Industrial Organization was formed by the major unions in 1938, and by mid-1939 it had evolved into a Trade Union Council comprising about ten affiliates with a total membership of over 11,000. This Trade Union Council was, in turn, transformed into the National Trade Union Congress in 1956 when six unions rejoined after breaking away in 1951 to form the Federation of Trade Unions. The Congress included the major unions representing in all about 40,000 workers.

The involvement of union leaders in politics often caused dissension within their organization and sometimes led to sectional breakaway and the formation of new unions. In addition, several unions were formed to provide electoral bases for political parties thereby diluting the effects of trade unionism, but the major unions remained independent of party politics.

In **Guyana,** to Critchlow's British Guiana Labour Union consisting mainly of waterfront workers was added in 1937 the Manpower Citizens' Association, a blanket union formed by Ayube Edun mainly from among sugar workers. Within a year it had called as many as 37 strikes on the Leonora Estate alone, and within five years its membership exceeded 20,000. By 1945, however, it had suffered some loss of faith through internal dissension, and another union, the British Guiana Workers' League had emerged to share recognition with it in the sugar industry. Meanwhile, certain government workers, chiefly railroad and ferry service employees, had been organized into a small but effective Transport Workers' Union. Other government employees were organized in a separate union called the Federation of Government Workers. Then there was the powerful and solidly organized British Guiana Bauxite Mine Workers' Union formed in the early 1940s, as well as a number of smaller unions which had emerged within two or three years after the riots. Indeed, when a Trade Union Council was formed in 1941 to settle jurisdictional boundary disputes among the overlapping unions, as many as 28 unions became members of it.

There was a tremendous growth in trade unionism in Guyana after the war. The British Guiana Labour Union under new leadership became more militant, and the M.P.C.A. broadened its base to include other workers such as the bauxite and electricity workers, though in the sugar industry its position was challenged by the politically motivated Guiana Industrial Workers' Union after 1948. A Civil Service Association (1948), a Clerical Workers' Union (1950) and a Federation of Unions of Government Employees were among some 60 new unions – many soon defunct – which were formed during the 1946–55 decade. Though some unions might be sympathetic towards certain political parties and though there might be some similarity of leadership, unions and parties tended to have separate existence.

St. Kitts and **Barbados** organized trade unions from their existing political organizations. The St. Kitts Workers League which already had elected representatives in the legislature, established a formal trade union in 1939 known as the St. Kitts-Nevis Trades and Labour Union. Both leaders and members of the League and Union were almost identical since the union was really the industrial arm of the political party. The Barbados Progressive League was similarly organized with separate political, social and economic arms, and in 1941 the economic arm was registered as the Barbados Workers' Union. After a somewhat disappointing start, the union began to flourish following a successful strike in 1944, and in early 1945 its 22 divisions numbered about 5,500 members, increased to over 11,000 by the end of 1947. Under Grantley

Adams as President and Hugh Springer as Secretary, both of whom were island scholars and graduates of Oxford University, the union achieved outstanding successes, so much so that the rival Congress Trade Union formed in 1944 was short-lived. An issue in 1954 as to whether a new leader to succeed Adams should come from within or from outside the trade union was decided in favour of one from within thereby permitting the development thereafter of autonomous trade unionism unaffiliated with and independent of any political party.

Antigua began its history in trade unionism with the formation in 1939 of the Antigua Trades and Labour Union with the advice and assistance of Sir Walter Citrine. Within three months its members numbered over 3,000, and by 1956 its 44 branches in industry and trade totalled 12,175 due-paying members including domestic servants, tradesmen, shop owners, teachers, civil servants and peasant farmers. The integrity and sincerity of leadership and the prompt and careful attention to workers' grievances won the loyalty of the workers. It was not until 1967 that a rival union – the Antigua Workers' Union, the industrial arm of the Progressive Labour Movement – emerged to challenge the monopoly of the A.T.L.U. and succeeded in gaining recognition in several spheres.

The Windward Islands were late in starting trade unions, and except for the Workingmen's Association in St. Vincent, no trade union was organized up to the end of the Second World War. Indeed, it was not until the disturbances of the early 1950s that trade unions emerged, three each in **St. Vincent** and **St. Lucia**, a situation which led to considerable factionalism, rivalry and jurisdictional overlapping and dispute worsened by the political activities of trade unions in these small islands. A similar plurality of trade unions emerged in **Grenada**, the most powerful and militant being the Grenada Manual and Mental Workers' Union (1950) under the charismatic leadership of Eric Gairy, followed by the weaker Grenada Technical and Allied Workers' Union, and the Waterfront Workers' Union. A Trade Union Council emerged later on but it was relatively ineffective. Windward Islands trade unions tended to become *de facto* political parties at election time and more industrially oriented thereafter.

With a total membership of about 200,000, some 150 trade unions were registered in the British West Indies in 1956, of which 14 with 100,000 members were in Jamaica, 60 with 41,000 members were in Trinidad, and 38 with 15,000 members were in Guyana. The strength of West Indian trade unionism was reflected in the formation of the Caribbean Labour Congress whose first meeting was held in Guyana in 1945. It was designed to co-ordinate union activity on a regional basis, but it collapsed in 1947 because of 'cold war' differences among delegates and was replaced in 1954 by the Caribbean Area Division of the

Inter-American Regional Division of the International Confederation of Free Trade Unions. The Caribbean Congress of Labour was formed in 1960.

4. Difficulties Experienced by Trade Unions

(a) Employer hostility to trade unions and favouritism towards non-union employees together with employers' associations in major industries, for example, the Sugar Producers Associations of Guyana and Barbados, constituted effective forms of opposition to union demands. In Guyana, differences between employers and union representatives in the sugar industry led the Labour Department to establish a Joint Estate Council consisting of seven elected workers' representatives and estate management, but the former proved weak and ineffective and the latter unwilling and unenthusiastic participants who refused to act on points brought up in discussion.

(b) The Second World War had a negative effect by muzzling the movement's militancy essential to its growth. In addition, Governor Richards of Jamaica applied temporarily the Defence (War) Regulations to bar the registration of trade unions comprising government employees but which were led by non-government employees. In Antigua the strike weapon was renounced in 1941 for the duration of the war, and workers sought employment on the United States naval base where unionism was made virtually impossible.

(c) The involvement of trade unions in politics tended to dilute their activities by promoting factionalism and partisanship and inter-union rivalry and friction. Where leadership of union and party was the same, leaders used union support for political expediency. Many so-called 'paper unions' were usually formed at election time and dissolved afterwards thereby retarding the development of legitimate trade unions.

(d) In a predominantly agricultural region such as the West Indies it was difficult to organize and mobilize agricultural workers because of their lack of precise status as wage earners. Except for bauxite in Guyana and oil in Trinidad, industries were few for a long time, and even when they appeared their work force was too small for effective organization.

(e) Potential union members from among negroes and East Indians with a background of slavery and indentureship respectively, were not very responsive to effective unionization, since opportunities for participation in communal activities were practically non-existent.

(f) In areas like Guyana and Trinidad with populations comprising different racial groups, it was more difficult to effect workers' unity; indeed, the different races were often engaged in different occupa-

tions and so were organized in different unions. In such a situation it might also have been easier for employers to use interracial suspicions and jealousies for their own ends.
(g) Where the loyalty of members was more for the leader than for the union, and where dues were collected only in small amounts, unions lacked the power to discipline members and to prevent fragmentation.
(h) The proliferation of trade unions, many of the blanket type, and the tendency of unions to fragment promoted jurisdictional disputes among them and weakened the bargaining power of the movement. Shifting worker allegiance among unions also prejudiced their interest. For a long time only St. Kitts, Antigua and Barbados did not suffer from worker fragmentation in several unions. In St. Vincent, St. Lucia and Grenada, charges and countercharges of graft, corruption, and surrender to the employers among the various unions competing on an island-wide basis for the same members, left workers confused and weak.
(i) The high degree of illiteracy among workers in the West Indies aggravated the problem of creating trade union understanding and made the organization of workers difficult. Ignorant workers were generally distrustful of the larger more firmly established unions. In these cases, workers turned to substitutes such as commission merchants for consultation and advice.
(j) Ideological differences within the labour movement between those who sympathized with and supported Soviet communism on the one hand and western capitalism on the other distorted workers' objectives and clouded basic issues and goals, and led to fragmentation within the ranks of trade unionists.
(k) Another difficulty was more peculiar to the larger territories where geographical conditions limited contact between union members and officers and made workers more subject to employer control. An outstanding example was found among the timber and quarry workers of Guyana.
(l) Unemployment, under-employment, seasonal employment, casual labour and disguised employment such as domestic service, limited organizing opportunities by preventing the creation of a viable economic base necessary for strong trade unionism.

5. Achievements of Trade Unions

The method usually adopted by trade unions was the strike followed by collective bargaining. Concerted action by workers revolutionized employer-employee relationships and workers with power to strike acquired status and dignity and became less submissive to employers.

Alternately, employers' awareness and acknowledgement of the new power of employees made them more willing to listen to employee needs, sometimes without a strike by employees.

As a result of workers' pressures, laws were passed in the colonies relating to workmen's compensation, minimum wages, protection against accidents, and the employment of women and young persons. Workers also benefited from such measures as overtime pay and paid holidays.

The effectiveness of organization at the sectional level in trade unions prompted organization at the national level in political parties to consolidate union gains and to seek further benefits through legislative action.

The association of trade unions with political parties and the exercise of the franchise by workers made both parties and governments more responsive to workers' demands for better housing, improved medical and sanitary facilities, better education, pure water supplies, and social and recreational facilities.

While contributing to the development of social democracy in the region and to a recognition of the dignity of the working class, unions assisted in the disintegration of colonial regimes which were denying the masses economic, social and political recognition, and in the promotion of self-government and independence.

B. POLITICAL PARTIES

1. The Background to the Development of Political Parties

The same dismal social and economic conditions which led to the formation of trade unions were also responsible for the organization of political parties. West Indians were convinced that it was only through political action that effective measures could be adopted to improve working and living conditions.

By and large effective political parties did not appear before the labour disturbances of the 1930s. However, the existence of labour-oriented nationalist organizations such as the Trinidad Workingmen's Association, the Barbados Democratic League and the St. Kitts Workers' League indicated by their broad reform programmes the direction which political parties ought to follow.

After the labour revolution of the 1930s, dedicated and inspired leaders emerged with education along the lines of western democratic and parliamentary practice but also with considerable 'grass-root' connections and sympathy with working class aspirations. To a large extent West Indians had become disillusioned with the middle class leadership which tended to side with vested interests.

The rising spirit of nationalism created among West Indians a new awareness of their social position and the desire to become fuller members of their society.

The organization of trade unions with mass support from the working class gave political parties an effective base from which to operate. In some cases, trade unions themselves created parties or simply assumed the character of political parties at election time.

The reintroduction of elected members into West Indian legislatures culminating in representative and ministerial government as well as the grant of universal adult suffrage were also powerful stimuli for the organization of political parties.

Of importance also for the rise of parties was the freedom to organize and to exert pressure for reform inherent in British democracy as well as the existence of an institutional framework and a political climate in which political parties were able to play meaningful roles.

2. The Rise of Political Parties

(a) Jamaica

Among the first political organizations in Jamaica was the Jamaican Political Reform Association founded in 1921 to work for constitutional reform in the island. Then in 1929 under the leadership of Marcus Garvey, recently returned from the United States, the People's Political Party was founded with a fourteen point programme. But though Garvey was twice elected to the Kingston and St. Andrew Corporation Council, he failed to secure election to the legislature.

Quasi-political parties founded in 1935 included the Elected Members Association and the Federation of Citizens' Association. Two years later a branch of the Jamaica Progressive League founded in New York by the distinguished Jamaican author, W. Adolphe Roberts, was established in Jamaica. The main objective of these organizations was a greater measure of self-government for Jamaica.

The movement of self-government, however, did not gain broadly based mass support until after the labour disturbances of May 1938 and the emergence of Alexander Bustamante and Norman Manley as champions of the working-man's cause. That same year the People's National Party (P.N.P.) was founded with Manley as leader, a position he held until his retirement in February 1969. The Jamaica Progressive League became a 'co-operative affiliate' of the new party. The P.N.P. was closely affiliated with the Trade Union Council (or Congress) but when the latter defected in 1952 the P.N.P. set up its own union, the National Workers Union.

Meanwhile, Bustamante had devoted his attention to labour activities and the formation of the Bustamante Industrial Trade Union. It was not until July 1943 that he launched his own political party called the

Jamaica Labour Party (J.L.P.). Somewhat earlier the relatively conservative Jamaica Democratic Party had been formed, and following the grant of universal adult suffrage in 1944 a number of new political parties appeared, namely, the Jamaica Liberal Party, the United Rent Payers Party, the Jamaica Radical Workers Union and the J. A. G. Smith Party. These were little more than party labels for independent candidates; at the 1944 general elections the J.L.P. won 22 seats, the P.N.P. 5 and Independents 5.

The two-party system was definitely established at the 1944 elections, and it has not been successfully challenged since then. For example, neither of the newly formed parties, the Agricultural Industrial Party formed by breakaway dissidents of the J.L.P. and the United Party of Jamaica, won any seats in the 1949 general elections while the J.L.P. won 17, the P.N.P. 13 and Independents 2. Since then victory at the polls has swung between the J.L.P. and the P.N.P. despite the continued appearance of new short-lived third parties.

(b) Trinidad

Trinidad's experience with political parties went back to 1894 when the Trinidad Workingmen's Association was formed by Alfred Richards. Though the Association was among the oldest political parties in the British West Indies it could hardly be very active politically before elected members were introduced into the Legislative Council. Even when this took place in 1924 the Association's activities were largely restricted to periods near elections. In 1932, Captain A. A. Cipriani, leader of the Association, changed its name to the Trinidad Labour Party (T.L.P.).

The extremely high qualifications for voters retarded the development of political parties; nevertheless, in 1936 Tubal Uriah Butler, recently expelled from the T.L.P. by Cipriani, founded the British Empire Workers' and Citizens' Home Rule Party otherwise called the Butler Party.

Political interest in Trinidad increased immensely in the 1940s due firstly to the introduction of an unofficial majority in the Legislative Council in 1941, secondly to the introduction of universal adult suffrage in 1945, and finally to the introduction of an elected majority in 1949. Several new political parties appeared to contest the 1946 general elections including the West India National Party which joined with the Federated Workers' Trade Union to form the United Front. The Trades Union Congress and the Socialist Party also participated in the elections but another association, the Progressive Democratic Party, did not.

The parties which contested the 1946 elections were mere labels to attract votes and appeared or were resurrected only for the elections. During the campaign emphasis was placed on personalities rather than on parties or programmes, and after the elections parties and party loyalties were inconsequential in the day to day operation of government.

What was true of the 1946 elections was also true of the 1950 elections contested by five political parties – the Butler Party, the Caribbean Socialist Party, the Political Progress Group, the Trinidad Labour Party and the Trade Union Council – and 91 Independents. It was not until January 1956, when Dr Eric Williams launched the People's National Movement (P.N.M.) and won a majority of the elected seats for the legislature in the general elections that year, that Trinidad began to experience genuine party politics.

The P.N.M.'s victory was achieved over eight other political parties among which was the People's Democratic Party (P.D.P.) led by Bhadase S. Maraj, head of the Cane Farmers and Sugar Workers Union. In August 1957 the P.D.P. joined with two other parties – the Trinidad Labour Party and the Party of Political Progress Groups – to form the Democratic Labour Party (D.L.P.). Though minor parties continued to appear briefly to contest elections since then, the D.L.P. has been the main opposition party to the P.N.M. which has continued to win subsequent general elections.

(c) *Guyana*

As in other British West Indian colonies, politically inclined groups existed in Guyana before the disturbances of the 1930s. There were, for example, the Reform Association which worked for the constitutional reforms of 1891, and the Popular Party which was active in the 1920s. However, constitutional limitations such as the very restricted franchise and the weak position of elected legislative members retarded the development of strong political parties.

Trade unions organized from the late 1930s, such as the Manpower Citizens' Association (M.P.C.A.) engaged in political activities, but it was not until 1946 as a result of an extended franchise that the first political parties of recent times were organized. These were the British Guiana Labour Party formed by Dr J. B. Singh, and the quasi-party called the Political Affairs Committee formed by Dr Cheddi Jagan, an East Indian dentist and treasurer of the M.P.C.A. However, independent candidates dominated the 1947 general elections.

The most dynamic political party in Guyana was the People's Progressive Party (P.P.P.) formed in January 1950 by Jagan and L. F. S. Burnham, a black lawyer, who was also president of the British Guiana Labour Union. In the general elections of 1953 based on universal adult suffrage, the P.P.P. won 18 out of the 24 elected seats in the legislature. Other parties formed just before the elections – the National Democratic Party (N.D.P.), the People's National Party (a splinter of the N.D.P.), the United Guiana Party, and the United Farmers' and Workers' Party – made a relatively poor show.

A significant development in the history of political parties in Guyana took place in 1955 when as a result of differences over tactics and a power struggle for leadership of the P.P.P. between Jagan and Burnham, the latter broke away to form his own party. This new party was at first also called the People's Progressive Party, but in October 1957 it was renamed the People's National Congress. Henceforth, Guyanese politics was to be dominated by the P.P.P. and the P.N.C. since they appealed to the two major races, East Indians and negroes respectively, for support. Because of this tendency, the P.N.C. was able to absorb the negro-supported N.D.P. in 1959.

Other minor parties continued to be formed to contest general elections only to disappear afterwards. These included the Guianese Independence Movement formed in 1958 by Jai Narine Singh, previously a member of the P.P.P. and then of the P.N.C.; the Progressive Liberal Party formed in 1959 by Fred Bowman previously of the P.P.P.; and the People's Democratic Movement in 1972 by Llewellyn John, a former Minister of the P.N.C. government.

The next significant landmark in party development took place with the introduction of proportional representation in the general elections of 1964. Under the simple majority or 'first past the post' system of election, the P.P.P. had won the general elections of 1957 and 1961; now the P.N.C. in conjunction with the United Force recently formed by businessman Peter D'Aguiar won a majority in 1964. The P.N.C. went on to win the 1968 and 1973 general elections without the United Force.

(d) Barbados

Though Barbados always had a completely elected Assembly, the severe franchise restrictions retarded the development of political parties. The first party in the island can be regarded as the Democratic League formed by Dr Charles Duncan O'Neale in October 1924. From time to time the League successfully supported candidates for the Assembly, but it disappeared when O'Neale died in 1936. By that time other groupings of politicians described as 'conservatives' and 'liberals' representing vested interests and workers respectively had emerged. The vast majority of successful candidates was always 'conservative', but in the 1937 elections the 'liberals' were successful in electing 9 out of the 24 members of the Assembly. The origins of the Barbados Progressive League can be traced to this early period.

The 1937 disturbances marked a political awakening of Barbadians generally, and the following year the Barbados Progressive League was formally launched by some past members of the Democratic League. Grantley Adams was its Vice-President the first year and its President continuously thereafter. By the early 1940s, the League was divided into three sections two of which were the Barbados Workers' Union and the Barbados Labour Party (B.L.P.) with Adams as Chairman of both. The connection between party and union was therefore close.

The lowering of franchise requirements in 1943 greatly expanded the number of eligible voters, and it was followed by the formation of two new political parties, namely, the Electors' Association and the West Indian National Congress Party.

At the general elections of 1944 and 1946 the legislative strength of the three existing parties was about equal, but in the 1948 elections the B.L.P. returned 12 of the 24 members of the Assembly, the Electors' Association 9, and the Congress Party 3. The introduction of universal adult suffrage in 1950 tripled the electorate and produced completely different results in the 1951 elections: the B.L.P. returned 16 members, the Electors' Association 4, the Congress Party 2, and Independents 2.

In May 1955 the newly organized Democratic Labour Party (D.L.P.) was officially launched by Cameron Tudor and Errol Barrow (previously of the B.L.P.) as well as O. T. Allder. They were joined by the elected members of the Congress Party shortly before the 1956 elections but the D.L.P. won only 4 seats to the B.L.P.'s 15. However, the situation was completely reversed at the 1961 elections when the D.L.P. won 14 seats to the B.L.P.'s 5. The Elector's Association still continued as the Barbados National Party, and the island retained the basic character of a three-party state. The D.L.P. subsequently led Barbados into independence and has held the reins of government since then.

(e) *Leeward and Windward Islands*

In contrast to Jamaica, Barbados, Trinidad and Guyana, the politics of the Leeward Islands was dominated by single parties. Wherever opposition parties developed they were generally middle class in orientation and were unsuccessful at the polls. The successful parties, on the other hand, were virtually identical with the leading island-wide trade unions from which they derived their support.

(i) In Antigua, the Antigua Labour Party organized by V. C. Bird in 1946 as the Political Committee of the Antigua Trades and Labour Union emerged victorious in every election for the next twenty-odd years despite challenge from the Antigua and Barbuda Democratic Movement. Later, the A.B.D.M. combined with a breakaway faction of the A.L.P. as the Progressive Labour Movement under the leadership of George Walter. In affiliation with the Antigua Workers Union, it successfully challenged and defeated the A.L.P. at the general elections in February 1971.

(ii) In St. Kitts-Nevis-Anguilla, the St. Kitts Workers League likewise dominated the politics of the group since its formation in 1932, moreso with the support of the St. Kitts-Nevis Trades and Labour Union, and more recently under the dynamic leadership of Robert Bradshaw. Ineffective opposition to it came at first from the St. Kitts Agricultural and Commercial Society and the Chamber of Commerce, and in 1957 from the St. Kitts Democratic Party. It was challenged in 1961 by the People's Progressive Movement under Morris Davis, and since 1965 by the People's Action Movement under Dr William Herbert but on every occasion without success due to the absence of union support. Such legislative opposition as there was, was based mainly on Nevis and Anguilla leading to an unstable political situation in the group.

(iii) In Montserrat, the dominant party was the Montserrat Labour Party formed in 1952 as the political arm of the Montserrat Trades and Labour Union. It won all the seats in the 1952 and 1955 elections, but in 1958 the electorate demonstrated unusual independence and elected candidates who were not members of the Labour Party, with a consequent weakening though not a negation of one-party domination.

The Windward Islands were among the last of the British West Indian colonies to develop meaningful political parties due in part to the fact that, as in the Leeward Islands, universal adult suffrage was not introduced until 1951. Before then political activities were left to trade unions. Unlike the Leeward Islands, the Windward Islands inclined towards the two-party system, and in all four vigorous opposition parties were represented in the legislatures.

(i) In St. Lucia, the St. Lucia Labour Party was formed in March 1949 and assumed the political activities previously performed by the St. Lucia Workers Union. In June of the following year the People's Progressive Party was founded with labour support but also with backing from the business community. A split in the Labour Party in 1961 led to the formation of the National Labour Movement under John Compton which went on to win future elections in St. Lucia as the United Workers Party.

(ii) Returning to Grenada from Aruba in 1949, Eric Gairy organized the Grenada Manual and Mental Workers' Union which proceeded to call labour strikes in 1950 and 1951. The Union also contested and won the 1951 general elections despite opposition from the Grenada Action Committee. It easily won again in 1954 when no political party but 23 Independents opposed it. In comparison, the 1957 elections were contested by four Parties – Dr John Watts' Grenada National Party, Eric Gairy's Grenada United Labour Party, the People's Democratic Movement, a loose grouping of candidates formed just for the elections, and the miniscule Grenada United Federal Labour Party – none of which secured a majority. The G.N.P. and the P.D.M. formed a coalition government, but defections the following two years from the P.D.M. and G.U.L.P. gave the G.N.P. a solid majority. Victories at subsequent elections were to alternate between the G.U.L.P. under Gairy and G.N.P. under Herbert Blaize.

(iii) St. Vincent was slow to develop political parties even after the introduction of universal adult suffrage in 1951. The St. Vincent Workingmen's Association engaged in political activities in the 1940s, and in the 1951 elections all the seats were won by the United Workers, Peasants and Rate Payers Union, a loose grouping of labour sympathizers, started in May 1951. After the elections, the island's first purely political organization was launched, namely, the People's Political Party of St. Vincent, by Ebenezer Joshua. The P.P.P. gradually built its support so that by 1961 it had emerged as the major Vincentian party. By that time too, the St. Vincent Labour Party (1954) had emerged under Milton Cato to form an effective opposition.

(iv) In Dominica, those political organizations which existed before 1951 were middle class oriented. Best known of these were the Dominica Taxpayer's Reform Association founded in 1932 and the People's Progressive Party formed at about the same time by J. B. Charles. The 1951 general elections were contested by labour organizations: the Dominica Trade Union which won a legislative majority, and the Dominica Progressive Workers' Union which won no seat. However, elected members operated independently of each other, and in the 1954 elections, all candidates ran as independents. In May 1955 Mrs Phyllis Shand Allfrey, a white middle-class woman, founded the Dominica Labour Party with working class support, and in 1957 the second political party called the People's National Movement was formed by Clifton Dupigny. The two parties, however, had to share political honours with independent candidates in the 1957 elections. In January 1958, the P.N.M. joined with other opposition groups to form the Dominica United People's Party which went on to exercise political control in Dominica.

3. Characteristics of Political Parties

Since the adoption of universal adult suffrage, the only parties which could hope to win a legislative majority were those which had the support of the working class or 'bare-footed man'; accordingly, most West Indian parties were connected in some way with a trade union or federation of trade unions. For many politicians union leadership was the only but sure way to political power.

The West Indian political party was invariably dedicated to the interests of the working class and to national aspirations whether it embraced capitalist or socialist ideology. Party manifesto programmes were promises to secure improvements in the social and economic condition of the people and to achieve self-government or independence for the territory.

The type of audience to which party leaders appealed, namely, the largely uneducated working class, and the programmes they supported, for example, social justice, meant that electioneering speeches were highly emotional with little intellectual appeal and few practical proposals for dealing with chronic social and economic problems.

Most West Indian parties, especially in the early years, were loosely organized. All had constitutions calling for a full complement of elected officers and central party and constituency organizations. These were mostly paper requirements; effective power rested with party leaders, principally the founder-leader who made the major decisions; rank and file members did little more than vote for the party at elections. Though parties espoused democratic causes, party organization was more truly demagogic than democratic.

The appeal of parties was due more to charismatic leadership than to policies advocated. Parties generally tended to support the same programmes, and so they attracted support according to the personality of their leaders. However, the more unchallenged and outstanding the leader, the less disposed he was to accept direction from his colleagues.

Party electioneering techniques based on extremely long, open-air, street corner, mass meetings held in the evening were fairly uniform throughout the West Indies. Such meetings were marked by political invective and innuendoes against political opponents. While campaigning for elections naturally took place close to election time it was not exclusively so, and political education of the electorate was conducted at all times through party newspapers.

In general West Indian parties have very little funds on which to operate since many supporters are not necessarily financial members. In any case, in many islands the electorate is very small and poor. Some parties, however, enjoyed considerable money gifts from individuals who were interested in the goodwill of the parties. Possible gain from parties winning elections was the main reason for such support. Some parties also obtained financial assistance from political sympathisers, both individuals and groups, resident overseas.

With the winning of self-government and independence, corruption in party politics has increased; party supporters have come to expect favours from the victorious party forming the government, and the tendency of governments to respond favourably to supporters' demands has caused much bitterness among other sections of the people. In Guyana this has led to much racial animosity since the major racial groups are closely identified with particular political parties.

4. Scope of Political Party Activities

Party programmes were subject to continuous change in order to attract support and varied from territory to territory according to local conditions. Nevertheless, there were certain points which were traditionally included in every party manifesto, and these created a similarity of outlook among the various parties. Manifestoes provided a general guide to legislative action, and the following were among the most important objectives:

(a) Programmes were geared to strengthen and reinforce party organization to ensure victory at the polls, to maintain unity in the legislature, and to effect legislation to implement social and economic objectives.

(b) Until these were achieved, the political objectives of parties would include proposals for constitutional advancement to secure elected majorities in the legislature, universal adult suffrage, a more equitable distribution of legislative seats, and internal self-government and independence. Before 1958 many parties also advocated federation of the British West Indies with Dominion Status.

(c) Various measures were advocated to improve the economic status of the territories including the stimulation of capital inflow, creation of central banks, increase in local food production in order to reduce imports, more equitable tax reform, industrial and agricultural expansion, possible nationalization of basic industries, and increase of overseas trade.

(d) With regard to social services, proposals were made to increase minimum wage, old age pensions, and sickness and unemployment benefits. Interest was expressed also in improving the quality and quantity of service relating to public health, water supply, education slum clearance and public housing.

(e) For those territories which have secured their political independence – Grenada, Jamaica, Trinidad, Guyana and Barbados –

party manifestoes would also cover such subjects as foreign relations, regional and international trade, membership of international organizations such as the United Nations and the Organization of American States, and diplomatic representation in foreign countries.

5. Problems Encountered by Political Parties

Crown Colony Government retarded the organization and progress of political parties for, so long as official members were responsible for policy formation and execution, party leaders were denied the opportunity to gain knowledge of the practical workings of the political system. Likewise, so long as members could be nominated, political parties were denied the services of outstanding individuals who were less likely to engage in party politics since they were assured of a place in the political process.

Since party organization tended to be loose and dependent upon charismatic leadership, the problem of maintaining discipline and cohesion was much more difficult. Loyalty to the founder-leader existed only as long as other members were unable to develop similar appeal. The charismatic nature of party organization meant that parties were constantly foundering on the rocks of personality.

Existing West Indian political parties were faced with the continuous problem of groups breaking away and establishing independent parties, thereby weakening the support and effectiveness of the parent party. A unique situation has developed in Guyana where the adoption of proportional representation has encouraged the fragmentation of political parties. However, the stronger and more established parties have become more or less institutionalized.

The tendency to over-organize on paper and to draw up endless party programmes and constitutions all roughly identical, has thrown prospective supporters as well as electorates into confusion. Also, the tacit acknowledgement and adoption by political parties of the spoils system has aroused unnecessary discontent and opposition thereby making it increasingly difficult for parties in power to govern, moreso since political favourites can prove inefficient workers.

The close connection between political parties and trade unions often resulted in demoralizing both. The attitudes and policies of political leaders were conditioned by the need to retain union support, and parties which had no effective working class support had difficulty in obtaining and maintaining a loyal body of dependable voters for themselves. Moreover, parties which depended for support through emotional appeal, as they did in their relations with the working class, found themselves without supporters when they lost that appeal.

6. The Relationship between Political Parties and Trade Unions

Both trade unions and political parties were basically in the formative stages in the 1930s, and both grew up together thereafter. The close connection between them can be explained by the common working class support on which they depended as well as by their almost similar objectives, namely, to enhance the social, economic and political status of that class.

The party-union connection originated in either of two ways. Firstly, some political parties began independently with appeal to all nationalists, but soon found it advisable to create trade unions in order to establish an effective base of support. Examples of such parties were the People's National Party of Jamaica, and the People's Progressive Party of Guyana.

Secondly, other political parties were created by trade unions in the hope that they might gain control over political institutions. In some cases, trade unions simply assumed the role of parties for the purpose of contesting general elections without making any attempt to provide separate organizations or personnel. Examples of parties formed in this way were the Jamaica Labour Party, the Antigua Labour Party, the Grenada United Labour Party, and the Montserrat Labour Party. In other cases, as with the founding of the St. Lucia Labour Party, a conscious effort was made to provide the party with a completely separate identity from the union.

Whether formed by trade unions or not, West Indian parties have maintained very close ties with the unions. A major result of this connection has been to blur the distinction between union and party activities and therefore to make it almost impossible to distinguish between them. The term 'trade union government' could be used to describe the political leadership provided by trade unionists when they were able to secure a majority of elected members in West Indian legislatures.

In the case of party-union combinations, it is the party which dominates because of the ultimate authority which it could wield. Greater power and prestige are attached to party leaders, and top union leaders gravitate towards political activities. In some cases, party leaders are also union leaders, but where this is not so, union leaders are subordinate to party leaders.

Except in the case of quasi-parties or electoral alliances created as vote-catching devices just before elections, party policies have been conditioned by the need to retain the support of union members. This practice has helped to sustain many parties, but such support has been guaranteed only so long as parties maintained their union appeal.

Conclusion

West Indian trade unions and political parties were the products of similar forces and developed basically from the need for social and economic improvement. The connection between them stemmed not only from their common objectives to improve the conditions of the labouring masses, but also from their common leadership. No political party was complete without its trade union, usually of the blanket type cutting across lines of craft and industry. Trade unions were, in the main, the electoral base or the industrial arm of political parties, and the ultimate objective of many labour leaders has been political power and control.

Trade unions and political parties together have brought to realization the quite justifiable demands of the West Indian peoples for immediate and badly needed improvements, especially in parliamentary democracy and social services. Together they have achieved gains in real wages and working conditions not only for their members but for the working class as a whole. However, in attempting to secure for West Indians a standard of living and employment similar to those of economically more advanced countries which they seek to emulate, they tend to retard development by straining limited resources and by restricting the expansion of employment opportunities, capital formation and government spending.

Revision Questions

1. What conditions have brought about the formation of trade unions and political parties?
2. To what extent did the riots and strikes of the 1930s mark a turning point in the formation of trade unions and political parties?
3. Trace the interrelationship between trade unions and political parties.
4. By what means have trade unions and political parties brought about an improvement in the living conditions of the working class in the West Indies?
5. What difficulties tend to limit the achievements of trade unions and political parties in the West Indies?
6. With reference to your own territory what would you say are the characteristics of the working class movement?

5. Constitutional Changes

Colonialism means dependence and in the area of politics it was expressed in the British West Indies in a colonial legislature subordinate to the British Parliament and subject to directions from the Colonial Office. Colonies had no control over external trade or defence and their legislation was subject to imperial powers of approval, disallowance and suspension.

Subordinate as the legislatures were, during the early post-emancipation period there was a further reduction of their powers. The constitutional form existing in most of the colonies at the time of emancipation was the old representative system which consisted of a Governor, a nominated Council and an elected Assembly. During the second half of the nineteenth century that system gave way to Crown Colony Government which, in its purest form, consisted of a Governor and a Legislative Council of official and nominated unofficial members.

Under Crown Colony Government the elective element had been completely removed or drastically reduced to a small minority. The Crown through the Governor exercised complete control. But Crown Colony Government failed to realize the expectations of its advocates, and West Indians generally came to feel that their welfare was being neglected or else sacrificed to that of vested interests. Constitutional reform was recognized as a necessary solvent of social ills and a requirement for economic progress. Organized in trade unions, political parties and other pressure groups, therefore, they successfully demanded the restoration and increase of elected representation in the colonial legislatures, and these representatives then demanded and secured a greater measure of self-government and eventually independence.

1. The Passing of the Old Representative System

The political system existing in most of the British West Indian colonies at the time of emancipation was the old representative system, a tripartite arrangement consisting of a Governor, a Council, and an Assembly.

The Governor was the representative of the Crown and head of the colonial government; in the former capacity he upheld imperial interests and executed imperial policy, and in the latter position he supervised all branches of the colonial administration. His situation made him subject to two masters – the British Government through the Secretary of State for the Colonies, and the local legislature – a condition which caused him endless trouble.

The Council consisted of members nominated by the Governor on behalf of the Crown from among the richest and most influential colonists, and served a double function; it served as an advisory body to the Governor and as the upper house of the colonial legislature. Generally, it tended to side with the Governor against the Assembly.

Compared with the Council, the Assembly was a representative body, its members elected by freeholders on a very restricted franchise. It exercised considerable legislative power, including the sole right to introduce money bills into the legislature. Its power brought it into continuous and sometimes bitter conflict with the Governor as well as with the Colonial Office whose policies he had to execute.

Under the old representative system power did not reside with responsibility, that is, while the Governor had full responsibility for administration, the power to make it effective rested with the Assembly. Also, while the Assembly could thwart and hinder the Governor at every turn, it could not actually control him except in matters of finance.

By the time of emancipation and continuing after it, the old representative system had been discredited in the eyes of the Colonial Office. As Henry Taylor of that Office summed it up: 'The West Indian legislatures have neither the will nor the skill to make such laws as you want made; and they cannot be converted on the point of willingness, and they will not be instructed'.

Colonies with representative assemblies had resisted British proposals to ameliorate the conditions of slaves; in contrast, the proposals had been easily introduced in the Crown dominated colonies of Trinidad and St. Lucia. It was the official belief that after emancipation representative Assemblies would be unwilling to educate the ex-slaves and improve their condition. Accordingly, it would be impossible to have settled government under the existing system.

While the old representative system, essentially a white oligarchy, had proved incapable of good, stable and orderly government, it was held that to give the vote to the ex-slaves would be to create a government which would be even more intolerant and more dangerous, because of its superior numbers, than the one in force.

Lack of competent candidates, widespread lack of interest in elections, and apathy in political matters were other negative characteristics of West Indian politics. For example, in 1854 there were in St. Vincent and St. Lucia respectively only 193 and 166 registered voters of whom just 130 and 43 actually voted. In some colonies, constituencies were unable to return elected representatives because of the complete lack of voters. In one case in Tobago in 1862, two members were elected by a single illiterate.

The British Parliament was not yet prepared to adopt the drastic policy of abolishing Assemblies. Indeed, when in 1839 the British Government tried to suspend the Jamaican Assembly for five years it was defeated and forced to resign. Following the introduction of responsible government in Canada in 1848–9, an attempt was made to effect reforms in the same direction in the West Indies. At first in Jamaica in 1854, and then in Tobago, St. Kitts, St. Vincent, Nevis and Antigua within the next five years, Executive Committees were appointed consisting in part of some of the elected members of the Assembly, in order to bridge the gap between the Governor and the Assembly to prevent conflict between them. However, the position of the Executive Committees was never clearly defined, and since they were neither wholly servants of the Crown nor agents of the legislatures they proved ineffective in fulfilling their expected functions.

The path away from representative government was laid in the British Virgin Islands where in 1854 the bicameral legislature (Council and Assembly) was replaced by a unicameral legislature of 6 elected and 3 nominated members, and where five years later the elected members were reduced to four. However, a fatal blow to the old representative system was given by the Morant Bay Uprising in Jamaica in 1865 after which the Governor Sir Edward John Eyre was able to persuade a recalcitrant and reluctant Assembly to pass a law abolishing the two chambers of the existing legislature and entrusting the task of prescribing a new constitution for Jamaica to the Crown. The way was paved for the adoption of Crown Colony Government.

2. The British West Indies under Crown Colony Government

Under Crown Colony Government, important changes were made in the mode of government as it existed under the old representative system. The basic change was that the Crown had the power to override all political opposition and dominated the colonial legislature which might be a purely nominated or a partially elected body.

Crown influence was exercised in the colonies by its local representative, the Governor, who was placed in control of all executive and policy-making decisions. In this he was assisted by an Executive Council which replaced the old Council. It was made up of senior administrative officials and a few unofficials nominated by the Governor, and it was reduced to a purely advisory capacity without legislative functions. The nominated unofficials were expected to be in general agreement with government policy; they had to be prepared to resign in case they differed seriously with it on important issues.

The Assembly was replaced by a Legislative Council consisting of a majority of senior government officials along with some unofficial members nominated from among the colonists by the Governor who presided over its meetings. Even when later some elected members were added to the Legislative Council, the official and nominated unofficial members were placed in a majority on it. The Legislative Council had no power to initiate legislation this being the sole responsibility of the Governor, but in some cases special powers over finance were given to the unofficial members.

'Pure' Crown Colony Government, that is, a Legislative Council without elected members, was first introduced in Jamaica in 1866 and thereafter rapidly in other colonies, so that by 1878 elected members sat in the legislatures of only Antigua, Dominica, Guyana and Barbados. Antigua and Dominica became pure crown colonies in 1898, but though Guyana became a crown colony in 1928, its legislature contained elected representatives. Barbados was never brought under Crown Colony Government because of local pride in the traditional political institutions.

The change from the old representative system to Crown Colony Government in the West Indies was encouraged by the Colonial Office for three main reasons: representative Assemblies had proved a barrier to good government; Crown Colony Government made possible a truer representation of all classes; and British aid to financially backward colonies required Crown control to direct expenditure. The new system was intended to operate as a relatively benevolent despotism to hold the balance between a selfish, inefficient and corrupt oligarchy, and an ignorant black populace.

Crown Colony Government corrected two serious defects in the old representative system: under it responsibility was clear and went with power, and it ensured more harmonious relations between the executive and legislative branches of government. The executive was in control of the legislature and could overcome opposition. Besides, the system ensured the participation of more qualified members in government than would otherwise have been obtained through the vote of an uneducated and uninterested electorate. Crown Colony Government could be used to secure legislative representation for all classes so that their interests could be safeguarded. The establishment of an effective method of co-operation between the executive and legislative branches of government made it easier to enact legislation, and in Jamaica, for example, as many as 97 laws were passed in 1867 and 1868 under the able and firm leadership of the Governor, Sir John Peter Grant.

However, Crown Colony Government in turn suffered from several serious defects. Officials and nominated unofficials could be required to vote on direction against their own judgement and conscience thus depriving them of initiative and making them shy of legislative activities. It is not surprising, therefore, that unofficial members developed the character of a more or less united opposition to official policies. The fact that nominated members did not have to answer to constituents led to another situation where power did not rest with responsibility. In this respect, one serious complaint against Crown Colony Government was that those who were taxed did not have any voice in the selection of the persons who taxed them. Even where elected representatives were allowed, their minority made them powerless and ineffective, and since they were not associated with the Executive Council, they obtained no experience in the practical working of government, and so could not offer practical alternative measures. Instead, their almost continuous criticism and opposition to official action often prevented constructive executive action and led to a static condition. Thus, while Crown Colony Government made the adoption of legislative measures easier the system failed generally to devise and implement vigorous schemes for the social and economic development of the British West Indian colonies. Governments remained dominated by vested interests, and only the representatives of such interests were successful in exercising influence.

3. Stages in the Constitutional Evolution of the British West Indies

There were several stages in the constitutional evolution of the British West Indies: from pure Crown Colony Government, back to representative government, to responsible government, to internal self-government, and finally to independence within the Commonwealth. The changes were quite distinct and occurred in the different colonies at different times. In some the final stage has not yet been achieved.

Crown Colony Government came under increasing attack during the twentieth century, in essence because it failed to improve significantly the social and economic conditions of the people. Self-government through elected representatives was seen as the only way by which improvements could be introduced.

Constitutional Evolution 117

First begun in Grenada in 1914 by T. A. Marryshow, Representative Government Associations were formed in several British West Indian colonies, often under the leadership of ex-servicemen returning from the war, to press for representatives in the Legislative Councils elected on a limited franchise, as well as for federation. They organized public meetings and prepared petitions to the Secretary of State for the Colonies, which were to some extent supported by middle-class businessmen and intellectuals as well as by the working-class.

It was partly in response to this situation of protest that the Hon. E. F. L. Wood (later Lord Halifax) was sent to the West Indies in 1921, and his Report became a landmark in British West Indian constitutional advancement towards representative government. Wood recommended that the elective principle should be advanced in stages in the colonial legislatures: firstly, while official members continued to be a majority, nominated unofficials should be reduced to make way for elected members; later, the unofficial members both nominated and elected should be placed in a majority over the official members.

Following the Wood Report constitutional evolution proceeded rather leisurely and wherever elected members were introduced the reform proved unsatisfactory to the advocates of representative government. Basically, elected legislators were mostly coloured representatives of middle class opinion and they tended to identify themselves with the power elite. Accordingly, after the labour revolution of the mid-1930s, more radical demands were made for universal suffrage, entirely elected legislatures, and Executive Councils responsible to the legislatures. Progress towards more representative legislatures followed rapidly: the official element was speedily reduced in those colonial legislatures where it was still substantial, and elected majorities were established. These changes were accompanied by an extension of the franchise culminating in universal adult suffrage and a lowering of the qualifications of candidates for election. The result was that political power passed substantially to the working class and their representatives, many of whom were of working class origin themselves. Nominated members continued to be appointed for some time longer to provide representation for important sectors of the community which could not hope to win seats in an election. Eventually, however, they also were replaced by elected members.

Representative government had been achieved but it did not satisfy West Indian politicians; the new demand was for responsible government to enable the elected members to play a constructive role in the initiation of policy. The first step in this direction was taken when a few elected members were appointed by the Governor to the Executive Council. The elected members, however, were in a minority and could not be very effective though they could evade responsibility for unpopular executive policies. Moreover, they ran the risk of being identified with the official and nominated members at the expense of popular support as well as of the confidence of their elected colleagues in the legislature.

The next step was to make the Executive Council responsible to the representative legislature and this was taken by at first introducing elected members in the Executive Council who were appointed and removable by the legislature. This element of responsibility was increased when an Executive Council was created with a majority of elected representatives appointed and removed on the advice of the leader of the majority party in the legislature, known as the Chief Minister.

The elected members of the Executive Council gained power not only over the initiation of policy but also over its administration. The adoption of the Committee System recommended by the Moyne Commission assisted in this development. Elected members of the Executive Council were appointed chairmen of committees which discussed and offered advice on the activities of various administrative departments. They then occupied the position of quasi-ministers as they had no real authority over the departments, but they were able to gain valuable administrative experience.

Ministerial status was achieved by the elected members when they were empowered with effective administrative authority over their departments and began to exercise genuine executive functions. Ministers were generally selected from the majority party in the legislature by the leader serving as premier.

Responsible government advanced into internal self-government. At first, only a few of the less critical subjects were assigned to the quasi-ministers or ministers, but gradually more and more departments were transferred to them from the chief administrative officials until they were in charge of all internal affairs.

Meanwhile, the Executive Council had evolved from an advisory body to the Governor to a cabinet of Ministers presided over by the premier and having final responsibility over the initiation of public policy. The Governor moved towards the position of a constitutional monarch functioning on the advice of his Ministers. His reserve powers were limited to matters prejudicial to the Royal prerogative and inconsistent with the colonial constitution or with international agreements.

The final stage in the constitutional evolution of the British West Indies was the attainment of independence. While the colonial governments had control over internal affairs, there were certain matters which continued under the jurisdiction of the British Government including defence, foreign relations and trade, and the colonial constitution. Independence enacted by the British Parliament brought these and all other matters under local control. In addition, the Crown-appointed Governor was replaced by a locally appointed Governor-General as head of state. By 1974 only Jamaica, Trinidad and Tobago, Guyana, Barbados and Grenada had gained their independence, though most of the other colonies have secured internal self-government. The independent states have become members of the Commonwealth of Nations, an international organization consisting of independent British and ex-British countries.

4. Constitutional Development in the British West Indies

(a) Jamaica

Following the Morant Bay Uprising in 1865, the old representative system gave way the next year to pure Crown Colony Government. Elections were abolished and a Legislative Council was introduced consisting of a Governor, 6 officials and an unspecified number of nominated unofficials. The Governor was to be advised by an Executive Council consisting of official and nominated unofficial members.

Many white and coloured middle class Jamaicans were dissatisfied with this arrangement from the very beginning and they agitated for reform. Accordingly, a measure of representation was reintroduced in 1884: in addition to 4 officials and 5 nominated unofficials, the Legislative Council was to consist of 9 members elected on a restricted franchise. In this 'balanced' legislature, the Governor was to have both an original and a casting vote to ensure a government majority since the nominated members were appointed on the understanding that they would always support the government. Noteworthy was the fact that the elected members were given financial powers over both taxing and spending in matters other than fixed administrative expenses: if 6 or more of them opposed a financial measure, the official votes would not count.

The 1884 reform did not satisfy Jamaicans for long, and they continued to press for an elected majority. Further reform in 1895 increased the number of elected members to 14, but they did not constitute a majority since the nominated unofficials were increased to 10. Initially, in order to pacify local opinion, the Governor left vacancies unfilled among the nominated unofficials to give the elected members a working majority, but in consequence of a political crisis over the tariff in 1899, this practice was abandoned.

Although Jamaicans continued to demand more representation after 1895, it was not until 1944, following the labour disturbances of the 1930s, that they experienced further reform. In that year, the single chambered Legislative Council was replaced by a bicameral legislature consisting of an entirely elected House of Representatives chosen on the basis of universal adult suffrage from single member constituencies, and a Legislative Council consisting of 3 officials and 10 nominated unofficials who could delay Bills passed by the House for only one year. The Governor was to be advised by a newly-created Privy Council of 4 officials and 2 nominated unofficials. The Executive Council was retained as 'the principal instrument of policy' with control over the introduction of Money Bills and Bills to implement government policy; the cabinet system was thus initiated. In addition to 3 officials and 2 nominated unofficials, the Executive Council was to consist of 5 members elected from and removable by the House of Representatives. An element of responsibility was thus introduced into executive-legislative relations, and the 5 elected Executive Council members or 'quasi-ministers' were empowered to represent certain departments in the deliberations of the Executive Council and House of Representatives.

Further reforms in 1953 provided Jamaica with an Executive Council consisting of a majority of 8 elected legislators who were to be appointed and removed on the advice of the leader of the majority party in the legislature known as the Chief Minister. Ministers were given real responsibility for policy decisions and were to be the effective political heads of their departments.

Reforms brought into operation in November 1957 replaced the Executive Council by a Council of Ministers consisting of 10 Ministers from the House of Representatives and 2 Ministers without Portfolio from the Legislative Council. Ministers were to be appointed by the Governor on the advice of the Chief Minister who was to call and preside over ministerial meetings. These reforms in effect gave Jamaica internal self-government, with the Governor reduced to the position of a ceremonial executive except in cases of emergency.

Following the withdrawal of Jamaica from the Federation of the West Indies as a result of an adverse referendum decision on 19 September 1961, talks were opened up with the British Government concerning the future political status of the island. On 6 August 1962 Jamaica became an independent nation within the Commonwealth of Nations, the first British West Indian colony to achieve this new status.

(b) Trinidad

Trinidad had been captured by the British from the Spaniards in 1797 and never experienced the old representative system, although Tobago did. The white British colonists in the island formed a tiny minority, and it was considered inadvisable by the British Government, despite the frequent requests of the colonists, to give the vote to freeholders since this would have enfranchised foreigners and a larger free coloured group. Besides, the existing system of government by Governor and cabildos, in essence Crown Colony Government, allowed the British Government to introduce desired regulations. After 1801 the Governor was advised by a Council of Advice consisting of five prominent inhabitants.

The first constitutional changes were introduced in 1831 when a Council of Government was established consisting of 6 officials and 6 unofficials nominated by the Governor who had both an original and a casting vote and served as its President. At the same time the Council of Advice was replaced by an Executive Council with advisory powers and consisting of the Governor and three senior officials. As under the old system, the Governor was a virtual autocrat.

As time passed, pressure mounted in Trinidad for an increase in local representation in government; gradually the nominated unofficial segment was enlarged so that by 1900, the Council of Government (now Legislative Council) consisted of 10 officials and 11 nominated unofficials. The Governor's position remained unchanged.

Agitation for constitutional reform by the black and coloured population increased, especially after the First World War. Fearing domination by the negro groups, some East Indian and white leaders opposed reform while other East Indians advocated communal representation. Two years after the Wood Report of 1922, elected representation was introduced into the Legislative Council which now consisted of 12 officials, 6 nominated unofficials and 7 elected members. Again, the Governor's position remained unchanged, but the Executive Council was reformed to contain one or more nominated unofficials from the Legislative Council in addition to the official members.

The high property qualifications for electors and candidates for election along with some language qualifications for electors meant that only six percent of the population qualified to vote, and those elected represented conservative vested interests. Nominated members also were appointed from the propertied class so that Trinidad's working class became firmly convinced that the government was the instrument of the rich to be used for their exploitation and suppression. Political agitation culminated in the labour disturbances of 1937.

Following the Moyne' Commission, further constitutional reforms were introduced in April 1941 increasing the number of elected members in the Legislative Council which now comprised 3 officials, 6 nominated unofficials and 9 elected members. The Governor was deprived of his original vote but retained his casting vote. The Executive Council was also given an unofficial majority, and it consisted of the Governor, 3 officials and 5 unofficials (3 nominated and 2 elected) from the Legislative Council, thereby introducing a measure of responsible government in the legislative process.

The next important reform took place in 1945 when universal adult suffrage was introduced without any property or language qualifications. In addition, the property qualifications of candidates for election were reduced by half. The net result was increased public political awareness expressed in the formation of political parties, as well as in the return of working class representatives to the legislature among whom the East Indian representatives were conspicuous.

Constitutional reform in the direction of control over policy by elected members was the next step and this was secured in 1950. The Legislative Council was reformed to consist of 3 officials, 5 nominated unofficials and 18 elected members, presided over by a non-voting nominated Speaker. The Executive Council consisted of the Governor with a casting vote, 3 officials, one nominated unofficial and 5 elected members chosen from among the members of, and removable by, the Legislative Council. Except in unusual circumstances, the elected members of the Executive Council would actually determine government policies and represent administrative departments in the legislature. These changes introduced the ministerial system.

Under the constitutional reforms of 1950, however, the Governor was given reserve powers to overcome opposition in both the Legislative and Executive Councils. In addition, only the Governor could assign departmental responsibilities to those Ministers elected by the Legislature, and much government business was still introduced and defended by official members to the discomfort of the elected Ministers. These conditions as well as the fact that the Legislative Council still contained nominated members, aroused opposition.

According to constitutional changes in 1956, more elected members were added to both the Legislative and Executive Councils. The former was modified to 2 officials, 5 nominated unofficials and 24 elected members, while the latter comprised the Governor, 2 officials and 7 elected members (the nominated unofficials being dropped). In addition, the elected members now chose the Speaker, previously nominated by the Governor, as well as a Chief Minister who directed the time and business of the Legislative Council and served as Government leader in the Executive Council. As yet, however, the Chief Minister did not choose the other Ministers though he had the right to advise the Governor on the assignment of Ministers to departments as well as their removal.

Following the victory of the People's National Movement under Dr Eric Williams in the general elections of 1956 in which it won 13 of the 24 elected seats, the Ministers were all chosen from this party, and

Williams as leader became Chief Minister. A significant innovation in 1956 also was the use of the nominated seats to give the P.N.M. a clear working majority in the Legislative Council.

The Executive Council gave way to the Cabinet in 1959 when the Governor was directed to call upon the elected member most likely to command a majority in the Legislative Council to form a Government. The appointment and removal of Ministers would be on the advice of the Premier who would normally preside over ministerial or cabinet meetings. The two officials in the Legislative Council were retained as non-voting members, but the following year agreement was reached on their total elimination.

Full internal self-government was attained after the general election of December 1961, when also a bicameral legislature was introduced consisting of a fully-elected lower House of Representatives and a fully-nominated Senate. The final stage in constitutional evolution took place the following year; on 31 August 1962 Trinidad and Tobago became an independent state within the Commonwealth of Nations.

(c) Guyana

The three Dutch colonies of Essequibo, Demerara and Berbice were captured by the British during the French Revolutionary War and retained after the Treaty of Amiens in 1802. The Dutch political institutions in the colonies consisting of a Court of Policy and a Combined Court were retained under the terms of capitulation. The Court of Policy was the legislative and executive body presided over by the Governor and comprised 4 officials and 4 planter representatives. The representatives were elected for an eight year term by the College of Kiezers (electors) who were in turn chosen for life by colonists owning 25 or more slaves. The Combined Court was responsible for financial matters and consisted of the members of the Court of Policy and six Financial Representatives indirectly elected every two years.

The three colonies were united as British Guiana in 1831, and thereafter there was a prolonged dispute over the precise legislative powers of the Court of Policy and the Combined Court. In addition, the elected representatives in the Combined Court were almost continuously at odds with the Governor who favoured an extension of Crown powers instead of more representation. A number of reform proposals were submitted by various groups but these proved abortive.

A political crisis occurred in 1887 when the Governor refused to suppress the Medical Inspector's Report which adversely criticized the living conditions of estate labourers, and the elected members withdrew from the Court of Policy thereby bringing legislative activity to a standstill. Constitutional reform took place four years later. The Court of Policy was increased to 7 official and 8 elected members presided over by the Governor who had both an original and a casting vote. The College of Kiezers was abolished, and the vote was extended to all colonists with an annual income of $480. The life of the Court of Policy was reduced to five years, and the Governor could dissolve it at any time. In addition, the Governor had the veto power over legislation and the exclusive right to originate ordinances. The Court of Policy lost its executive powers to a newly created Executive Council consisting of the Governor, 4 officials and 3 nominated unofficials. The Combined Court comprising the members of the Court of Policy and six Financial Representatives was retained with considerable power over taxation since it could strike out items.

Further constitutional reform followed recurring budgetary deficits between 1920 and 1927 and a commission of enquiry in 1926. An Act of the British Parliament in 1928 abolished the Combined Court and replaced it with a Legislative Council composed of the Governor as president with a casting vote only, 10 officials, 5 nominated unofficials, and 14 members elected on a restricted franchise but with the vote extended to women also. Since a government majority could be obtained in the legislature, the net effect of the reform was to introduce Crown Colony Government.

The Legislative Council was reformed in 1943 to effect a relative increase in the elective element; thereafter it consisted of the Governor, 3 officials, 7 nominated unofficials and 14 elected members. At the same time, the unofficials were given a majority in the Executive Council which now consisted of the Governor, 3 officials, and 5 unofficials nominated by the Governor from the Legislative Council. The pre-ministerial advisory committee system was also introduced in 1943.

Two years later voting qualifications were lowered and the franchise was extended to adults literate in English who owned land worth $150 or had an annual income of $120.

Three years after the Waddington Commission of 1950, Guyana experienced further constitutional reform. A bicameral legislature was introduced consisting of a State Council of 9 nominated members, and a House of Assembly of 3 officials and 24 elected members, the latter elected on the basis of universal adult suffrage from single member constituencies. The Executive Council now included the Governor, 3 officials, and 7 Ministers of whom 6 were elected by the Assembly and one without portfolio was from the State Council. The six Assembly Ministers were assigned portfolios by the Governor, and they could be removed by him or by the Assembly.

Under the 1953 Constitution, senior officials controlled security, the Civil Service and foreign affairs, and no Money Bill could be introduced without the approval of the Governor who, in addition, exercised reserve powers.

The 1953 Constitution was suspended within a few months on the grounds that the majority People's Progressive Party was trying to subvert it. During the next three years, Guyana was governed under a modified Crown Colony system consisting of an entirely nominated single chamber legislature and an Executive Council consisting of the Governor, 3 officials, and 7 nominated unofficials, two of whom were given ministerial portfolios.

The Renison Constitution was introduced in 1956 providing for a unicameral legislature of 3 officials, 11 nominated unofficials and 14 elected members. After the 1957 elections, the Governor chose to fill only six of the nominated unofficial seats thus giving the legislature an elected majority. In addition, the ministerial system was reintroduced: the Executive Council was to consist of the Governor, 3 officials, and 5 Ministers chosen from among the elected legislative members.

In August 1961 the colony was given a new constitution providing for full internal self-government but with safeguards concerning the police and Civil Service; defence and external relations remained under British control. Independence was achieved on 26 May 1966; a significant innovation was the introduction of proportional representation in place of the previous 'first past the post' as the system of voting at general elections. Provision was also made for the future introduction of republican status, and on 23 February 1970 Guyana was declared a Co-operative Republic. However, the country has remained a member of the Commonwealth of Nations since its independence.

(d) Barbados

Among the British colonies in the Eastern Caribbean, Barbados alone retained the old representative system of government consisting basically of a Governor, a nominated Legislative Council and an elected Assembly. Barbados was never brought under Crown Colony Government.

The only important change in the nineteenth century was the adoption in 1891 of an Executive Committee consisting of the Governor, 2 senior officials, and 5 nominated members (four from the Assembly and one from the Council). The Executive Committee exercised power until 1954, and it had the sole responsibility for initiating Money Bills.

As elsewhere in the British West Indies, the years between the First and Second World Wars saw the demand for constitutional reform by such political organizations in Barbados as the Democratic League and the Progressive League.

The first reform was effected in 1944 through a Bill introduced by

Grantley Adams as leader of the Labour Party in the Assembly. The Bill when passed reduced property qualifications for voting by almost one-half and extended the franchise to women with the result that the electorate was increased from about six thousand to almost thirty thousand.

A quasi-ministerial system was introduced and responsible government initiated two years later when Governor Sir Henry Grattan Bushe announced that the elected member who was a party or coalition leader able to command a majority in the Assembly would nominate three other elected members to sit on the Executive Committee, and that these four members would represent specific administrative departments in the Executive Committee and Assembly. From 1946, therefore, Barbados was governed under a system by which the elected majority party exercised executive power in policy-making except in unusual circumstances.

The 'Bushe Experiment' was useful in creating a closer link between the Assembly and Executive Committee, but the quasi-ministers did not have any real authority to direct departmental policies or even the salary to devote full time to departmental business.

The power of the elected Assembly was increased vis-à-vis the nominated Council in 1947 when the latter's legislative power was reduced to a one year suspensory veto. Four years later, universal adult suffrage was introduced, property qualifications of candidates for election were abolished, and the life of the Assembly was extended from one to three years.

The Ministerial system was adopted in 1954; henceforth the governor would ask the majority leader, or leader able to command a majority in the Assembly, to become Premier and then propose four other Assembly members as Ministers. The Ministry so formed would have almost complete control over policy-making, and only through it could Bills, including Money Bills, be introduced in the Assembly.

The reforms of 1954 advanced Barbados towards the Cabinet system though official and nominated unofficial members from the Council continued to sit on the Executive Committee. The existence of a nominated Council also created an anomalous situation. Therefore, in 1959 the Premier was empowered to nominate a member of the Council to serve as Minister Without Portfolio on the Executive Committee and leader of government business in the Council. He and the other Ministers would meet as a cabinet under the chairmanship of the Premier and make all executive decisions except those reserved for the Governor-in-Council. Internal self-government was introduced by these changes. Barbados finally achieved independence in November 1966, and like Jamaica, Trinidad and Guyana, it became a member of the Commonwealth of Nations.

(e) The Leeward and Windward Islands

By 1898 all the British colonies in the Leeward and Windward groups had been given Crown Colony status with Legislative Councils composed of officials and nominated unofficials but without elected members. Four years later, the legislature of the British Virgin Islands took a unique step and legislated itself out of existence and transferred political power over the Presidency to the Governor and Federal Legislature of the Leeward Islands.

The first step towards the restoration of representative government in the Leeward and Windward Islands was taken after the First World War, though changes were introduced slowly. An elected minority was introduced into the Legislative Councils of all the Windward Islands in 1924 following recommendations of the Wood Report, but not until 1936 in the Leeward Islands (St. Kitts-Nevis-Anguilla, Antigua and Montserrat). A further change in 1936 reduced the official and nominated unofficial members in the legislatures of both the Windward and Leeward Islands to create an unofficial majority of nominated and elected over official members.

Further constitutional advances came in 1951. The four Windward Islands were given legislatures of the same composition, each to consist of the Administrator as president with a casting vote only, 2 officials, 3 nominated unofficials, and 8 members elected from single member constituencies by universal adult suffrage with no literacy test. The Leeward Islands, except Montserrat and the British Virgin Islands, were given a similar system. Montserrat received a smaller Legislative Council of 2 officials, 2 nominated unofficials, and 5 elected members, while the British Virgin Islands, returning to the mainstream of constitutional government, had a restored Legislative Council of 2 officials, 2 nominated unofficials and 4 members elected by literate adults.

In 1951 the Windward and Leeward Islands were also given Executive Councils each consisting of 2 officials, one nominated unofficial from the Legislative Council chosen by the Governor, and 3 elected representatives from the same body chosen by their elected colleagues.

The very same year, the committee system was implemented in the Windward and Leeward Islands in order to familiarize the elected members of the Executive Council with the practical operation of administrative departments.

The ministerial system was introduced in 1956 when the elected members of the Executive Council were placed in charge of groups of departments as Ministers. Since these Ministers comprised a majority in the Executive Council, they could control policies, but the Governor held reserve powers in cases of emergency.

Three years later, it was agreed that the elected Executive Council members should be selected by the member of the Legislative Council most likely to command a majority in that body. This reform in effect introduced the cabinet system of ministerial government.

A final constitutional change took place in the Windward and Leeward Islands (except the British Virgin Islands) following the collapse in 1962 of the Federation of the West Indies of which they formed a part. Britain tried to keep the seven islands together in a smaller federation, but when this failed a new status of independent statehood in association with Britain was given in 1967 to Antigua, St. Kitts-Nevis-Anguilla, St. Lucia, Grenada, Dominica and, in 1969, to St. Vincent. Montserrat remained aloof from this arrangement and so did Anguilla when in 1967 it broke its political connections with St. Kitts-Nevis.

5. Associated Statehood

Following the break-up of the Federation of the West Indies, political development among the participating units took two main directions – independence and associated statehood. Independence was the direction taken by Jamaica, Trinidad and Barbados, while associated statehood was the direction given by Britain to Antigua, St. Kitts-Nevis-Anguilla, St. Lucia, Grenada and St. Vincent, through an imperial enactment of 1966.

Associated statehood stemmed from the too small and too poor nature of the islands to maintain the responsibilities of independence. However, the associated states have full control over their internal affairs and can even pass laws amending their own constitutions. Political control in each state is exercised by a Premier and a cabinet of Ministers drawn from the party capable of commanding a majority in the local legislature. A Crown appointed Governor plays a largely ceremonial and politically powerless role in government. Constitutional provision has been made to safeguard the fundamental rights and privileges of the people within a democratic system.

Under associated statehood Britain cannot pass laws affecting the states without their consent. However, Britain has retained authority over their foreign relations and external defence. In these two areas there is some measure of shared responsibility.

In foreign relations Britain cannot act unilaterally to bind the states in any international agreement or obligation: the states must first give their approval. In addition, the states have been empowered to seek membership in international organizations, to negotiate trade agreements, and to conclude technical assistance programmes with other independent countries.

Britain has undertaken to defend the associated states against external attack on condition that they provide the necessary military facilities. In addition, the states cannot allow another nation the use of their territory or facilities without British consent. British forces stationed within an associated state can be used by the local government with British consent to suppress civil disorders such as riots.

The associated states generally seem satisfied with this new status: it guarantees maximum self-government and foreign representation without the responsibility of defence. While they are thus free of heavy financial burdens they can still rely upon British financial subsidies and trade preferences. Besides, the status is not permanent; each state is free at any time to sever its relationship with Britain. Political independence can still be achieved.

Two important changes in the constitutional relationship of the associated states have taken place since the introduction of the new arrangement in 1967. The first change has been the secession of Anguilla from political union with St. Kitts-Nevis because of the previous neglect of its affairs by the central government in St. Kitts and the desire for more local autonomy. The island thereafter reverted to a more distinctly colonial status under the British Government but with a Council of its own having combined executive and legislative powers. The second change has been the political independence of Grenada on 7 February 1974 despite widespread local demonstrations of discontent with the government of Premier Eric Gairy.

6. The Aftermath of Independence

While the smaller British West Indian territories were moving towards associated status and increasing self-government under continued British control, the larger territories achieved their political independence: Jamaica and Trinidad in August 1962; Guyana in May 1966 and Barbados in November 1966. For these territories, the post-independence period was marked by new initiatives in foreign relations as well as in domestic affairs.

Independence gave the new Caribbean nations complete control over their foreign affairs for the first time. While retaining traditional ties especially in trade relations, new connections were made. All four decided to enter the Commonwealth of Nations – an international organization comprising independent British and ex-British countries. As a result of this membership Jamaica, Trinidad, Guyana and Barbados are often referred to as the Commonwealth Caribbean. The association has facilitated co-operation, the frank discussion of problems, technical assistance and preferential trade agreements.

Independence has also brought about membership of two other international bodies – the United Nations and the Organization of American States. Membership in these organizations has made available to the Commonwealth Caribbean a wide range of technical and financial assistance for economic development and the improvement of social services while opening new avenues of friendship and for the redress of grievances. While all four new states have become members of the United Nations with a vote each in the General Assembly, to date only Guyana has been excluded from the Organization of American States because of its border dispute with Venezuela which claims almost five-eighths of the country. Within the world body, the Caribbean states have aligned themselves with the Afro-Asian bloc of so-called 'Third World' countries, to work against international political and social injustices such as colonialism and racial discrimination.

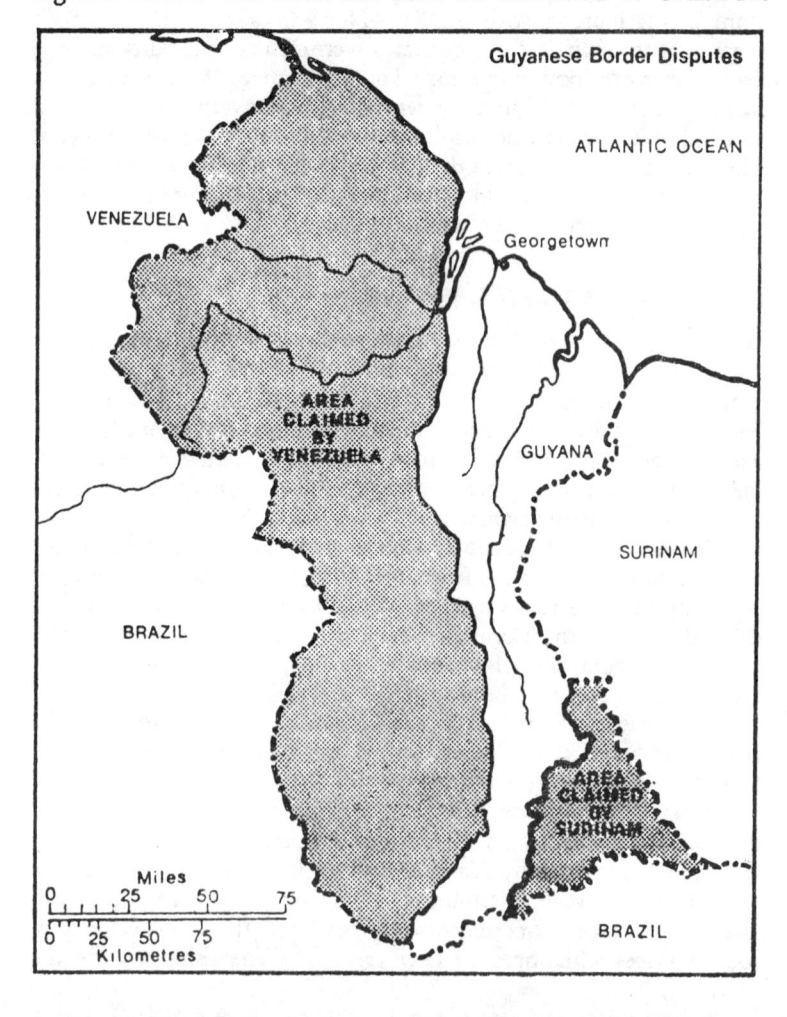

Nearer home, independence has led to new moves to establish closer ties among West Indian territories themselves, whether independent or dependent, British or non-British, in an effort to resolve problems of a regional nature. The result has been the formation of CARIFTA (which later gave way to the Caribbean Common Market and Community) and the Regional Development Bank, and intensified co-operation in various educational, social, economic, scientific and technical areas. Co-operation has developed to such an extent as to lead to a resumption of discussions concerning the possible formation of some kind of political union among Caribbean territories. A dramatic development recently has been a growing friendship and contact between the Commonwealth Caribbean and Cuba despite the political estrangement between the latter and the United States.

In domestic affairs, independence witnessed an increasing search for the realities of nationhood and this quest was demonstrated in the intensification or evolution of new political, economic and social forms.

After independence the Commonwealth Caribbean countries continued their commitment to the democratic process expressed in universal adult suffrage, representative legislatures and the two-party state. Generally there has been greater emphasis on pragmatic rather than on ideological politics. In each of the states a Governor-General, representative of the British monarch though himself a citizen of the particular Caribbean state, served as head of state. The significant departure from this practice took place in February 1970 when Guyana was proclaimed a Co-operative Republic with a President as its head of state.

In other political matters, governments have been concerned with combating divisiveness within the society. The need to create national unity has been particularly evident in Guyana and Trinidad because of the various ethnic groups there, though division also exists in the other states because of preferential treatment based on party politics. In addition, governments have expressed a concern for greater national awareness among the people and have sought to create it partly through the adoption of a local honours system to replace the British system.

Economically, there has been an upsurge of activity since independence in the search for economic viability. Private initiative has been encouraged and it has expanded, but governments have also been very active. Economic diversification has been sought, and development corporations have been formed to promote both agriculture and industry. Port facilities have been developed, roads and other infrastructures built, and airports and airport installations expanded. Central banks have been established, feasibility surveys have been undertaken, development plans have been prepared, and foreign capital investment encouraged. Wherever possible, without danger to employment, improved technology has been introduced. Lastly, there has been a continuous search for wider and better markets in which to buy and sell.

STATISTICAL ABSTRACTS OF THE BRITISH CARIBBEAN DURING THE PERIOD OF SELF-GOVERNMENT AND INDEPENDENCE

Country	Area (sq. mls.)	Population 1960	Population 1970	Revenues* 1960	Revenues* 1970	Expenditures* 1960	Expenditures* 1970	Imports* 1960	Imports* 1970	Exports* 1960	Exports* 1970
Barbados	166	232,327	238,141	26.0	76.8	22.7	89.5	83.3	235.0	43.9	79.2
Grenada	133	88,677	104,188³	8.1	14.3³	7.7	14.2³	14.8	26.3³	7.2	10.0³
Guyana	83,000	575,270	714,000	56.2	162.7⁵	50.7	135.0⁵	147.6	268.2	127.3	268.0
Jamaica	4,411	1,609,814	1,890,700	191.85	247.4	187.5	256.4	372.0	437.8	272.0	283.1
Trinidad & Tobago	1,980	827,959	1,026,750	186.7	348.4	191.7	389.1	504.6	1,084.8	491.8	960.3
Antigua	170½	54,354	63,000⁴	9.6	—	9.6	30.4⁵	15.6	39.1³	4.3	5.0³
British Virgin Islands	59	7,338	10,500	0.3	6.4	0.8	6.8	1.7	10.2	0.4	0.07
Dominica	305	59,916	70,352	5.0	15.0	6.1	16.5	10.0	31.3	6.2	11.7
Montserrat	39	14,538¹	12,300	2.0	4.0	2.0	3.9	—	8.8	—	0.5
St. Lucia	238	94,720	101,064	6.1	—	5.9	18.5	12.0	41.5⁴	5.6	11.4⁴
St. Kitts-Nevis-Anguilla	136	56,591	34,492	6.7	11.3	6.7	12.2	12.1¹	23.5	9.6¹	8.3
St. Vincent	150	79,948	89,129	5.1	12.2	4.6	18.2	13.0	30.5	6.0	6.6

*In millions of dollars (B.W.I.)   ¹1959; ²1967; ³1968; ⁴1969; ⁵1971

Socially, there has been a concerted effort to improve the nature and quality of social services. For example, low and middle-income housing has been constructed at government expense and either sold or rented to workers. Medical facilities have been expanded partly through the construction of more hospitals and rural clinics and in the training and employment of more doctors and nurses. Besides, governments have instituted birth-control programmes to reduce the birth-rate and limit population growth in an attempt to ease the problems of high population density. In education, more schools have been built, teacher training expanded, and free secondary education extended to more students. Moreover, greater emphasis has been placed on technical and vocational education, and while no new university has been started since independence, those in existence have been retained and expanded.

Compared with the long colonial period, tremendous strides have been made since independence to deal with the large variety of outstanding problems. Political independence has been justified, but much is left to be accomplished in the face of very great difficulties. All of the independent territories lack adequate capital most of which can be obtained from metropolitan countries only at high rates of interest. Skilled workers, managerial and supervisory personnel, technicians and specialists are in short supply and their numbers are continuously being reduced by the 'brain drain'. Besides, control of economic enterprises by foreign capitalists results in a flow of profits away from the territories rather than being reinvested here for overall development.

Conclusion

By the early 1970s the British Caribbean territories were in different stages of political evolution. Five of them, Jamaica, Trinidad, Guyana, Barbados and Grenada, have become independent, most of the Windward and Leeward Islands have attained internal self-government in association with Britain, and a few others like Anguilla and the British Virgin Islands have retained a greater measure of the traditional colonial status.

Self-government and independence have given West Indians control over their own affairs and have enabled the adoption of policies and measures more relevant to the West Indies. They have permitted a more energetic approach towards demands for public welfare as well as greater control over external affairs than was possible under the earlier governmental systems. Within the context of West Indian society, greater autonomy has contributed to social cohesion and self-respect, and it has enhanced the public spirit and interest in community welfare. The promotion of parliamentary democracy has created a closer bond between leaders and the people while it has halted the tendency towards autocracy and oligarchic tyranny inherent in Crown Colony Government. Moreover, it has done much to stimulate nationalism and to erode the feeling of helpless dependence upon a superior external power.

Even in the fully independent territories, however, several conditions have operated to limit their sovereignty. External agencies still prevail leading to overseas economic dominance: substantial local resources including land, mineral deposits, export commodities, transportation facilities and banks are foreign owned and controlled. The persistence of the traditional commercial ties between the territories and the metropolitan powers results in strategic accommodations which reduce the exercise of sovereign powers. Tax free incentives encourage reliance on foreign capital, and West Indians must buy from those to whom they sell. Moreover, they are still heavily dependent culturally upon the more dominant nations and subservient to metropolitan norms and values.

In the associated states and the other colonies, Britain is still largely responsible for defence and foreign relations. Even in the independent Commonwealth Caribbean, however, as Dr David Lowenthal has indicated, 'great power strategic aims, global economic patterns, the diffusion of technology and of expectations, and the endurance of colonial attitudes all subvert true independence.' The task remains to make self-government more complete and meaningful and to remove all traces of colonialism where it still exists.

Revision Questions

1. Give an account of the old representative system of government.
2. What conditions gave rise to the adoption of Crown Colony Government?
3. Why were West Indians dissatisfied with the working of the Crown Colony system?
4. Trace the progressive constitutional development of the West Indies from Crown Colony Government to full independence.
5. In what ways has political independence proved of advantage to Caribbean territories? What conditions have retarded progress?
6. Trace the constitutional advancement of your own territory since emancipation.

6. Closer Association

The presence of a group of islands with a common imperial affiliation and in somewhat close proximity to each other has always been a challenge to create some form of political or administrative union among them. The desire for closer association has been particularly attractive during periods of economic decline in the hope that such unity would result in greater economy through more efficient administration.

Administrative union has been fairly common in the British West Indies but in the three hundred and fifty year history of the islands only three federations have been formed among them and these lasted for varying lengths of time. A federation of the Leeward Islands in 1674 resulted from action taken by their common governor, but it did not function very effectively and passed quietly out of existence. A more formal federation of the Leeward Islands was organized in 1871 by the British Government; its unpopularity led to demands for defederation, and it was finally dissolved in 1956 in preparation for a wider federation of the Leeward Islands along with Jamaica, Barbados and Trinidad two years later. The federation of 1958 was due largely to the efforts of West Indians themselves but with support coming from the British Government. However, it collapsed four years later when Jamaica and later Trinidad withdrew from it.

Political federation was only one aspect of closer association among the British West Indian territories; several forms of social and economic co-operation also developed among them during the twentieth century. It is hoped that some form of political union will eventually emerge from such co-operative enterprise among West Indians.

1. Attempts at Unification up to 1900

Attempts to unify the British West Indian colonies in the seventeenth and eighteenth centuries had the common objective of producing more efficient administrations in view of the limited economic resources and relatively small population to maintain all the offices of government in each colony. Until 1900 several attempts were made to unify the colonies in various combinations with varying degrees of success. These may be summarized as follows:

(a) From the beginning of English colonization in the Caribbean, attempts were made to group the colonies under a single government. The governor of St. Kitts, the first colony to be settled in 1624, was also made governor of the other settled English Leeward Islands. This was an executive union; from the late 1630s colonies began to develop their own separate legislatures.

After 1663 the Leeward Islands – St. Kitts, Nevis, Antigua and Montserrat – were governed from Barbados, but a separatist movement developed in the former colonies and their Assemblies persuaded the English Privy Council to appoint a separate governor for them in 1671. The formation of this separate Leeward Islands administration broke down the executive unity of the Lesser Antilles and began the series of regional groupings.

(b) It was in the Leeward Islands that federalism was first tried. The governor was empowered by an ambiguous clause in his Commission to call General Assemblies, and in 1674 Governor William Stapleton did so. The vulnerability of the islands to attacks from strong neighbours was the main reason, and the General Assembly remained viable for 37 years during which it legislated on matters of common concern for the Leeward Islands – between 1690 and 1705 no less than 35 Acts were passed. After 1711 the General Assembly lapsed chiefly because of the particularist beliefs of the islands; it was revived for one brief session in 1798 during which some legislation was passed, and it then completely ceased to function. (This federation is discussed more fully in the next section.) In 1816 the British Government revoked the authority of the governor of the Leeward Islands to summon General Assemblies. Furthermore, the islands were divided into two separate administrations with one Governor for Antigua, Montserrat and Barbuda, and another for St. Kitts, Nevis, Anguilla and the British Virgin Islands.

(c) Meanwhile an attempt had been made in 1764 to establish a federal government for Dominica, St. Vincent, Grenada, and Tobago which had been ceded by France to Britain the previous year. The islands were grouped under Governor Robert Melville who was resident in Grenada and he was authorized to organize local and federal governments. Once local Councils and Assemblies had been established in each island, however, the colonists contended that a federation was undesirable and unnecessary and used their new legislatures to obstruct its formation. They were supported by the West India Interest in London, and the British Government instructed Melville to forego the proposed federal legislature.

Dominica secured its own legislature in 1770, followed by St. Vincent in 1776, while Tobago was returned to the French in 1783 and retaken in 1802. Even the executive union came to an end when a separate governor was assigned to each island remaining after the American War of Independence.

(d) Even while they were under Dutch control the then separate colonies of Essequibo and Demerara were united: in 1730 they were given one Directeur-General, in 1789 their Councils were fused into a Combined Council, and in 1792 they became a United Colony. In 1803 the Colony was transferred to the British along with Berbice, and in 1831 Essequibo, Demerara and Berbice were united as the 'Colony of British Guiana'.

(e) In 1833, under a general policy of consolidation, Grenada, St. Vincent, Tobago and Barbados were placed under one governor resident in Barbados; St. Lucia and Trinidad, acquired by Britain during the French Wars, were added two years later. Each island, however, retained its own governmental machinery, the only change being that the chief executive, now called Lieutenant-Governor, had to communicate with the Imperial Government through the Governor in Barbados. Trinidad was given a partial exemption from this requirement, and in 1842 it was made separate with its own governor. A joint appeal court for the Windward Islands was established in 1859.

The Leeward Islands were also reunited in 1833 and Dominica was added to the group; directions given to Governor Evan J. M. MacGregor to summon a General Assembly were resisted by the island legislatures.

(f) The next attempt to restore the Leeward Islands federation was initiated in 1837 by the governor Sir W. M. G. Colebrooke who saw in it a means of obtaining effective legislation governing apprenticeship. With the approval of Lord Glenelg, Secretary of State for the Colonies, writs of election were issued in 1837. The local legislatures protested and were supported by the West India Interest, but Colebrooke went forward with elections to the General Assembly, and nominated two members from each island to the General Council. Responding to pressure, however, Lord Glenelg ordered him to relinquish the plan, and although some representatives were already on the way to Antigua, Colebrooke dissolved the General Assembly before it met. Subsequent unsuccessful efforts

were made by Colebrooke in 1840 to get the federation established.
(g) British Honduras which had been under the nominal jurisdiction of Jamaica since its settlement in the seventeenth century was declared a colony in 1862 and given a Lieutenant-Governor subordinate to the governor of Jamaica, a connection which lasted until 1884.
(h) The initiative for the next attempt to federate the Leeward Islands was taken by the British Government in 1869, no doubt inspired by the Canadian example two years before. Its successful outcome owed much to the persuasive arguments of the governor Sir Benjamin Pine with reluctant Assemblies. The federation of Antigua, St. Kitts, Nevis, Dominica, Montserrat and the British Virgin Islands was created by the Leeward Islands Act passed by the British Government in 1871, which outlined the respective legislative responsibilities of the federal and unit governments. In 1882, the Presidencies of St. Kitts and Nevis were amalgamated, and Anguilla was added to the union the following year. The federation was unpopular from the beginning and continued so since it failed to produce the expected economy and efficiency of government. Eventually Dominica was separated from it in 1940 and placed under the executive authority of the Governor of the Windward Islands, and the federation itself was dissolved in 1956 to make way for the federation of the West Indies. (The Leeward Islands Federation of 1871 is discussed more fully below.)
(i) In the early 1870s the Colonial Office contemplated a confederation of the Windward Islands (St. Vincent, St. Lucia, Dominica, Grenada and Tobago) and Barbados modelled after the Leeward Islands Federation of 1871. However, Barbados was jealous of its political system, and when Governor John Pope-Hennessy tried to bring about the federation he was vigorously resisted by the Barbadian Assembly. Local demonstrations developing into the so-called Confederation Riots occurred in the island in 1876 in protest against the proposed federation and several people were killed and much property destroyed. Pope-Hennessy was subsequently made governor of Hong Kong following a request of the Assembly for his transfer.

The scheme for the federation of the Windward Islands was finally abandoned; instead in 1885 Barbados was given its own governor while each of the other islands received an administrator under a common governor located in Grenada. Furthermore, in 1889 Tobago was brought under the direct authority of the Governor of Trinidad, and when ten years later it was converted into a Ward or local government district of Trinidad with a single representative in the Trinidad and Tobago Legislative Council the amalgamation was complete.

2. The Leeward Islands Federation of 1674

The Leeward Islands were created a separate administrative unit with its own governor in 1671 following the protest of the Assemblies of St. Kitts, Nevis, Antigua and Montserrat to the Privy Council that their interests were being neglected by the governor in Barbados.

The Commission of the new governor of the Leeward Islands contained a vague clause empowering him to convene General Assemblies for the four islands. Nevertheless, in 1674 Governor William Stapleton took the initiative and summoned representatives from each island legislature, though for consultation only. Other meetings followed on a legislative basis. The Commission of Stapleton's successor, Sir Nathaniel Johnson, made definite provision for calling General Councils and Assemblies.

The general legislature of the Leeward Islands was designed to overcome the difficulties of administering four separate islands each with its own administrative and legislative system. Besides, from 1672 to 1713 the West Indies was the scene of almost continuous warfare and the vulnerability of the Leeward Islands to enemy attack made concerted action for defence necessary.

The federal legislature consisted of two chambers: the General Assembly to which the individual islands sent elected representatives, and the General Council which consisted of members nominated by the island Councils, and after 1705 by the governor. Though constitutions were adopted governing the powers and composition of the federal legislature, there was no definite partition of functions between it and local legislatures. Besides, there was no federal budget, and the federal legislature met only when summoned by the governor, and that irregularly.

Even though there were no regular sessions, the federal legislature was fairly productive, and between 1690 and 1705 as many as 35 Acts were passed. The majority of the legislation concerned defence – the drafting of articles of war, the provision of naval stores, and the erection of fortifications. It was generally recognized that the federal Acts once approved by the Imperial Government were binding on all the units, but after 1692 an island could contract out of a federal measure if a majority of its Assembly wished.

The local legislatures jealously preserved their control over expenditure and this contributed to the breakdown of the federal idea. Also responsible was local particularism fostered by the distance and poor communications between the separate units, and the fact that after 1713 the threat of war was absent. Even when war broke out again in 1739, Britain relieved the colonies of the main responsibilities for their defence. There was fear also that Antigua, which was rapidly becoming the richest of the Leewards, might dominate the federal legislature. Moreover, the colonists tended to regard the federal legislature as an extraordinary body superimposed by the Imperial Government so that it might more easily impose its will on the four islands.

The success of the federal legislature depended very much on the quality of leadership provided by the governor; the Codringtons (1689–1704) were popular while their successors Daniel Parke and Walter Douglas were not. After 1705 the federal legislature seldom met and in fact did not do so between 1728 and 1798. In the latter year it was called to deal with a resolution passed by the British House of Commons concerning slavery, and an Act was passed to improve the conditions of slaves in the Leeward Islands. Two other Acts subsequently disallowed by the Crown were passed, one to remove the civil disabilities of Roman Catholics and the other to abolish the $4\frac{1}{2}$ percent duty levied by the British Government on Leeward Islands exports.

After 1798 the federal legislature again ceased to function, and in 1816 the power to convene it was removed from the Commission of the Governors of the Leeward Islands.

3. The Leeward Islands Federation of 1871

The federation of the Leeward Islands was undertaken to overcome the problems created by the existence of too many and too expensive governments among islands suffering from economic decline and unable to support adequately all the offices of government in each. Besides, it was becoming increasingly difficult to find people of ability and leisure to participate in the government of the colonies. Administrations were inefficient, the legal system, for example, being slow and often capricious. It was hoped that federation would reduce the cost and increase the efficiency of administration by providing certain common services.

The original plan to revive federation in the Leeward Islands stemmed from the Colonial Office, but it was Governor Sir Benjamin Pine who by hard work and persuasive argument was able to overcome the 'spirit of self-importance and narrow patriotism' of reluctant island legislatures which formed the major obstacle to federation. After eighteen months of negotiations agreement was reached, and the federation of the Leeward Islands was created by an Act of the British Parliament in 1871.

The Act established a federation consisting of six Presidencies – Antigua, St. Kitts, Nevis, Dominica, Montserrat and the British Virgin Islands – subsequently reduced to five when St. Kitts and Nevis were amalgamated in 1882. The federal government, based in principle on the Crown Colony system, was to consist of an Executive Council nominated by the governor, and a Legislative Council of 20 members, half of whom would be nominated officials and the other half elected by the unofficial members of the local legislatures from among themselves. The government was located in Antigua, the governor's official residence, but he was instructed to visit the other islands frequently, and the Legislative Council was to meet alternately in Antigua and St. Kitts. The expenses of the federal government were to be met by the units, each contributing in proportion to the number of its representatives in the federal legislature, though in reality payments fluctuated according to the expenses incurred for special services.

The federal legislature was to meet annually and for three-year terms, and its power was restricted to specified subjects – personal property, criminal law, the supreme court and court procedure, militia and police, the post office, currency and audit, quarantine, immigration, education, prison and lunatic asylum – and residual powers were lodged with the local legislatures which also had the right of concurrent legislation on the specified subjects. In case of conflict between local and general enactments the latter were to prevail. Moreover, the federal government could legislate on any matter referred to it by any local legislature, and this proved a most productive source of additional power for it.

The Leeward Islands federation was unpopular from the start and remained so largely because the expected reduction in government expenditure did not materialize. The savings made by having one Attorney-General, one Auditor-General and one Colonial Secretary for all the islands were offset by the new charges for the judiciary and salaries of the local executives. To islanders their contributions seemed too large for services received, and they complained of neglect by the governor and federal officials. Local legislatures jealously guarded their fiscal autonomy; they refused to relinquish the power of taxation to the federal legislature, and they kept financial contributions to a minimum. As local and federal legislatures did not often agree on policies obvious difficulties and frustrations ensued. Administration was not markedly more efficient than before despite some useful work done by federal officials.

The federal government acquired and retained the reputation of being a costly impediment to good government. It is not surprising, therefore, that 'defederation' became a political catchword in the Leeward Islands. Slight modifications were made with regard to representation and budgetary appropriations, but official Commissions which commented on the federation in 1884, 1894, 1897 and 1922 did not recommend any substantial changes, and the existing system was preserved in all its essentials. Most of the Commissions agreed that Dominica should be separated from the federation, but it was not until 1940 that the separation was effected.

By that time the end of the federation was fast approaching. The Standing Closer Association Committee discussing federation of the West Indies in 1949 recommended that the Leeward Islands should enter it as individual units rather than as a group. The following year, the federal Legislative Council passed a resolution calling for the abolition of the Leeward Islands federation. The London Conference of 1953 agreed on a plan for West Indian federation, and in preparation for it an imperial Act of 1956 defederated the Leeward Islands and converted the units into separate colonies under a single governor.

4. Proposals for Closer Union in the West Indies after 1871

Of great importance were the official reports because of their intrinsic significance, the greater publicity attendant upon them, and the discussion they generated.

(a) The Royal Commission of 1882 appointed to investigate the financial condition of certain British West Indian colonies with a view towards the introduction of more economic administrations, urged joint consultation and common action on the part of all the West Indian colonies in order to achieve uniformity in certain matters. It envisaged some form of federation ultimately.

(b) Sir Robert Hamilton appointed as sole Commissioner in 1894 to enquire into the unsettled state of affairs in Dominica expressed himself in favour of a West Indian federation. However, he did not think that the step should be taken immediately since the islands were 'not yet sufficiently advanced.'

(c) The Royal Commission of 1896-7 saw no value in political federation, or even in a unified West Indian civil service, though it recommended improved communications among the islands.

(d) The Royal Commission of 1910 on Canada-West Indies Trade Relations declared in favour of closer union of West Indian colonies since it had been shown that negotiations between a large country and a number of small separate governments were cumbersome.

(e) After a tour of investigation of the British West Indies in 1921, Major Wood (later Lord Halifax) then Under-Secretary of State for the Colonies, reported that public opinion, especially in Barbados, was not favourably disposed towards federation. He reported the immense obstacles to be overcome such as a diversity of culture and economic organization, and the difficulties of communication. However, he proposed the closer association of Trinidad and the Windward Islands. Later discussions took place on this proposal but no progress was made.

(f) The West Indian Sugar Commission of 1930 also stopped short of federation, but it recommended an administrative association of the

Leeward and Windward Islands as being more conducive to agricultural progress and prosperity.

(g) The Closer Union Commission of 1932 composed of General Sir Charles Fergusson and Sir Charles Orr rejected the idea of a large West Indian federation but stressed the possibilities of co-operation in agriculture. It considered the feasibility of forming a closer union of the Leewards and Windwards to achieve greater economy and efficiency in administration. Grenada rejected the proposal, but a conference of the other territories held in St. Lucia endorsed the recommendation, again with negative results.

(h) The Moyne Commission of 1938 advised caution with regard to a general federation; it favoured treating the area as an administrative unit and recommended a unified West Indian civil service and development and welfare programmes on a regional basis. It proposed a federal union of the Leewards and Windwards as a useful prelude to a larger federation of all the British Caribbean colonies.

In addition to the official comments on closer union, a number of unofficial proposals for federation were made in the nineteenth and twentieth centuries, which were prompted in part by the official reports. The most important of these were made by C. S. Salmon and Nicholas Darnell Davis in 1888 and 1890 respectively following the report of the Royal Commission of 1882, and by Gideon Murray, J. Meikle, G. R. Rippon and Sir Norman Lamont all in 1912 on the occasion of the Royal Commission of 1910 on Canada–West Indies trade relations.

Between the First and Second World Wars the question of federation was taken up by radical political and nationalist movements. Following the proposal of Sir Edward Davson, President of the Associated Chamber of Commerce of the West Indies, for 'federation by conference,' West Indian Conferences were held in London in 1926 and in Barbados in 1929 which promoted the idea of closer union though no direct political issues were discussed.

When in January 1926 labour leaders from Trinidad, Guyana and Surinam met in Georgetown for the first British Guiana and West Indies Labour Conference, federation occupied a prominent place in their speeches. The Conference adopted, with only one negative vote, a resolution calling for the federation of Guyana and the British West Indies.

In preparation for the visit of the Closer Union Commission of 1932 a West Indian Unofficial Conference was held in Roseau, Dominica, in October 1932. The Conference was called on the initiative of the Dominica Taxpayer's Reform Association (DTRA) and its chairman was Cecil Rawle, an eminent Dominican lawyer and President of the

DTRA. Delegates from Representative Government Associations and other kindred groups attended from Trinidad, Barbados and the Leeward and Windward Islands. The Unofficial Conference marked the first occasion on which leaders of the Eastern Caribbean met and made a concerted demand for federation and self-government backed by a draft constitution by which the federation could be effected. Lastly, the Conference created the West Indian National League to propagate the principles of West Indian nationalism in each colony and 'to secure common political action in matters of common interest.'

The federal ambitions of the Unofficial Conference did not come to fruition, but interest in federation continued. Following the labour disturbances of the mid-1930s, the cause of federation became identified with the rapidly developing labour movement expressed in trade unions and political parties. The federal movement gained more mass support and became more powerful. Another draft federal constitution prepared by Grantley Adams of Barbados was adopted by the British Guiana and West Indies Labour Conference meeting in Trinidad in 1938 to prepare a set of proposals to put before the Moyne Commission.

The desire for federation had been greatly stimulated by both the official and unofficial lines of action, but progress seemed threatened by the outbreak of the Second World War in 1939. Besides, the caution shown in recommending closer association and the failure to effect a federation were due to various factors inherent in the West Indian situation.

5. Conditions Retarding the Adoption of Federation

Among the conditions which retarded the adoption of the federal idea in the late nineteenth and twentieth centuries can be mentioned, firstly, the geographical separateness of the various colonies. Stretching in an arc from Guyana in the east to Jamaica in the west, the colonies are separated by a wide expanse of sea. For example, from Trinidad or Barbados to Jamaica is more than 1,100 miles in a straight line, and still more by shipping routes.

The problems created by distance were aggravated by the backward state of inter-colonial communication both by steamer and by cable telegraph. As far as ocean travel was concerned, West Indian colonies could be more easily reached from Britain, the United States and Canada than from each other. Partly because of inadequate communications, the exchange of visitors and news among the several colonies was infrequent thereby contributing to the ignorance West Indians had of each other.

Inter-colonial understanding and co-operation were further retarded by the absence of trade among the colonies. All were primary producing, and most of them produced similar commodities. West Indians had few goods to exchange with each other, there was no mutual dependence for supplies, and most of their trade was with North America and Europe.

It was not unusual for the separate colonies to experience periods of prosperity and of depression at different times from each other. The idea that the financial resources of one colony might be diverted through the action of a federal government to relieve the distress of another did not appeal to West Indians.

From the middle of the nineteenth century, the economies of the West Indian colonies developed in somewhat different directions. Thus, Barbados and Guyana continued as predominantly sugar-producing plantation colonies, St. Vincent and Grenada had largely abandoned plantation agriculture for peasant holdings, and Trinidad represented a more even mixture of plantations and small-holdings, and had, in addition, become mineral producing. Again, while the Leewards, Windwards and Barbados had little room for economic expansion, the same was not true of Jamaica, Trinidad and Guyana. Differences in economic organization were reflected in different attitudes towards federation.

The past development of the islands more or less in political isolation from each other encouraged the spirit of particularism caused by lack of contact. By the later nineteenth century, the colonies had attained different levels in their political evolution. They were a medley of representative, semi-representative and Crown Colony governments, for which a federal government seemed an inappropriate constitutional device to achieve unity and co-operation.

6. Conditions promoting Federation in the twentieth century

Despite the various factors which operated against federation, a number of other conditions created the need for such a political organization.

(a) Social and economic conditions in the colonies were in a dismal state as reflected in extremely low wages, high unemployment, and poor educational, medical and housing facilities. Moreover, the best lands were unfairly concentrated under foreign absentee ownership and control. Through joint political action it was believed that a more satisfactory and fairer system could be established.

(b) After emancipation West Indian affairs were generally neglected by Britain since the colonies did not have much to offer by way of raw materials and markets. This neglect was an additional source of anxiety and unrest among West Indians. Gradually the idea deve-

loped among intellectual groups that their problems could be more readily solved by themselves through closer union or federation.
(c) Federation could allow for greater progress in regional economic development. West Indians already had the example of the functioning of other regional institutions such as the Imperial Department of Agriculture to show them the positive values of co-operation.
(d) West Indians were aware that united action could increase their bargaining power in international negotiations and thereby secure for them better terms in world trade.
(e) The resurgence of United States imperialism in the Caribbean in the twentieth century, expressed by military intervention in and political control over several West Indian territories, suggested the need for a strong and viable nation, such as a federation could produce, to deal more effectively with the colossus to the north.
(f) The federations of Canada and Australia provided clear examples of political unions within the British empire; the existence of these new states strengthened the desire for self-government among West Indians and increased the impetus towards federation.
(g) In the Caribbean itself, the direct representation of Martinique and Guadeloupe in the French National Assembly, and the proposed Dutch scheme to join the Netherlands Antilles into a single self-governing federation constituted a challenge to British West Indians to develop in the same direction towards political consolidation.
(h) The experiences of West Indians resident and educated abroad created a new awareness of the value of political independence and co-operation. Moreover, they acquired the knowledge necessary to operate political systems.
(i) For a long time federation was seen as a necessary first step in the direction of an advanced political status for West Indian colonies and for their eventual achievement of dominion status and independence.

7. Steps towards the Federation of 1958

Developments during the Second World War, such as the expansion of transportation facilities and the setting up of the Colonial Development and Welfare Organization and the Anglo-American Caribbean Commission, gave West Indians the opportunity to work together on a regional basis, and led to an increased consciousness among them of belonging together.

Federation itself was again advocated in 1944 by the meetings of the British Guiana and West Indies Labour Conference in Georgetown and the Associated West Indian Chambers of Commerce in Barbados. The following year, unofficial legislators from the Windward Islands meeting in Grenada proposed the federation of the Leeward and

Windward Islands as a test of the advantages of a wider union. However, that same year, the first session of the newly-organized Caribbean Labour Congress demanded that a conference, to be held in the West Indies, should be called for the purpose of considering a West Indian federation. It was this action which initiated a number of discussions and led eventually to the federation of 1958.

(a) *The Montego Bay Conference, 1947*

Delegates from all the British Caribbean colonies met at Montego Bay in Jamaica to discuss closer union; it was decided that if agreement in favour of a federation was reached then another conference could be held in the West Indies or in London to discuss it further.

The Conference passed fourteen resolutions which reflected the general mood of the participants: the principle of federation on the Australian model was adopted, but it was understood that federation was not to prejudice or hinder the constitutional advancement of member territories. Delegates created committees to work out the detailed organization of the federation, the two most important being the Regional Economic Committee and the Standing Closer Association Committee.

(b) *The Standing Closer Association Committee Report, 1949*

The S.C.A.C. was composed of members from all the territories represented at the Montego Bay Conference. Its report (popularly known as the Rance Report after the Committee's chairman, Sir Hubert Rance) was published in 1949 and contained concrete proposals for financing the federation and for its constitutional organization. It was received with wide acclaim in the West Indies since federation now seemed a clear possibility; to many the time for resolutions had passed and the time for action had arrived. Moreover, as Professor Lloyd Braithwaite has stated, 'The ideology of the report was completely acceptable to West Indians. The purpose of the federation was to ensure the shortest possible path to political independence and responsible Dominion status.' Only Guyana and Belize rejected the report thereby indicating their intention not to participate in any federation.

(c) *The London Conference, 1953*

This conference was called in April 1953 to deal with the problems and disagreements which had arisen from the Rance Report. Delegates made a detailed examination of specific problems – raising of loans, freedom of movement, unit representation, imperial financial aid, constitutional amendment – and the Rance Report which formed the basis for discussion was substantially amended into a new document called 'The Plan for a British Caribbean Federation.'

(d) The Conference on Freedom of Movement, 1955

It was generally assumed that with federation West Indians would be free to move from one unit to another. However, at the London Conference of 1953 serious difficulties had arisen over the question of migration thus requiring a separate conference to deal with them.

At the Conference of 1955, held in Trinidad, a compromise agreement was reached whereby units were to control immigration on the grounds of health and security, while the federal and local governments would be jointly responsible otherwise. Also, the conference agreed that the federal constitution should state in its preamble that freedom of movement in the area was one of the main aims of the federation. In effect, a definite solution was postponed.

(e) The London Conference, 1956

The final agreement on West Indian federation was worked out at this conference though serious differences developed among the West Indian delegates relating mainly to the questions of customs union and the site of the federal capital. Eventually, a decision on the first was postponed while the second was referred to a Site Commission.

(f) The Standing Federation Committee Meeting, 1957

The main decision pertained to the site of the federal capital; shortly before, the Site Commission had reported Barbados, Jamaica and Trinidad as its choices in order of preference, and the Standing Federation Committee selected Trinidad as the best location for communication and for drawing upon essential services.

The Committee also adopted the title 'The West Indies' to describe the federation, completed the last details of the federation, and approved the final draft of the federal constitution.

8. The Federation of the West Indies

An Act of the British Parliament was passed on 2 August 1956 for a federation of the West Indies to consist of Jamaica, Barbados, Trinidad and Tobago, the Leeward Islands (Antigua, St. Kitts-Nevis-Anguilla, and Montserrat) and the Windward Islands (Dominica, St. Vincent, St. Lucia and Grenada).

The federal constitution provided for a Council of State consisting of a Governor-General as its president, a Prime Minister and ten other Ministers, a Senate of 19 members (two from each unit except Montserrat which had one) nominated by the Governor-General, and a House of Representatives of 45 members elected by universal suffrage from the various units. Provision was also made for a compulsory review of the constitution within five years.

Lord Hailes, Chief Whip of the Conservative Party in the British House of Commons, was appointed Governor-General of the federation, and elections to the House of Representatives were held in March 1958, along party lines. With support from the leading parties in the major participating units, the Federal Labour Party secured a slight majority over the opposing Democratic Labour Party, and Grantley Adams its deputy leader became Prime Minister. The Federal Parliament was opened by Princess Margaret on behalf of Queen Elizabeth II on 22 April 1958.

The federal government was responsible for 18 areas of legislation indicated in an exclusive list including audit, borrowing, defence, exchange control, immigration and emigration, the public service, federal agencies, and the University College of the West Indies. The functions which it shared with the unit governments on the concurrent list were more extensive and covered 39 areas including customs and excise, movement of persons, postal services, trade unions, weights and measures and aliens. In case of conflict, federal laws were to supersede local laws, but unit governments had residual powers not mentioned on the exclusive and concurrent lists. The British Government could issue Orders-in-Council regarding defence, external relations and the financial stability of the federation.

The federal government had no powers of taxation; instead, its expenses were to be met by a levy imposed on the units: Jamaica to pay 43 percent, Trinidad 39 percent, Barbados 9 percent, and the others much smaller amounts. However, total revenue for any one year was not to exceed $9,120,000 (B.W.I.).

Most of the energy of the federal legislature was dissipated by continuous wrangling over issues aroused by differing conceptions of federation and by local self-interest. Because of the importance of Jamaica and Trinidad, their attitudes were crucial for the future existence of the federation.

Jamaica which was becoming more industrialized and economically more viable by the late 1950s wanted a weak federation which did not have the power of taxation lest Jamaica be made to carry a greater share of the financial burden of the federation. Fears were aroused when in January 1959 Adams threatened to impose retroactive taxation as soon as the federation obtained the power to tax. Moreover, Jamaica stood opposed to a customs union since this would involve it in a yearly loss of £4 million in customs revenue and hamper the development of new industries.

Trinidad, under Premier Eric Williams, was in favour of greater federal control as the only way to make the federation effective. However, Trinidad stood opposed to freedom of movement since, as the most prosperous of the Eastern Caribbean colonies, it was attractive to labourers from the nearby Leeward and Windward Islands. Already by 1959, Trinidad's police were rounding up and deporting immigrants at the rate of 25 a week, much to the displeasure of the other members of the federation.

Another source of concern for the major units was their under-representation in the federal House of Representatives. Since Jamaica and Trinidad were represented by 17 and 10 elected members respectively, their representation was not proportional to their financial contribution. On the other hand, Barbados with five, Montserrat with one, and the others with two members each, were over-represented.

Hampered by differences among the constituent parts as well as by inadequate finances, the performance of the federation was inglorious. The most noteworthy achievements were the Defence Bases Agreement with the United States whereby the latter agreed to release parts of the land it held in Trinidad, St. Lucia, Antigua and Jamaica, and the preparations made to train future federal diplomats. Other activities included the distribution of Colonial Development and Welfare grants, the administration of the West India Regiment, and the support of the University College of the West Indies.

In order to resolve some of the problems of the federation, the constitution was amended by an Order-in-Council in August 1960 to give the federation a greater measure of internal self-government. The Council of State was replaced by a Council of Ministers, and the federal government was given full control over all matters provided by the constitution though defence and external relations remained within the jurisdiction of the British Government.

An Inter-Governmental Conference held at Port-of-Spain in May 1961 reached agreement on a revised system of representation by abolishing the disproportion of seats favouring the small islands. However, a new revised constitution formulated in London shortly after left the federation extremely weak with little control over finances, while complete freedom of movement and a customs union were postponed for nine years.

By this time the federation was in great danger; in June 1960 the Jamaican government had decided to call a referendum on federation and with the approval of the federal government this was conducted on 19 September 1961. The result was a vote of 54 percent against and 46 percent for federation, which was endorsed by the British Government as final.

The continuation of the federation now depended upon the attitude towards it of the Trinidadian government, but following a resounding victory in the general elections of December 1961, Dr Eric Williams announced the following month Trinidad's withdrawal from the federation with an invitation to the smaller islands to join it in a unitary state. Subsequent suggestions for a federation of the remaining colonies, 'the little eight', came to nothing and on 23 May 1961 a final Order-in-Council brought the federation to an end.

9. Causes for the Failure and Collapse of the Federation of the West Indies

Various reasons have been given for the failure of the West Indian federation. Some of these are:

(a) The absence of a sufficiently strong political and ideological commitment to the primary concept or value of federation, for example, federation to promote national greatness. A common colonial past and similarity of culture among the West Indian colonies were necessary but not sufficient reasons for federation.

(b) In the West Indies there were neither politically agreed goals of federation nor the leaders able to develop a federal ideology. Intellectuals like Dr Eric Williams of Trinidad and Norman Manley of Jamaica preferred local to federal politics since they were debarred by the federal constitution from concurrent participation in both.

(c) Politicians were dominated by insular patriotism which retarded co-operation for the benefit of the region. The crisis of the federation can be regarded as a failure in leadership.

(d) The federal government had too weak powers and lacked sufficient finances to be effective, and it was unable to create a noticeable impact on the everyday life of the people. Generally, West Indians found it difficult to identify themselves with the federation; the impression had been created of a useless union and this undermined its existence. It is not surprising, therefore, that a majority of the Jamaican voters in the referendum opposed it.

(e) The centralism of federation proved too weak to overcome the isolationism of the units fostered by traditional nationalist attitudes and geographical separateness.

(f) The islands' economies were not complementary but competitive, and as in the case of bananas in Jamaica and the Windward Islands, and cement and oil-refining in Trinidad and Jamaica, competition bred conflicts among the units which the federal government was unable to reconcile.

(g) Contact among the constituent units of the federation was hampered by inadequate and expensive means of transportation and communication. Most of the islands' trade was with Britain, the United States and Canada, and only about two percent of the federation's total trade was among its units. Lack of meaningful contact elevated the prevailing insular nationalism above regional nationalism.

(h) A federation between the larger islands (Jamaica and Trinidad) and the smaller islands was one of comparatively well-off islands with poverty-stricken ones; the two groups showed great diversity in revenue and per capita income, and in rate of economic growth. Moreover, industrial Jamaica and Trinidad were trade-oriented towards the United States while the others, largely agricultural, were commercially closer to Britain. The long federal negotiations between 1947 and 1958 proved detrimental to the federation by widening the economic gap between the two groups. Economic differences accentuated the difficulties of political federation.

(i) To Jamaica and Trinidad continued participation in the federation meant severe losses in terms of slower economic development and in having to share their assets with poor islands.

(j) The federal structure had too few regional and political associations to reinforce it. Labour unions were essentially island-based, and inter-island competition led union leaders to agitate against the growth of regional ties. The federation's political parties had been organized only when the federation was formed and were weak alliances of existing island parties; as soon as the federal elections were over, the party alliances began to fall apart.

(k) It was found that independence and dominion status, two dominant reasons for the federation, could be achieved without federation.

(l) Neither the federal government, poor in budget, initiative and leadership, nor the unit governments, engaged in a deliberate effort to educate the federal electorate into the meaning and value of federation. Public apathy signalled the death knell of the federation.

(m) The use of coercive power was never contemplated by the British or by the federal government to prevent or reverse the secession of Jamaica and Trinidad. Indeed, the federation did not have the military means to do so.

10. Regional Co-operation and Integration

In addition to the political federation of the British West Indies, the territories engaged in certain limited forms of functional co-operation suggested by their common geographical and economic situation.

Because of the primacy of agriculture in the economy of the British West Indies, it is not surprising that early attempts at co-operation and integration were directed towards its improvement. The Imperial Department of Agriculture founded in Barbados in 1898 was designed to develop by means of research and experimentation improved varieties of sugar cane more suited to West Indian conditions, as well as alternative crops to sugar cane.

The Department of Agriculture was superseded in 1922 by the Imperial College of Tropical Agriculture located in Trinidad with the three-fold purpose of undertaking special research schemes, providing advisory services, and initiating training schemes, all relevant to the area. The College concentrated on postgraduate research for expatriate students, but its graduation of West Indians with diplomas in agriculture opened positions for them in the administration of agriculture in their homelands, which would otherwise have been closed. In 1960 the College was absorbed into the University College of the West Indies as its Faculty of Agriculture, and its teaching scope was expanded.

Because the production of sugar, the main West Indian staple, was subject to international regulation and dependent upon a protected market, organizational action on a regional basis was important. Accordingly, the British West Indies Sugar Association was formed in 1941 to bargain with buyers on behalf of sugar producers. Besides that, Trade Commissions were appointed to Canada in 1934 and to Britain two decades later to promote the sale of West Indian products in those markets. These offices came to an end when the federation was dissolved, and their functions were later assumed by the High Commissioners of the independent territories.

As early as 1917, on the initiative of Sir Edward Davson, son of an Englishman with business interests in Guyana, the Associated Chambers of the West Indies was organized to deal with general matters relating to West Indian commerce. Through discussions and proposals it promoted the idea of a customs union and federation for the region. The organization later came to be called the Incorporated Chambers of the Commonwealth Caribbean.

The Second World War resulted in greater West Indian co-operation in foreign exchange control, and in the bulk purchasing and bulk sale of products. It also witnessed the establishment of the Regional Oils and Fats Conference which gave impetus to local production and control of marketing.

The war period also witnessed the establishment of the Colonial Development and Welfare Organization created and maintained by Acts of the British Parliament in 1940, 1945 and 1955. Under the Acts, a Comptroller assisted by a technical and research staff was responsible for helping British West Indian governments in framing schemes for social and economic development to be financed from imperial sources. Between 1940 and 1958 as much as £27,924,205 had been thus spent. When the federation of the West Indies was formed, the functions of the organization were taken over by it.

An association to encourage and strengthen social and economic co-operation among imperial nations with colonies in the West Indies was the Caribbean Commission. It was set up in 1942 by Britain and the United States, and expanded a few years later to include France and the

Netherlands. During the war the Commission organized a schooner service among the Eastern Caribbean colonies, but its more regular function was to provide colonial governments with technical assistance and advice, and to circulate research information among them. The Commission was transferred from imperial to West Indian control in 1959 and renamed the Caribbean Organization, and six years later it became the Caribbean Economic Development Corporation (CODECA), in effect an agency of the Puerto Rican government with only indirect participation by the other regional governments. CODECA achieved very little and in 1971 it ceased to function.

Partly to promote inter-territorial co-operation and partly to avoid confusion caused by having separate currencies, a Caribbean Currency Board was set up in 1946, which successfully harmonized the currency situation in the Eastern Caribbean. However, a common currency for the entire British West Indies was never achieved, and even that for the Eastern Caribbean eventually disintegrated as Trinidad, Guyana and Barbados became independent and instituted their own separate currencies.

The foundation of the University College of the West Indies in Jamaica in 1948 in association with the University of London was a major landmark in West Indian education. Supported financially by regional governments with some outside assistance, it opened the avenue to higher education to many West Indians who would otherwise have been denied it. It became a full-fledged university in 1962, and campuses were opened in Trinidad and Barbados also. Of importance have been a number of research institutes associated with it in social and economic studies, trade unionism, international relations and education. The University has been plagued by financial and other problems which have limited its performance, but its achievement in developing ideas and programmes for regional advancement cannot be doubted.

From the outset a University College Hospital was established in conjunction with the University College to train nurses and doctors for the region and it developed an international reputation in tropical medicine.

Another significant step in co-operative education was taken in April 1972 when after a decade of discussion the Caribbean Examinations Council was brought into operation to introduce secondary school-leaving examinations relevant to local needs.

Co-operation in transportation was less noticeable because of the small volume of inter-territorial trade, and such trade as there was, was handled by the schooner service of individual territories. Inter-territorial transport was also facilitated by British and Canadian shipping services, and by the subsidized steamship *West Indian*.

During and after the federation, two vessels donated by the Canadian government, the *Federal Palm* and *Federal Maple*, provided regular passenger and cargo services among the federal units under the control of the West Indies Shipping Corporation. The *Federal Palm* was sold in 1972 and plans were initiated to replace it.

In air transport, radio communication and the press, the several territories tended to operate independently, and such co-operative organizations as the Air Transport Council, the Caribbean Broadcasting Union, and the Caribbean Press Association, have not materially improved the quality of services on a regional basis.

Two other regional organizations which also merit consideration are the Caribbean Meteorological Service and the Caribbean Hotels Association embracing, like the Caribbean Commission, a wider political area than the British West Indies, though they are of more recent origin. The former was important for its study of climatic conditions, enabling the adoption of precautionary measures when bad weather was predicted, while the latter worked to co-ordinate policies among its members for the promotion of tourism.

Among the most important West Indian professional associations can be mentioned the Caribbean Union of Teachers (1935), the Federation of the Civil Servants of the West Indies (1944), the Caribbean Medical Association (1948) and the Caribbean Bar Association (1952). At another level, labour problems were dealt with by the British Guiana and West Indies Labour Conference, afterwards by the Caribbean Labour Congress, and yet later by the Caribbean Congress of Labour. All of these professional and labour organizations sought through periodic meetings and discussion to promote their particular interests, and to develop common approaches to common problems, but, whenever possible, they discussed other matters of regional concern. Because of their tendency to follow, their lack of dynamism, and the many governments with which they had to deal, they were not very effective, though the social background of their members ensured more elitist support for West Indian nationalism.

Within the separate legal systems of the British West Indies, Barbados, Tobago and the Windward Islands shared a common Windward Islands Appeal Court which was replaced in 1919 by a West Indian Court of Appeal with a wider jurisdiction to include Trinidad, Guyana and the Leeward Islands also. After the demise of the federation in 1962, the West Indian Court of Appeal was dissolved, and while the Windward and Leeward Islands have maintained a common judiciary and Court of Appeal, the independent territories have established their own Courts of Appeal. However, appeals to the Judicial Committee of the Privy Council have continued, and plans are presently under consideration for a Caribbean Court of Appeal.

The two most important experiments at regional co-operation and integration undertaken recently have been the Caribbean Free Trade Association (CARIFTA) and the Regional Development Bank (R.D.B.). Brought into operation in 1968 with headquarters in Guyana, and including all the members of the former federation as well as Guyana and Belize, CARIFTA sought to promote trade in the products of member territories to lead ultimately to a Caribbean Common Market. Its operation was not markedly successful and it caused severe discontent among the smaller Windward and Leeward Islands; nevertheless, in April 1973 an agreement was reached at the Heads of Government Conference in Georgetown for the introduction of the Caribbean Community (CARICOM) on July 4 of that year.

Located in Barbados, the R.D.B. was brought into operation in 1970 with membership open to all Caribbean territories, and with an operational capital of $50 million (U.S.) from which loans were to be provided to member territories for infrastructural development and integration of industries. Both CARIFTA and the R.D.B. are seen as the prelude to some form of political union among the Caribbean territories.

Conclusion

The federation of the West Indies collapsed and passed out of existence in 1962, but the desire for unity among West Indians has not died. The search for a common political identity goes on spurred by the economic dangers of separation in a steadily contracting world and the growing influence of multinational economic communities and multinational corporations. Political integration could facilitate the adoption and implementation of policies and measures to deal effectively with external interests which threaten to subvert West Indian independence and identity.

Pending political federation co-operation among West Indian territories is expressed in various forms of social and economic enterprise. Foremost among these are the Caribbean Free Trade Association (CARIFTA), the Caribbean Community (CARICOM) and the Regional Development Bank. These organizations have been established to show the economic benefits of closer association in the hope that they would lead to some form of political union. Since 1964 West Indian heads of government have been meeting regularly at 'Summit' Conferences to work out common strategies to deal with common internal and external problems. Because of improved means of communication and transportation West Indians are now much more familiar with each other than they have ever been before.

Friendship exists among West Indians, but another federation seems remote. The animosities, jealousies and mutual distrusts of 1958-62 are still fresh in people's memory, and these raise doubts about the wisdom of a new federation. Besides, many of the personalities involved in the federation of 1958 are still engaged in local politics making political integration questionable. Since 1962, Jamaica, Trinidad, Guyana, Barbados and Grenada have become independent, and other Leeward and Windward Islands have secured internal self-government through associated statehood. The spirit of independence runs strong among them, and there might be unwillingness to share political power with a federal government.

While some individuals may desire federation, the movement towards it can hardly be called popular. Besides, suspicion still lurks among the leaders. For example, no sooner had the Prime Minister of Guyana and the Premiers of Grenada, St. Lucia, Antigua and St. Kitts-Nevis agreed on the Grenada Declaration to initiate some form of political union among them than Premier Compton of St. Lucia announced his withdrawal from fear of the preponderant influence of Guyana in such a union. Only if one of the larger territories joined would he be willing to reconsider unity. However, political leaders of Barbados and Jamaica have declared against a new federation, favouring economic co-operation instead.

Revision Questions

1. What conditions would suggest to West Indians the need for closer co-operation and association?
2. What attempts at closer union were made between the seventeenth and nineteenth centuries? How far were they successful?
3. Outline the attempts made before 1958 to form federations and associations in the West Indies.
4. Why did the withdrawal of Jamaica and Trinidad from the Federation of 1958 result in the breakup of that federation?
5. What obstacles are in the way of Caribbean unity?
6. Do you think that West Indians are seriously in favour of another federation? Why?

7. The United States and the Caribbean

By the end of the eighteenth century, the Caribbean had been under European domination for fully three centuries. The region had been a centre of colonization and trade as well as a base for expansion into North, Central and South America. It was also the arena for almost continuous rivalry and conflict among European nations as they vied with each other for naval and territorial supremacy.

By the end of the Napoleonic Wars in 1815, Britain had emerged over Spain, France and the Netherlands as the most viable imperial and naval power in the West Indies. However, its supremacy was to be short-lived. An effective challenge to it came from the United States of America, a new nation which had emerged on the world scene in 1783 when the thirteen British North American colonies finally won their independence from Britain.

The growth in influence of the United States was to shift the balance of power in the Caribbean; from being the cockpit of European struggle in the western hemisphere, the Caribbean Sea became in effect nothing more than an American lake.

1. Reasons for United States Interest in the Caribbean

A primary consideration which influenced the policy of the United States in the Caribbean was national defence and security or, as it has been termed, 'protective imperialism'. The intention was to create a situation which would safeguard the United States against enemy attack. For this reason, among other actions taken, the United States constructed military bases and centres and maintained military training facilities in the Caribbean.

North Americans had developed trading and commercial interests in the region even before the Declaration of Independence in 1776, and such contacts continued afterwards even though for a time the navigation laws of imperial nations tended to prohibit or restrict them. However, the repeal of the navigation laws and the growing freedom of Caribbean territories to govern themselves served to stimulate United States commercial relations with the region.

Apart from their expenditure in shipping, United States capitalists also had investment in the Caribbean of economic or strategic importance, including sugar in Cuba, petroleum in Trinidad, and bauxite in Jamaica and Guyana. Protection of these vital interests necessitated the creation of a favourable political situation in the territories concerned, even if that meant military intervention and control.

As far as trade and investment were concerned, the territorial ambitions in the Caribbean, real or imagined, of such nations as France and Germany were of concern to the United States which felt its own potential for expansion in the region threatened.

The scheme to construct a canal across Central America in both its conception and accomplishment exerted a profound influence on the global and regional policies of the United States in terms of trade and military strategy.

In their relations with the Caribbean also, Americans harboured missionary and humanitarian impulses to spread some of the benefits of their 'superior' civilization to their 'backward' southern neighbours – to build schools and hospitals, to eradicate disease, to improve agricultural methods and techniques, to improve communications and other public works, and to make for more efficient and honest administration.

From around the beginning of the twentieth century when Britain became less able to maintain its world-wide control of the seas, it in effect yielded strategic control over the Caribbean to the United States.

As the foremost champion of democracy, especially since the First World War, and particularly because of the ideological conflict called the 'cold war' between the United States and the Soviet Union after 1945, the United States was naturally interested in solid foundations in the western hemisphere, and Americans opposed any movement which threatened to undermine them, and with them the national security of the United States.

The independent Caribbean territories are of great importance to the United States; as members of the United Nations, their votes there in support of the United States are seen as being especially useful in the light of 'cold war' politics.

Lastly, it is the belief of some Americans that the denial or curtailment of United States influence in the Caribbean would be difficult to reconcile with the maintenance of the United States as a world power or with any attempt to extend American ideas and institutions to other parts of the world.

2. United States Involvement in the Caribbean in the nineteenth century

During the first decades of the nineteenth century, the United States acquired Louisiana and Florida and thereby obtained an open door in the south to the entire Caribbean. These acquisitions did not mark the beginning of United States contact with the Caribbean since, long before the Declaration of Independence in 1776, the mainland colonies had developed a flourishing trade with this region. Rather, they indicated the beginning of an intensified relation in an attempt by the United States to establish its hegemony in the western hemisphere through the elimination of European influence.

After 1815 a struggle ensued between Britain and the United States for the carrying trade of the British West Indies. The United States had long supplied the West Indian colonies with their essential supplies of lumber and provisions in return for sugar and molasses, and it wanted to continue this trade. The British, however, were determined to maintain their shipping monopoly and sought to enforce the Navigation Laws which forbade trade between British colonies and foreign nations such as the United States had become since their independence. In reply to the British action, in 1817 the United States introduced measures excluding from American ports British ships sailing to and from the West Indies. The trade war hurt everyone involved, including the British, and in 1822 some West Indian ports were opened to certain goods imported in American ships, though they were subject to a ten percent discriminatory import duty.

While the trade war was going on, the United States became involved with Britain in a dispute over trade supremacy in Cuba, a quarrel which was dropped due to American preoccupation with internal problems.

American concern was also expressed over the struggle of the Spanish American colonies for independence which the reactionary powers of Europe wanted to suppress by force of arms. In December 1823, President James Monroe issued the famous statement which warned European powers that any attempt to interfere with the independence of any territory in the western hemisphere recognized by the United States would be regarded 'as the manifestation of an unfriendly disposition towards the United States.' The Monroe Doctrine became the corner-stone of the Caribbean policy of the United States.

After a temporary lapse, United States interest in the Caribbean revived in the 1840s under the impact of 'Manifest Destiny', that is, the belief in an ultimate voluntary union within the United States of all suitable states. Between 1844 and 1848, Texas, California and Oregon were added to the United States, and questions were raised over the possible acquisition of Cuba, Mexico and other Central American territories.

With the beginning of the gold rush in California in 1849, discussions were begun about a possible canal in Central America to facilitate the passage of men and goods from the eastern United States to that state because of the difficulties of overland communication. The result was the Clayton-Bulwer Treaty between Britain and the United States which provided for a neutralized canal under the control of neither of them.

The revival of United States interest in acquiring Cuba led to filibustering attempts under Narcisso Lopez in 1849–51 to seize the island. The failure of these attempts, together with the demands of internal United States politics culminating in four years of civil war (1861–5), diverted American attention away from West Indian affairs. The most significant action taken was the formal recognition of Haiti and Santo Domingo as independent states in 1862 and 1865 respectively.

Even after the civil war, American attention was directed towards internal social and economic reconstruction. The anti-imperialist attitude of the country was reflected in the failure in 1870 of a treaty to purchase the Danish islands of St. Thomas and St. John, and of a Senate Bill to annex Santo Domingo. When the Ten Years' War began in Cuba in 1868, Americans were content to regard it merely as a struggle for liberation rather than as an opportunity to annex the island.

In the later nineteenth century there was reawakened United States interest and involvement in Caribbean affairs. A remarkable economic recovery and industrial over-production suggested the need for wider markets to take care of surpluses. Expansion was also influenced by an intensification of imperialism among western European nations as the United States was afraid that the Caribbean and Latin America would fall under their spheres of influence and domination.

From the mid-1870s there was an increase in private American investment in Central America and the Caribbean in such enterprises as railway construction, mining, banana growing and sugar cane cultivation. Economic investment was particularly noticeable in Cuba. Trade expansion followed and by the early 1890s Americans were clearly dominant in the markets of Cuba, Puerto Rico, Haiti, the Dominican Republic, Salvador and Honduras. The diversification of the economy of Jamaica was so closely associated with United States trade as to provoke discussion of a possible political union between them.

A turning point in United States–Caribbean relations came in 1889 with the holding of the first Pan-American Conference to discuss matters of common concern to the United States and the Caribbean and Latin American states. A few years later, as champion of the independence of states in the western hemisphere, the United States became involved in two incidents, namely, the Venezuela–British Guiana boundary dispute and the Cuban War of Independence.

In the Venezuela–British Guiana boundary dispute, on the threat of war in 1895 the United States President Cleveland demanded of Britain and secured an international boundary commission which reached a settlement of the issue. With regard to the Cuban War of Independence, the United States intervened in 1898 on behalf of the Cubans against harsh Spanish colonialism as well as to protect endangered American interests in the island. The immediate cause of intervention was the blowing up of the United States battleship *Maine* in Havana harbour with the loss of 260 lives, responsibility for which has never been fixed. In the ensuing war with Spain which lasted just a few weeks, the United States emerged victorious and secured Puerto Rico, along with the Philippine Islands in the Pacific, from Spain. The Spanish–American War marked the beginning of a new relationship between the United States and the Caribbean.

3. Extension of United States Influence in the twentieth century

United States relations with the Caribbean underwent important changes in the twentieth century governed by two basic doctrines, namely, the Platt Amendment and the Roosevelt Corollary to the Monroe Doctrine. The Platt Amendment was an agreement exacted from the Cuban government in 1903 after a four year military occupation of Cuba by the United States following the Spanish–American War, whereby the latter secured the right to intervene in Cuban affairs for the preservation of order and good government. The Corollary to the Monroe Doctrine enunciated by the United States President Theodore Roosevelt in 1904 provided that in order to prevent the intervention of European creditor-states in Caribbean territories, the United States would intervene to regulate the financial and other affairs of the Caribbean states concerned.

The Platt Amendment and the Roosevelt Corollary governed the so-called 'big stick' policy of President Theodore Roosevelt as well as the 'dollar diplomacy' of President Taft's administration, and provided the justification for United States intervention in the internal affairs of Panama, the Dominican Republic, Cuba and Haiti.

United States interest in Panama increased during the Spanish–American War which emphasized the need for a short route between the Atlantic and Pacific Oceans for the transfer of warships and troops.

After the war the United States became anxious over the growing German commercial interest in the area. The Clayton-Bulwer Treaty with Britain was set aside and President Theodore Roosevelt formulated an agreement with Columbia for the construction of a canal across the Isthmus of Panama which was then Columbian territory. When the Columbian senate rejected the agreement, Roosevelt supported a revolutionary movement in Panama against Columbia which resulted in an independent Panama Republic. A treaty was speedily negotiated with the new government for the construction of the canal, and years later Roosevelt boasted 'I took Panama'.

United States intervention in the Dominican Republic took place in 1905 when financial insolvency threatened the island with foreclosure by its European creditors. Roosevelt placed an American receiver-general in charge of the Dominican revenues and made successful arrangements for paying off the debt. The United States sphere of influence was subsequently enlarged in 1916 when President Wilson ordered the military occupation of the island. Intervention in Cuba was effected in 1906 upon the request of the Cuban President Estrada Palma; a provisional government was established under American authority, new elections were held, and the island was eventually evacuated in 1909. Further intervention in Cuban affairs took place in later years as in 1912 when President Taft despatched marines to the island, but these were more for the sake of maintaining stability than to erect a 'protectorate'. In Haiti, revolutionary disorders in 1914 led to the occupation of the island by United States marines in 1915.

The same concern for the national interest which governed the United States attitude towards the independent Caribbean states led to the conclusion of a treaty with Denmark in August 1916 for the purchase of the Danish West Indian islands of St. Thomas, St. John and St. Croix for $25 million. The islands were important for their strategic position and were seen as vital to the national security of the United States which was seemingly threatened by Germany following the outbreak of the First World War in 1914.

Fundamental changes in the Caribbean policy of the United States took place from the 1920s culminating in the so-called 'good neighbour' policy of President Franklin Roosevelt in the 1930s. In a series of Pan-American Conferences, conventions were adopted which outlawed wars of aggression, provided for the arbitration of all disputes, called for the removal of trade barriers, and renounced the doctrine of intervention. The new outlook was dramatized by the end of the military occupation of the Dominican Republic in 1924 and by the repeal of the Platt Amendment ten years later. In 1934 also the United States evacuated its troops from Haiti though it retained a measure of control over Haitian customs until 1936.

The policy of non-intervention coincided with the United States' adoption of the New Deal programme to fight the economic and social dislocations caused by the Great Depression (1929–32). As much as the New Deal was extended to the Caribbean, however, it was confined to the United States territories of Puerto Rico and the Virgin Islands, and it was expressed in measures to improve social services and to develop the economies of the islands.

The United States had hitherto abstained from interfering in the West Indian colonies of European nations, but the Second World War which the United States entered in 1941 led to the lend-lease agreement by which the United States transferred fifty over-age destroyers to Britain in return for the right to establish military bases in Guyana, Trinidad, St. Lucia, Antigua, the Bahamas, Jamaica and Bermuda.

Also during the war, the United States joined with Britain to form the Anglo-American Caribbean Commission (later joined by France and the Netherlands) in an effort to solve some of the area's pressing social and economic problems on a regional basis.

After the war the Caribbean became involved in the ideological conflict known as the 'cold war' between the United States and the Soviet Union. The United States' response to the Soviet threat of world communism was the Truman Doctrine of March 1947 which stipulated that unless the United States was willing to help free peoples everywhere to maintain their free institutions, international peace would be threatened and hence the security of the United States. After 1947 the United States was determined on the global containment of communism, and in the Caribbean this led to action in Cuba, Guyana and the Dominican Republic.

The United States became involved in Cuba after Dr Fidel Castro had ousted the dictator Fulgencio Batista as President in 1958, established a communist state and adopted a policy to introduce communism to all Latin America. Through the Central Intelligence Agency (C.I.A.), the United States gave assistance to anti-Castro forces in the United States – leading to the Bay of Pigs episode in 1961 which ended in fiasco for the insurgents. A more acute crisis developed the next year when it was discovered that the Russians had constructed missile launching bases in Cuba aimed at the United States. President Kennedy immediately deployed warships in the area and ordered the Russians to remove their weapons; Russian compliance averted possible war. In other respects, the United States broke off diplomatic relations with Cuba, imposed trade sanctions upon it, and suspended it from the Organization of American States.

The United States intervened in Guyana in 1964, again through the C.I.A., to prevent the return of the Marxist-oriented Premier Cheddi Jagan in favour of Forbes Burnham. The following year, the outbreak of revolt in the Dominican Republic and the possibility of a communist takeover led to the landing of American troops in April 1965, and their retention there for more than a year until the political situation became more stable.

Intervention was not the only way by which the United States handled Caribbean problems; indeed, unilateral intervention was both unpopular and illegal. In the decades after the Second World War greater emphasis was placed on consultation and co-operation expressed chiefly in the Organization of American States (O.A.S.), chartered in 1948 to replace the older Pan-American Union (1910), but with wider powers. Independent Caribbean nations are qualified for membership and to date only Guyana has been excluded, because of the renewed boundary dispute with Venezuela, while Cuba has been suspended.

Other organizations such as the Agency for International Development and the Inter-American Development Bank were established and brought into operation within the general programme called the Alliance for Progress launched by President Kennedy in 1961. Under the Alliance agreement, the United States promised the greater portion of $10 billion to provide financial and technical advice to accelerate the modernization of social and economic life in the Caribbean and Latin America. The programme was designed to create a situation more receptive to the United States presence and influence in the Caribbean. In addition, the Central American Common Market (C.A.C.M.) and the Latin American Free Trade Association (L.A.F.T.A.) have been organized to promote industrialization and to draw Latin America and the Caribbean states closer together within the orbit of United States influence in the sphere of trade relations. Lastly, the creation in September 1961 of the Peace Corps consisting of dedicated young American men and women willing to give voluntary and direct service to improve the standard of living in the Caribbean has probably been the most gracious and generous attempt at international co-operation.

4. Impact of the United States presence on the Caribbean

Either directly or indirectly, by example and precept, the United States has promoted the spread of democracy in the Caribbean. At various times, though not consistently, it has refused to recognize and support rulers who have secured power by revolution or by illegal means, and it has made the granting of aid such as that offered under the Alliance for Progress subject to the improvement and strengthening of democratic institutions.

The United States presence in the Caribbean served as a stimulus to the demand for self-government by several colonies, but by demanding conformity with its democratic principles, the United States has stifled the principle of national self-determination and the natural growth of political institutions among the complex and varied territories.

With the loss of Cuba and Puerto Rico at the end of the Spanish-American War in 1898, Spain ceased to be a colonial power in the Caribbean after 400 years.

The progressive expansion of United States influence in the Caribbean promoted successively by the Monroe Doctrine, the Roosevelt Corollary, the 'good-neighbour' policy and the Alliance for Progress, has meant the reduction of European influence in the area, even of those nations such as Britain and France which still have territorial possessions here. The result, in short, was to turn the Caribbean into an American sphere of influence.

The injection of enormous amounts of United States capital and technical advice and supervision into an area otherwise lacking in these resources, whether directly through military occupation, or through loans and grants, has allowed for tremendous improvements in economic development, standards of living and political stability.

(a) United States military occupation of Cuba, the Dominican Republic and Haiti was followed by impressive achievements. In all three islands the periods of occupation were periods of stable government, though democracy did not survive in any one of them.

In Cuba, public buildings were repaired and more public works introduced, a school system was inaugurated and the University reorganized. Measures were adopted to suppress yellow fever, reform prisons, reorganize the judiciary, introduce *habeas corpus*, and organize municipal self-government. Besides, the collection of taxes was improved, Church and state were separated, and the railway regulated.

In the Dominican Republic and Haiti, the finances were reorganized on a more efficient basis to enable the more regular payment of the public debt, important road building programmes were undertaken, and the school systems were completely reorganized. In addition, the problems of public health were tackled energetically – hospitals and free clinics were built, school children were medically inspected, a good water-system was laid, and street cleaning services were begun. In Haiti, a Central School of Agriculture was established to improve agriculture.

(b) The extension of the agencies of the New Deal to the United States Caribbean territories witnessed the establishment of the Virgin Islands Company for the economic and industrial development of the Virgin Islands to ease the heavy unemployment there, while interest in Puerto Rico was to mature in the 1940s into the massive industrial programme known as 'Operation Bootstrap'. Both the Virgin Islands and Puerto Rico were developed as showpieces of democracy in the western hemisphere.

(c) The construction of United States military establishments in various Caribbean territories created a widespread demand for labour and eased the pressures of unemployment and, moreso, brought West Indians into direct contact with American living standards and labour practices. Together they stimulated working-men to organize in trade unions and political parties to work towards the adoption of similar values on a territorial scale.

(d) The Caribbean Commission created during the Second World War provided maritime connections, built roads and improved local food production for the duration of hostilities, but afterwards it expanded its economic and social activities.

(e) The Alliance for Progress has promoted social and economic reconstruction and so have the other financial agencies. For example, in the Leeward and Windward Islands money obtained through the Agency for International Development (AID) has been used to provide road equipment, well drilling equipment, agricultural projects, electricity and airports and school buildings. In the decade after 1962 AID provided more than $314 million to the Dominican Republic for its development programmes. In 1971 Jamaica received a loan of $6.2 million from the Inter-American Development Bank to finance a farm improvement programme.

(f) Peace Corps volunteers have been employed mainly as teachers in the various territories and as such they have rendered valuable service in areas lacking in sufficient and adequately trained personnel.

United States capital investment was most noticeable in the Caribbean sugar industry. Large plantations were developed under American control; in Cuba six companies owned over two million acres of land while in Puerto Rico and the Dominican Republic large American corporations dominated the sugar industry. In terms of production, the resulting increase was phenomenal; for example, under American direction, Cuban sugar output increased from 447,000 tons in 1860 to over five million tons in 1925.

Investment was not confined to sugar production but extended to lesser though important enterprises like tobacco and banana cultivation, mining and railway construction. Hotels have also been constructed by American investors to support tourism. Estimates show that by the 1930s American investment amounted to $166 million in Cuba, $41 million in the Dominican Republic and $10 million in Haiti. By 1968 investment in the last two territories was estimated at

$150 million and $51 million respectively, while investment in all the West Indian islands and Guyana totalled $4,756 million of which $2,440 million was in Puerto Rico, $900 million in the Bahamas and $500 million each in Trinidad and Jamaica.

Agricultural expansion created an increased demand for labourers, and in the early decades of the twentieth century there was a considerable migration of labourers from other West Indian colonies to Puerto Rico, the Dominican Republic, Haiti and, moreso, Cuba to take advantage of the favourable job opportunities there.

The United States has long attracted West Indians looking for better employment opportunities elsewhere. Recent official statistics show that under United States immigration laws, between 1958 and 1967 as many as 295,977 West Indians entered the United States (154,257 from Cuba alone, due no doubt to the Castro revolution); in addition, an indefinite number entered illegally. Such emigration benefited the West Indies by reducing the high unemployment here, by lessening the strain on existing social services and public facilities, and by providing revenue through remittances from the United States. On the other hand, however, it contributed to the 'brain drain' thereby depriving the region of people whose talents and skills are necessary for sustained development.

In terms of trade, the Caribbean has been considerably affected by contact with the United States in having ready markets for its produce as well as by obtaining adequate supplies of essential items. In 1968, West Indian and Guyanese exports to and imports from the United States totalled $2,454.3 million and $2,516.5 million respectively. However, as indicated by these figures, the balance of payment was against the West Indies.

Contact with Americans, including tourists, has stimulated rising expectations among West Indians; new tastes have been acquired for American music, food, clothes and culture generally, as well as the desire to secure them through appropriate action.

5. Local Response to the United States in the Caribbean

Partly because of the social and economic improvements brought about in the West Indies by American capital, West Indian public opinion is in large measure favourably disposed towards the United States. Also, the large number of West Indians permitted yearly to enter the United States, and the commitment of West Indians to the democratic process have added to the attraction of the powerful Republic. Besides, many West Indians look to the United States for financial and technical assistance in order to plan future developmental strategies.

The fact that the United States has assumed the role of protector of western hemisphere countries against external aggression has significantly reduced the need for West Indian nations to develop alternative military measures except to maintain internal security.

Inasmuch as the United States has proven helpful to West Indians, the very power of the 'colossus to the north', and the way that power was exercised, has aroused the apprehension of many West Indians, in some cases to a very acute state. Despite their admiration of United States scientific and technological achievement, wealth and business efficiency, West Indians have been unwilling to become mere satellites of that superpower.

United States financial assistance has been both necessary and desirable, but even so loans have often been given at high rates of interest while a certain stigma with connotations of charity and inadequacy has been attached to 'aid'. The United States use of aid as reward or penalty for the recognition or rejection of American policies by the recipient nations and the American tendency to use such aid to protect and subsidize American economic interests adds to its unpopularity.

American companies investing in mining and agriculture in the West Indies have paid wages and taxes substantially higher than those offered by local investors. Nevertheless, concern has been expressed over their overall contribution to national development. The opinion prevails that national resources should benefit the national interest, and attempts have been made to restrict the outflow of profits to encourage their reinvestment within the territory of origin. Some West Indian planners envisage the transfer of control over regional resources from foreign multi-national corporations to local majority ownership or to regional companies.

The development of tourism supported mainly by United States citizens has contributed in various ways to the economic and social development of the West Indies, but among peoples whose forebears had experienced centuries of enslavement, the fear exists of being reduced to a servile status. The assertion of national pride and dignity takes precedence over material advancement.

United States military intervention in West Indian states promoted political stability therein, but assertion of national sovereignty resulted in strong objections to such intervention. For example, local resentment at United States intervention in the Dominican Republic in 1905 and in Haiti in 1915 developed into guerrilla warfare which American marines had to suppress by force of arms. To a large extent the adoption of a policy of non-intervention, or alternatively intervention with the approval and support of the Organization of American States, has been forced upon the United States by the widespread unpopularity of intervention among Caribbean and Latin American states.

Conclusion

The progressive rise of United States influence in the Caribbean since the beginning of the nineteenth century was achieved at the expense of the traditional colonizing European nations. In the process, the United States itself became an imperial nation after being in the vanguard of anti-imperialism in the western hemisphere.

Even before the construction of the Panama Canal, and especially after it, official United States policy towards the Caribbean was governed by two main considerations, namely, the protection of vital economic interests and national security. Economic relations in the form of investment, raw material supplies and markets had begun even during the colonial period of American history, and more recently, in the twentieth century, tourism, migration and cultural exchanges have stimulated American interest in the area.

Of equal if not more importance than economic interests has been national security, and in this respect the Caribbean, from its strategic position, has been vital to United States defence and protection. Fear of Germany dictated the acquisition of Puerto Rico in 1898 following the Spanish-American War, and the purchase of the Virgin Islands from Denmark in 1917. More recently, the threat of communist domination by the Soviet Union became evident to the American public as a result of the Cuban Missile Crisis in 1962. The importance of the Caribbean as a strategic sphere of influence has been reduced but not nullified by the development of supersonic jet aircraft and intercontinental ballistic missiles.

The United States attitude towards the Caribbean was expressed in such declarations as the Monroe Doctrine, the Roosevelt Corollary and the Truman Doctrine, the essence of which was military intervention, such as took place in Cuba, Haiti and the Dominican Republic at various times, in defence of American interests. Because of the unpopularity of intervention, the United States has more recently emphasized co-operation and financial assistance, mainly through the Alliance for Progress, to retain control in the Caribbean. The area is still very much under the American security umbrella; providing support is received from the Organization of American States, United States military intervention in the internal affairs of Caribbean states cannot be completely ruled out in certain circumstances.

Revision Questions

1. What historical reasons are there for United States involvement in West Indian affairs?

2. How did the Monroe Doctrine influence the attitude of the United States towards the West Indies?
3. To what extent did the American Civil War affect United States relations with the Caribbean?
4. Compare the 'big stick policy' of Theodore Roosevelt with the 'good neighbour policy' of Franklin D. Roosevelt.
5. By what methods did the United States try to establish its control and influence over Caribbean nations?
6. Do you think that the West Indies have benefited through association with the United States?

List of Short Note Topics

The following topics have been selected from past examination papers. They are included here to encourage students to find out facts for themselves and as a revision aid for examinations. They should be useful to both teachers and students.

A few of the subjects listed below are not covered in this book and will require outside reading. Students should write brief notes on each topic. These notes will serve as useful revision material and examination preparation.

1. The Economic Background

1. The Sugar Duties Act, 1846
2. Labour-saving devices after emancipation
3. The Free Village Movement
4. Hucksters and higglers
5. The Encumbered Estates Act, 1854
6. Cuban Sugar
7. The production of beet sugar
8. Banana Production in Jamaica
9. Jamaica's banana trade
10. Captain Lorenzo Baker
11. The United Fruit Company
12. The Royal Commission to the West Indies, 1896
13. The foundation of the Imperial Department of Agriculture
14. Joseph Chamberlain as Secretary of State for the Colonies
15. The Brussels Convention, 1903
16. The Imperial College of Agriculture
17. The Empire Marketing Board, 1926
18. The Moyne Commission
19. The Commonwealth Sugar Agreement
20. The International Sugar Agreement

2. Immigration and Emigration

1. The labour crisis of 1834–8
2. The 'Gladstone experiment'
3. Chinese immigrants to the West Indies in the nineteenth century
4. East Indian immigration in the nineteenth century
5. William des Voeux
6. The Commission of Enquiry, 1870
7. Asian immigration into Guyana

3. The Public Welfare

1. The Negro Education Grant
2. The Mico Charity
3. Missionary bodies of the period 1834 to 1850
4. Harrison College
5. Carnegie Libraries
6. Mary Seacole
7. The Marriot-Mayhew Report, 1933
8. Jamaica Welfare Ltd.
9. University College of the West Indies

4, 5 and 6. Organization for Development, Constitutional Changes and Closer Association

1. Governor Sligo of Jamaica
2. The Executive Committees
3. Crown Colony Government
4. Sir John Peter Grant
5. Sir Benjamin Pine
6. The Leeward Islands Act, 1871
7. Federal Attempts in the 1870s
8. Governor Pope-Hennessy
9. Attempts at federation before 1900
10. The Representative Government Associations
11. Marcus Garvey
12. Cecil Rawle and the West Indian Unofficial Conference of 1932
13. Captain Arthur Cipriani
14. Alexander Bustamante
15. Uriah Butler
16. Trade Unionism in the West Indies
17. The Montego Bay Conference
18. Dr Eric Williams
19. Forbes Burnham
20. The Commonwealth
21. The Caribbean Free Trade Area

7. The United States and the Caribbean

1. The Monroe Doctrine
2. The Spanish-American War, 1898
3. The Platt Amendment, 1901
4. The Panama Canal
5. 'I took Panama'
6. The American Virgin Islands
7. The U.S. 'Good Neighbour' Policy

8. F. D. Roosevelt's policies in the Caribbean and Latin America
9. Dr Fidel Castro
10. Cheddi Jagan
11. Chaguaramas

A Select Bibliography

This list is by no means exhaustive. It consists only of some of the primary and most important sources used in the preparation of this text. Three general works on West Indian history are given first. Thereafter the more specialized studies are given in alphabetical order by authors.

General Works;

1. Sir Alan Burns, *History of the British West Indies* (George Allen & Unwin, Ltd., London, 1954).
2. Agnes M. Whitson and Lucy F. Horsfall, *Britain and the West Indies* (Longmans, Green and Co., 1948).
3. Eric Williams, *From Columbus to Castro: The History of the Caribbean 1492–1969* (Andre Deutsch Ltd., London, 1970).

Special Studies:

1. R. W. Beachey, *The British West Indies Sugar Industry in the late 19th Century* (Oxford, Basil Blackwell, 1957).
2. Paul Blanshard, *Democracy and Empire in the Caribbean. A Contemporary Review* (New York, The Macmillan Company, 1947).
3. Robert D. Crassweller, *The Caribbean Community. Changing Societies and U.S. Policy* (Published for the Council on Foreign Relations by Praeger Publishers, New York, 1972).
4. G. E. Cumper (Ed.), *The Economy of the West Indies* (Printed for the Institute of Social and Economic Research, University of the West Indies by United Printers Ltd., Kingston, 1960).

5. Noel Deerr, *The History of Sugar* (2 volumes) (Chapman and Hall Ltd., London, 1949-50).
6. Emanuel de Kadt, *Patterns of Foreign Influence in the Caribbean* (Published for the Royal Institute of International Affairs by Oxford University Press, London, New York, Toronto, 1972).
7. *Developments towards Self-Government*: A Symposium held under the auspices of the Netherlands Universities Foundation for International Co-operation at the Hague, September, 1954. (W. van Hoeve Ltd., The Hague, Bandung, 1955).
8. Gisela Eisner, *Jamaica, 1830-1930: A Study in Economic Growth* (Manchester University Press, 1961).
9. Shirley C. Gordon, *A Century of West Indian Education* (Longmans, 1963).
10. Douglas Hall, *Five of the Leewards 1834-1870* The major problems of the post-emancipation period in Antigua, Barbuda, Montserrat, Nevis and St. Kitts. (Caribbean Universities Press, 1971).
11. Zin Henry, *Labour Relations and Industrial Conflict in Commonwealth Caribbean Countries* (Columbus Publishers Ltd., Trinidad, 1972).
12. William H. Knowles, *Trade Union Development and Industrial Relations in the British West Indies* (University of California Press, Berkeley and Los Angeles, 1959).
13. K. O. Laurence, *Immigration into the West Indies in the 19th century* (Caribbean Universities Press, 1971).
14. David Lowenthal (Ed.), *The West Indies Federation. Perspectives on a New Nation* (Columbia University Press, New York, 1961).
15. John Mordecai, *The West Indies. The Federal Negotiations* (George Allen & Unwin Ltd., London, 1968).
16. Carleen O'Loughlin, *Economic and Political Change in the Leeward and Windward Islands* (Yale University Press, 1968).
17. Ceri Peach, *West Indian Migration to Britain: A Social Geography* (London, Oxford University Press for the Institute of Race Relations, 1969).
18. Dexter Perkins, *The United States and the Caribbean* (Harvard University Press, Revised Edition, 1966).
19. Roy Preiswerk, *Regionalism and the Commonwealth Caribbean*. (Institute of International Relations, University of the West Indies, Trinidad, 1968).
20. T. S. Simey, *Welfare and Planning in the West Indies* (Oxford, at the Clarendon Press, 1946).
21. Hugh W. Springer, *Reflections on the Failure of the First West Indian Federation* (Published by the Center for International Affairs, Harvard University, July 1962).
22. Hume Wrong, *Government of the West Indies* (Oxford, at the Clarendon Press, 1923).

Examination Questions

The following questions have been selected from past General Certificate of Education examination papers. Though an attempt has been made to classify them according to subject matter it should be noted that in some instances questions refer to several topics. Answers should make allowance for this.

1. The Economic Background

1. 'The present distress far exceeds any that ever before occurred in the West Indies' (from the Report of the Select Committee on the West Indies in 1848). Illustrate and explain the causes of the distress at that time and show what steps were taken to deal with it during the 1850s and 1860s. (London, Summer 1966)

2. What is meant by *Free Trade*? Explain why Britain adopted this policy in the nineteenth century and how it affected the West Indies. (London, January 1971)

3. 'In 1863, 5 percent of the United Kingdom's sugar imports were in the form of sugar beet; by 1893 beet sugar accounted for 70 percent of the United Kingdom's sugar imports.' How do you account for this great increase? What were its effects upon the West Indies? (London, January 1967)

4. Show how sugar production in the British islands in the second half of the nineteenth century was affected by (a) the free trade policy of Great Britain; (b) competition from foreign producers. (Cambridge, June 1972)

5. Write a letter to a West Indian newspaper from a sugar planter protesting against the British Government's Sugar Duties Equalization Act of 1846. (Cambridge, Summer 1973)

6. Assess the effects on sugar production in British West Indian possessions in the nineteenth century of *three* of the following: the emancipation of slaves; the arrival of new immigrants; Britain's free trade policies; the cultivation of beet sugar. (London, June 1974)

7. Why did the British West Indies find it increasingly difficult to compete in the production of sugar after 1846? (Cambridge, June 1968)

8. For what reasons did the sugar industry decline in the West Indies in the century before 1939 and what alternatives were developed in industry and agriculture? (London, January 1969)

9. What alternatives to sugar production were developed in the West Indies in the first quarter of the twentieth century and what was their importance? (Cambridge, June 1969)

10. Why was the Imperial government so unpopular in the 1930s? (London, January 1968)

11. Describe briefly the events leading up to the appointment of the Moyne Commission in 1938. What were its chief recommendations, and how far were these important in the history of the British West Indies? (Cambridge, June 1971)

12. Why was the Moyne Commission appointed in 1938? Outline the principal points made in the Commission's Report. What actions had Britain taken in these matters by 1958? Why was the Report called a 'hoax'? (London, January 1974)

13. State what facts were reported concerning the West Indies and what recommendations were made by *at least one* of the Royal Commissions of 1882, 1896, 1938. (London, June 1974)

14. Give an account of the chief economic developments which have taken place in the West Indian territories since 1945. (Cambridge, June 1971)

15. What parts of the Caribbean, in your opinion, are at the present time the most industrialized? How has this industry developed? Why is it considered essential that there should continue to be industrial development? (London, January 1973)

16. What natural advantages favoured the growth of industry in the West Indies in the twentieth century? Describe some of the problems that face industrialists and businessmen at the present time. (London, Summer 1971)

17. How has industrialization changed the West Indies in the twentieth century? (London, January 1974)

2. Immigration and Emigration

1. What reasons do you suggest for the influx of people from abroad to work in Jamaica, Trinidad and British Guiana in the middle of the nineteenth century? (London, January 1964)

2. Give an account of the attempts made to obtain estate labour from outside the West Indies from 1841 to 1870. (Cambridge, June 1968)

3. Describe the attempts to solve labour shortages by the introduction of Chinese and Indian labour in the nineteenth century. (London, Summer 1965)

4. Account for the failure of attempts to use foreign labour on the West Indian sugar estates between 1838 and 1870. (Cambridge, Summer 1973)

5. Show the importance of immigrant labour in West Indian history in the nineteenth century. (London, January 1967)

6. Why was there migration from Asia to the West Indies in the nineteenth and twentieth centuries? What arrangements were made for these immigrants and what were the effects of their arrival upon the West Indies? (London, Summer 1970)

7. What were the difficulties in the use of immigrant labour on the sugar plantations after emancipation? (Cambridge, June 1970)

8. How have the immigrations of the nineteenth and twentieth centuries influenced the social structure and culture of any *one* West Indian territory? (Cambridge, June 1972)

9. By what main stages did the islands of the Caribbean become multi-racial? In what ways, in 1973, does this sort of society have (a) advantages and (b) disadvantages? (London, January 1973)

10. Give an account of the life of an Indian labourer in Jamaica *or*

Trinidad *or* British Guiana during the latter half of the nineteenth century. (Cambridge, June 1971)

11. Write a history of Indian immigration into Guiana and Trinidad. Assess the consequences of that immigration at the present time. (London, Summer 1972)

12. Why has there been emigration from the West Indies in the twentieth century? To what parts of the world have West Indians emigrated and what difficulties have arisen as a result? (London, Summer 1969)

13. Give an account of migration from the West Indies to American countries between 1904 and 1924. What were the main effects when West Indians were no longer admitted by these countries? (Cambridge, Summer 1973)

14. How has *your own territory* been affected by emigration during the past twenty years? (Cambridge, June 1970)

3. The Public Welfare

1. What measures were taken by the British to help former slaves in the ten years after emancipation and how far were they successful? (London, January 1965)

2. Outline the main developments in education in the West Indies from 1835 onwards. (London, January 1971)

3. Why was it necessary to make provision for the education of former slaves? What had been done in this matter by the end of the 1830s? (London, January 1974)

4. Describe what was done in the nineteenth century to extend education to more children in the West Indies. (London, June 1974)

5. What were the problems in the development of education in the West Indies *after* the end of the negro education grant in 1845? (London, Summer 1964)

6. Show the extent to which there has been educational advance in the West Indies in the last hundred years. What more, in your opinion, remains to be done? (London, January 1970)

7. Outline the gradual transformation of West Indian education with special reference to (a) State Schools, (b) Denominational Schools and

(c) Colleges and the University College of the West Indies. (London, Summer 1971)

8. Describe what has been done during the last ten years to improve the provision of education *in your territory*. What other improvements would you suggest? (Cambridge, June 1971)

9. What proposals did the Moyne Commission make regarding health services, housing and slum clearance, the encouragement of land settlement and greater opportunities for work in the islands of the West Indies? (London, January 1968)

10. Outline the main developments since 1835 affecting the British West Indies in two of the following: communications; education; trade unionism. (London, Summer 1970)

11. What problems made West Indian educational advance such a slow process? (London, January 1972)

4. Organization for Development

1. Trace the growth and show the importance of Trade Unions in the West Indies to the year 1939. (London, January 1968)

2. Trace the growth and show the importance of Trade Unions in the West Indies. (London, January 1970)

3. Trace the development of trade unions in your territory. How have they affected its history? (London, Summer 1963)

4. Describe the conditions which gave rise to the development of trade unions in the West Indies. What have the unions achieved? (London, January 1973)

5. Describe the development of trade unionism in the West Indies and show how *at least one* union leader became prominent in political affairs. (London, June 1973)

6. Describe (a) how industry has developed in the West Indies in the twentieth century and (b) how trade unionism has come to be important in *at least one* West Indian state. (London, June 1974)

5. Constitutional Changes

1. What do you understand by 'Crown Colony Government'? Do you think the British Government was justified in wanting to set up Crown

Colony Government in the West Indies? Give your reasons. (London, Summer 1964)

2. Why was the Crown Colony system of government introduced after 1865? How did it differ from the system of representative government which previously existed in the British West Indies? (Cambridge, June 1972)

3. Explain the changes which resulted from the coming of Crown Colony government to most British West Indian territories, limiting your consideration to the latter part of the nineteenth century. (Cambridge, June 1970)

4. What problems would you have faced had you been sent to an island in the West Indies in the nineteenth century as a British governor? Illustrate your answer by reference to the work of *up to three* such governors. (London, Summer 1970)

5. What criticisms of Crown Colony government arose in the years 1919–39? (Cambridge, June 1968)

6. 'Since 1944 the movement towards a greater share of West Indians in their government has gone forward fairly steadily.' What facts about any one West Indian territory would you use to prove this statement or deny it? (London, January 1968)

7. Name the various countries in the Caribbean at the present time and describe their systems of government. What changes have occurred since 1960? (London, January 1969)

8. Assess what have been (a) the principal advantages and (b) the principal disadvantages for the West Indians of association with Britain in the twentieth century. (London, Summer 1970)

9. What changes have occurred in the system of government of former British colonies in the Caribbean during the last hundred years? (London, January 1971)

10. Trace the history of Guyana (formerly British Guiana) from 1796 to the present day. (London, June 1973)

11. Give an account of the political changes *your territory* has experienced since 1958. (Cambridge, June 1968)

12. Outline the history since independence of *two* of the following: Barbados; Guyana; Jamaica; Trinidad (and Tobago). (London, June 1974)

6. Closer Association

1. Argue the case for and against federation in the West Indies. (London, Summer 1967)

2. What attempts were made to promote co-operation and unification between West Indian islands (a) before 1939 and (b) after 1945? (London, January 1969)

3. Trace the rise and decline of the idea of federation in the West Indies in the twentieth century. (London, Summer 1969)

4. Explain the term *Federation*. What attempts have been made since 1871 to set up federations in the British West Indies, for what reasons and with what results? (London, Summer 1970)

5. Why and with what results were attempts made in the period 1869 to 1899 to link together West Indian islands? (London, January 1974)

6. Why was a West Indian Federation set up in 1958? Why did it break up? (London, January 1970)

7. Describe the movement for federation in the British West Indian territories *either* in the period 1869-76 *or* in the period 1947-58. Explain (a) the difficulties experienced and (b) the success achieved in the period of your choice. (Cambridge, Summer 1973)

8. Describe the movement after 1947 leading to the establishment of a federation of the British West Indian territories. What support still remains for the idea of federation? (Cambridge, June 1970)

9. Why was *Federation* thought to be desirable in the West Indies after the Second World War? Trace the steps by which the Federation of the West Indies was set up. Why did it not last beyond 1962? (London, June 1974)

10. Account for the rise and fall of the Federation of the West Indies. What other associations have West Indians formed in the years since 1962? (London, January 1973)

11. Describe briefly the agencies which now exist for co-operation between the English-speaking territories in the Caribbean. What difficulties stand in the way of closer co-operation? (Cambridge, June 1971)

7. The United States and the Caribbean

1. Trace the development of American interference in the West Indies from 1812 to 1902. (London, January 1971)

2. Show how the United States of America became increasingly involved in West Indian affairs from the late nineteenth century to the Slump of 1929. (London, January 1974)

3. Give an account of the extension of the influence of the U.S.A. in the Caribbean in the twentieth century. (Cambridge, Summer 1973)

4. Describe the main events which led to the United States interest in the Caribbean area. Which Caribbean territories were most influenced by United States policy before 1939? (London, January 1964)

5. 'The United States has become a force in the Caribbean during the last hundred years'. How and why has this happened? (London, Summer 1970)

6. Describe and assess the importance of the involvement of the United States of America in the Caribbean from 1889 to the present day. (London, Summer 1972)

7. Explain (a) the advantages and (b) the disadvantages for the West Indies of the interest in the area shown by the U.S.A. from the election of Theodore Roosevelt (1900) to the death of Franklin D. Roosevelt (1945). (London, January 1973)

8. Give an account of the ways in which the culture and policies of the United States have influenced the Caribbean since 1939. (Cambridge, June 1970)

Index

Adams, Grantley 34, 95–6, 104, 126, 144, 149
Agency for International Development 165, 167
Agricultural Departments 28
Air Transport Council 155
Allder, O. T. 104
Allfrey, Mrs Phyllis Shand 106
Alliance for Progress 165, 166, 167, 170
Alves, Bain 90
amalgamation of estates 15
Andrews, C. F. 60
'Angel Gabriel' Riots 61
Anguilla 40, 105, 127, 128, 129, 133, 136, 138, 148
Antigua 10, 11, 12, 20, 22, 26, 28, 29, 30, 39, 41, 47, 64, 71, 73, 84–5, 96, 98, 104–5, 114, 115, 127, 128, 136, 137, 139, 140, 141, 148, 150, 157, 164
Anti-Slavery Society 50, 59
artisans 11, 24, 61, 68
Assembly, Chapter 5, *passim*
associated statehood 128–9

Baden-Powell, George 22
Bahamas 64, 164, 168
Baker, Captain Lorenzo 27
Balak Sahaita Mandalee 84
bananas 9, 27, 39, 78, 151, 161, 167
Bank of British Guiana 14
Baptist ministers 12
Barbados 10, 11, 12, 15, 20, 22, 26, 29, 31, 33, 34, 37, 38, 41, 47, 63, 69, 72, 73, 77, 80, 85, 91, 92, 95–6, 97, 98, 103–4, 108, 115, 125–6, 128, 129, 133, 135, 137, 138, 144, 145, 146, 148, 149, 150, 154, 155, 156, 157
Barbour, Sir David 25
Barbuda 136
Barrow, Errol 104
Batista, Fulgencio 164
bauxite 28, 40, 97, 159
beet sugar 9, 17–19, 26, 28, 45
Belize 40, 138, 147, 156
Bentinck, Lord George 21
Bermuda 164
'big stick' policy 162
Bird, V. C. 104
Blaize, Herbert 106
Boards of Health 79–80
Boston Fruit Company 27
Botanical Stations 39
Bradshaw, Robert 105
'brain drain' 65, 133, 168
Britain 44, 128, 144, 151, 152, 153, 158, 160, 166
British East Indies 15–16
British Virgin Islands 24, 40, 114, 127, 133, 136, 138, 140
Brown, Major Orde 92
Brussels Convention 19, 28, 30
Burnham, L. F. S. 102, 103, 164
'Bushe Experiment' 126
Bushe, Sir Henry Grattan 126
Bustamante, Alexander 33, 100
Butler, Uriah 33, 101

cabildos 121
cable telegraph 78, 144
Calcutta 53, 54

Index

Canada 26, 28, 29, 64, 77, 114, 138, 144, 146, 151, 153, 155
Canada-West Indies Trade Relations 142, 143
Canadian Presbyterian Mission 58, 73
Caribbean Bar Association 155
Caribbean Broadcasting Union 155
Caribbean Commission 37, 146, 153–4, 155, 164, 167
Caribbean Common Market 132, 156
Caribbean Community 132, 156
Caribbean Congress of Labour 97, 155
Caribbean Currency Board 154
Caribbean Economic Development Corporation 154
Caribbean Education Council 75
Caribbean Examinations Council 154
Caribbean Free Trade Area 78, 130–2, 156
Caribbean Hotels Association 155
Caribbean Labour Congress 96, 147, 155
Caribbean Medical Association 155
Caribbean Meteorological Service 155
Caribbean Organization 154
Caribbean Press Association 155
Caribbean Union of Teachers 155
cash crops 9, 13, 27–8, 38, 39, 40
Castro, Dr Fidel 41, 164
Cato, Milton 106
Central American Common Market 165
central factories 20, 26, 28, 38
Central Intelligence Agency 164
centrifugals 14, 20
Césaire, Aimé 32
Chamberlain, Joseph 25, 26
charitable organizations 68, 86, 87
Charles, J. B. 106
Chief Minister, Chapter 5, *passim*
Chimman Lal 60
Cipriani, Captain Arthur A. 90, 91 101
Citrine, Sir Walter 34, 92–3, 96
Clayton-Bulwer Treaty 161, 163
Closer Union Commission 143
Codrington, Christopher 140
Codrington Grammar School 69, 72
coffee 27, 28
'cold war' 159, 164
Colebrooke, Sir William W. G. 137
College of Kiezers 123, 124
Colonial Bank of the West Indies 14
Colonial Development Corporation 37
Colonial Development Fund 30

Colonial Development and Welfare Organization 37, 81, 86, 146, 150, 153
Colonial Office 21, 59, 113, 115, 138, 140
Colonial Sugar Certificates 30
Combined Council 137
Combined Court 123, 124
Commission to Enquire into the Treatment of Immigrants in British Guiana 57
Committee System 118
Commonwealth Immigration Acts 64
Commonwealth of Nations 120, 123, 125, 126, 129
Commonwealth Sugar Agreement 38
communication 22, 24, 26, 76–9, 132, 144, 154–5, 159, 166, 167
Compton, John 105, 157
Comptroller 35, 37, 153
Confederation Riots 138
consignee merchants 14
constitutional reforms
    old representative system 113–14
    Crown Colony government 114–16
    stages in 116–19
    in Jamaica 119–20, 133
    in Trinidad 120–3, 133
    in Guyana 123–5, 133
    in Barbados 125–6, 133
    in Leeward and Windward Islands 127–8, 133
Co-operative Republic of Guyana 125, 131
Costa Rica 27, 63
cotton 27, 28, 40
Council, Chapter 5, *passim*
credit 14, 15, 16
Critchlow, Hubert Nathaniel 91, 95
Crosby, James 58
Crossman, William 22
Crown Colony Government 32, 71, 89, 109, 112, 114–16, 119, 124, 127, 134, 140–1, 145
Cuba 16, 19, 27, 29, 31, 38, 41, 63, 64, 131, 159, 160, 161, 162, 163, 164, 166, 167, 168, 170
Cuban Missile Crisis 164, 170
curriculum 31, 71, 74
customs duties 22, 23–4, 84
customs union 148, 153

D' Aguiar, Peter 103

Index 187

Daily Meal Society 84–5
Danish West Indies 63, 161, 163
   See also U.S. Virgin Islands
Davis, Morris 105
Davis, Nicholas Darnell 143
Davson, Sir Edward 143, 153
Defence Bases Agreement 150
Departments of Agriculture 15
Des Voeux, George William 57
Dharamsala 84
diseases 31, 46, 55, 56, 79, 80, 82–3, 166
doctors 81, 82
'dollar diplomacy' 162
Dominica 11, 12, 26, 28, 39, 47, 49, 106, 115, 128, 136, 137, 138, 140, 142, 143, 148
Dominican Republic 27, 32, 63, 161, 163, 164, 165, 166, 167–8, 169, 170
Douglas, Walter 140
dual control 71, 73, 75
Dupigny, Clifton 106

East Indians 9, 14, 24, 40, 66
  immigration 49, 50–1
  reasons for 46, 51–3
  recruitment and transoceanic crossing 53–5
  working and living conditions 55–9
  end of immigration 59–60
  impact on society 60–1
  education 72, 74
  social welfare 84
  as trade unionists 97
  in politics 121, 122
economic diversification 26, 27, 36, 39–42, 61, 132
education 11, 31, 35, 36, 58–9, 61, 65, 66, 73, 87, 98, 99, 108, 133, 145, 166
  elementary 70, 73
  during slavery 69
  19th century developments 69–72
  20th century developments 73–5
  problems in 75–6
Edun, Ayube 95
emigration 13, 31, 44, 63–4, 67, 168, 170
Emigration Agent 53
Empire Marketing Board 29–30
Engledow, Professor Frank 34
European Economic Community 39
evictions 10–11
Executive Committees 114
Executive Council, Chapter 5, *passim*

Eyre, Sir Edward John 114

federation 23, 24, 25, 34, 37
  attempts before 1900 136–8
  of Leeward Islands (1674) 135, 136, 139–40; (1871) 135, 138, 140–2
  proposals for 142–4
  conditions retarding 144–5
  conditions promoting 145–6
  of West Indies (1958) 78, 108, 120, 128, 135, 138, 142
  steps towards 146–8
  operation 148–51
  collapse 151–2, 156
  future prospects 156–7
Fergusson, General Sir Charles 143
fertilizers 14, 20, 21, 38
financial problems 13–15
food crops 9, 27
forestry 39, 40
free trade 15–17, 25
free village movement 12
Frere, W. E. 57
friendly societies 84
functional co-operation 152–6

Gairy, Eric 96, 105–6
Garvey, Marcus 32, 90, 100
'Gladstone experiment' 50
'good neighbour' policy 163, 164
governor, Chapter 5, *passim*
Grant, Governor John Peter 116
Great Depression (1929–32) 31, 164
Grenada 10, 11, 12, 13, 22, 28, 30, 39, 47, 49, 50, 59, 80, 96, 98, 105–6, 108, 116–17, 128, 129, 133, 136, 137, 138, 143, 145, 146, 148, 157
Grenada Declaration 157
Grey, Sir Edward 25–6
Guadeloupe 146
Guyana 10, 11, 12, 15, 20, 22, 28, 29, 32–3, 38, 40, 41, 42, 46, 47, 48, 49, 50, 52, 54, 55, 56, 57, 60, 61, 64, 67, 71, 72, 73, 74, 77, 79, 80, 91, 94, 96, 97, 98, 102–3, 104, 108, 115, 123–5, 129, 130, 133, 143, 144, 145, 147, 154, 155, 156, 157, 159, 164, 168

Hailes, Lord 149
Haiti 63, 161, 163, 166, 167–8, 169, 170
Hamilton, Sir Robert 142
Harrison's Free School 69
hawkers 13

health services 31, 35, 56, 65, 76, 79–83, 108, 166
Herbert, Dr William 105
higglers 13
Hincks, Sir Francis 58
Hindu Society 84
hospitals 80, 81–2, 83, 84, 85
housing 31, 35–6, 55, 56, 57, 58, 65, 81, 85, 86, 99, 108, 133, 145
hucksters 11, 13, 61
hydro-electricity 42

immigration 14, 17, 24, 65
  reasons for 44, 45–6
  of Europeans and Portuguese 44–5
  of West Indians 47–8
  of Africans 48–9
  of Chinese 49–50
  of Indians 49, 50–60
imperial aid 21–6, 87
Imperial College of Tropical Agriculture 36, 39, 74, 152–3
independence 34, 73, 107, 108, 112, Chapter 5, *passim*
Indian National Congress 60
industrial education 26, 72
industries 9, 39, 40–1, 42
Inter-American Development Bank 165, 167
Inter-Governmental Conference 150
International Courts of Mixed Commission 48
International Sugar Agreement 30, 38

Jagan, Dr Cheddi 102–3, 164
jails 86
Jamaica 10, 11, 12, 20, 22, 23, 27, 29–31, 33, 34, 38–41, 46–51, 54, 56, 63, 65, 69–73, 77, 78, 80, 84, 85, 90, 94, 96, 97, 100–1, 104, 108, 114, 115, 116, 119–20, 128, 129, 133, 135, 144, 145, 148, 149–52, 157, 159, 164, 168
Jamaica Welfare Ltd. 85
Johnson, Sir Nathaniel 139
Joint Estate Council 97
Joshua, Ebenezer 106

Labour Advisers 93
Labour Departments 93, 97
labour-saving devices 13, 14, 16, 17, 21, 38, 39
labour shortage 9, 10–11, 24, 44–5, 65
labour unrest of the 1930s 31–4, 40, 64, 99

Lamont, Sir Norman 143
landownership 11–13, 31, 51
land-settlement 30
Latin American Free Trade Association 165
Latrobe, Charles 70
Leeward Islands 11, 22, 23, 24, 47, 72, 104–5, 127–9, 133, 135, 136, 137, 138, 139, 143, 144, 145, 146–7, 148, 155, 157
Legislative Council, Chapter 5, *passim*
lend-lease agreement 164
Leonora Estate 33, 57
liberated Africans 48–9
limes 28, 39
livestock 11, 12, 39
loans 14, 22, 169
London Conference (1953) 142, 147; (1956) 148
Lopez, Narcisso 161

MacGregor, Governor Evan J. M. 137
Mackenzie, George 48
McNeill, James 60
Madeira 46–7
Madras 53, 54
Madras Presidency 53
Manifest Destiny 160–1
Manley, Norman 34, 85, 94, 100, 151
manures 20, 21
Maraj, Bhadase S. 102
markets 15, 16, 27, 28, 29, 31, 145, 158–60, 168
Marryshow, T. A. 116
Martinique 20, 146
Mauritius 15, 16
medical services 55, 58, 60, 79–82, 99, 133, 145
Meikle, J. 143
Melville, Governor Robert 136
metayer (*or* metairie) 13
Mico Charity 69–71
minerals 9, 28, 39, 40, 41, 77, 151, 161, 167, 169
Minor Keith 27
missionary societies 69–70
Mitchell, Dr Charles 57, 58
Monroe Doctrine 160, 166, 170
Monroe, President James 160
Montego Bay Conference (1947) 147
Montserrat 10, 11, 13, 22, 39, 65, 84, 105, 127, 128, 136, 138, 139, 140, 148, 150
Morant Bay Uprising 114, 119

Morris, Dr D. 25
mosquito control 80, 82–3
Moyne Commission 34–7, 68, 85–6, 87, 92, 121, 143, 144
Murray, Gideon 143
muscovado sugar 16, 17

National Association for the Advancement of Coloured People 32
national insurance 86
natural gas 40
Navigation Laws 16, 160
Negro Education Grant 69–70
Netherlands Antilles 64, 105, 146
New Deal 164, 166
non-intervention policy 163–4
normal schools 70, 71
Norman, Sir Henry 25

oil 28, 40, 97, 151
old-age pensions 86
old representative system 89, 112–14
Olivier, Sydney 26
O'Neale, Dr Charles Duncan 103
Organization of American States 109, 129–30, 164, 165, 169, 170
Orr, James Sayers 61
Orr, Sir Charles 143

Palma, Estrada 163
Panama 32, 63, 162–3
Panama Canal 163, 170
Pan-American Conference 161–2, 163
Pan-American Union 165
'paper unions' 97
Parke, Daniel 140
'payment by results' 71–2, 73, 75
Payne, Clement 33
Peace Corps 165, 167
Pearson, W. W. 60
peasant farming 9, 11–13, 24, 26, 27–8, 30, 36, 38, 39–40, 51, 56, 61, 68, 76, 145
petroleum 159
pimento 27, 28
Pine, Sir Benjamin 138, 140
plantations abandoned 12, 13, 16, 19
Planters' Bank of Jamaica 14
Platt Amendment 162, 163
political parties 34, 67, 89, 112, 152, 167
    background 99–100
    growth of 100–6
    characteristics 107–8

scope of activities 86, 108–9
    problems encountered 109
    relations with trade unions 110
poor relief 68, 84, 85
Pope-Hennessy, Governor John 138
population 31, 81, 86, 87, 133
Portuguese 46–7, 61, 66
preferential treatment 29, 36
Princess Margaret 149
proportional representation 103, 109, 125
Protector of Immigrants (or Agent General) 55, 58
Puerto Rico 19, 29, 154, 161, 162, 164, 166, 167, 168, 170

quarantine 79
quasi-parties 110
Queen Elizabeth II 149
Queen's College 72
Queen's Collegiate School (Queen's Royal College) 72

radio 78
Rance, Sir Hubert 147
Rawle, Cecil 143
reafforestation 40
Red Cross 83
referendum 120, 150
refrigeration 27, 78
Regional Development Bank 132, 156
Regional Oils and Fats Conference 153
religious denominations 69, 71
remittances 65
Renison Constitution 125
representative government 34, 87, 100, Chapter 5, *passim*
Representative Government Associations 116–17, 144
Reynolds Company Ltd. 40
rice 40, 61
Richards, Alfred 90, 101
Rippon, G. R. 143
roads 76–7, 87, 132
Roosevelt Corollary 162, 166, 170
Roosevelt, Franklin D. 163
Roosevelt, Theodore 162
Royal Commissions
    (1882–3) 22–5, 142
    (1896–7) 20, 25–6, 30, 142
    (1910) 142, 143
    (1929) 30
    (1938) *See* Moyne Commission

St. Helena 49
St. John Ambulance Brigade 83
St. Kitts-Nevis 11, 12, 13, 20, 22, 28, 29, 30, 32, 39, 40, 47, 49, 84, 91, 95, 98, 105, 114, 127, 128, 129, 136, 138, 140, 141, 148, 157
St. Lucia 10, 11, 12, 13, 15, 20, 22, 28, 30, 32, 39, 49, 50, 59, 64, 70, 92, 96, 98, 105, 113, 114, 128, 137, 138, 143, 148, 150, 157, 164
St. Vincent 10, 11, 22, 26, 28, 30, 32, 39, 47, 49, 50, 59, 91, 98, 106, 114, 128, 136, 137, 138, 145, 148
Salmon, C. S. 143
Salvation Army 84
Sanderson Committee 59
sanitary inspectors 80
sanitation 79–80, 99
secondary education 72, 73
Select Committee of Enquiry (1847–8) 20, 21–2
self-government 34, 36–7, 65, 73, 74, 100, 107, 108, 112, Chapter 5, *passim*
sewage disposal 82
Sierra Leone 48, 49
Singh, Jai Narine 103
slave compensation 13–14
social services 10, 32, 60, 65, 83–6, 87, 99
Social Welfare Officers 86
soil conservation 40
Spanish-American War 19, 162, 166, 170
Springer, Hugh 96
squatting 12
Standing Closer Association Committee 142, 147, 148
Stapleton, Sir William 136, 139
steampower 20
steamships 78
Stockdale, Sir Frank 37
stone-quarrying 40
strikes 57, 89
sugar
    foreign colonial 9
    collapse 9, 13–14, 15–16, 17–19, 28–9
    technical improvements 9, 19–21, 27, 28–9, 36, 37–9, 60, 167
    prices 12, 13, 16, 17, 19, 29
    exports 17, 18–19, 29
    non-profitability 19
Sugar Duties Act (1846) 14, 15–17, 21, 50
Sugar Producers Association 97
sulphate of ammonia 21
'Summit' Conferences 156

Taft, William H. 162, 163
Taylor, Henry 113
teacher training 72, 73, 75
technical institutes 74
television 79
timbers 27, 40, 77
Tobago 10, 11, 12, 13, 22, 28, 114, 136, 137, 138, 148, 155
tourism 9, 41, 42, 167, 169, 170
Trade Commissions 153
trade unions 10, 32, 36, 65, 86, 89, 112, 152, 167
    early beginnings 90–2
    conditions influencing development 92–3
    developments since 1930s 93–7
    difficulties experienced 97–8
    achievements 98
transportation 76–9, 87, 132, 146
Trinidad 10, 11, 12, 15, 20, 22, 28, 29, 30, 31, 33, 36, 38, 39, 40, 41, 46, 47, 48, 49, 50, 52, 54, 55, 56, 57, 60, 61, 64, 67, 70, 71, 72, 73, 74, 77, 79, 85, 94–5, 96, 97, 101–2, 104, 108, 113, 120–3, 128, 129, 133, 135, 137, 138, 142, 143, 144, 145, 148, 149, 150, 151, 152, 154, 155, 157, 159, 164, 168
Trinidad Leaseholds Ltd. 33
Trinidad Oilfield Company Ltd. 40
Truman Doctrine 164, 170
Tudor, Cameron 104

unemployment 31, 64, 76, 98, 145, 168
UNESCO 76, 81
UNICEF 76, 81
United Fruit Company 27, 85
United Nations 109, 129, 159
United Nations Sugar Conference 38
United Negro Improvement Association 32
United States 15, 16, 19, 25, 27, 28, 29, 30, 31, 32, 38, 41, 44, 47, 63, 64, 93, 131, 146, 151, 152, 153, 158
    reasons for Caribbean interest 158–60
    19th century involvement 160–2
    20th century involvement 162–5
    impact on Caribbean 165–8
    Caribbean response 168–9

United States Virgin Islands 64, 164, 170 *See also* Danish West Indies
universal adult suffrage 34, 36, 100, 101, 105, 106, 107, 108, Chapter 5, *passim*, 149
universities 73
University (College) Hospital 81, 154
University (College) of the West Indies 74-5, 81, 93, 149, 150, 152, 154
University of Guyana 74

vaccinations 79
vacuum pans 14, 20
Venezuela 63
Venezuela-British Guiana boundary dispute 162
Virgin Islands Company 166-7
voluntary organizations 68, 86, 87

Waddington Commission 124
wages 10, 11, 13, 16, 31, 32, 45, 47, 48, 52, 55-6, 63, 71-2, 73, 145, 169
Wages Boards 36
Walter, George 105
Wars
  American Civil (1861-5) 17, 28
  American Independence (1776-83) 137, 160
  Crimean (1854-6) 17
  First World (1914-18) 28, 31, 44, 60, 63, 65, 73, 84, 89, 90, 92, 121, 127, 143, 159, 163
  French Revolutionary (1793-1802) 123
  Napoleonic (1803-15) 17, 158
  Second World (1939-45) 37, 38, 41, 64, 65, 77, 78, 81, 93, 97, 143, 144, 146, 153, 165
water conservation 40
water-supply 80, 82, 108, 166
wells 80
West India Bank of Barbados 14
West India Interest 136
West Indian Court of Appeal 155
West Indian Department of Agriculture 21, 26, 28, 39, 74, 146, 152
West Indian Sugar Commission 30, 142-3
West Indian Unofficial Conference 143-4
West Indian Welfare Fund 35
West India Regiment 150
West Indies Encumbered Estates Act 15, 24
Williams, Dr Eric 102, 122, 149, 150, 151
Wilson, Woodrow 163
Windward Islands 11, 22, 23, 24, 39, 47, 50, 59, 72, 92, 96, 105-6, 127-9, 133, 138, 142, 143, 144, 145, 146-7, 148, 151, 155, 157
Windward Islands Appeal Court 137, 155
wireless telegraph 78
Wolmer's School 69
Women's Societies 84
Wood, E. F. L. 77, 117, 142
World Health Organization 76, 81

yellow fever 63
Y.M.C.A. 84
Young, Sir George 57
Y.W.C.A. 84